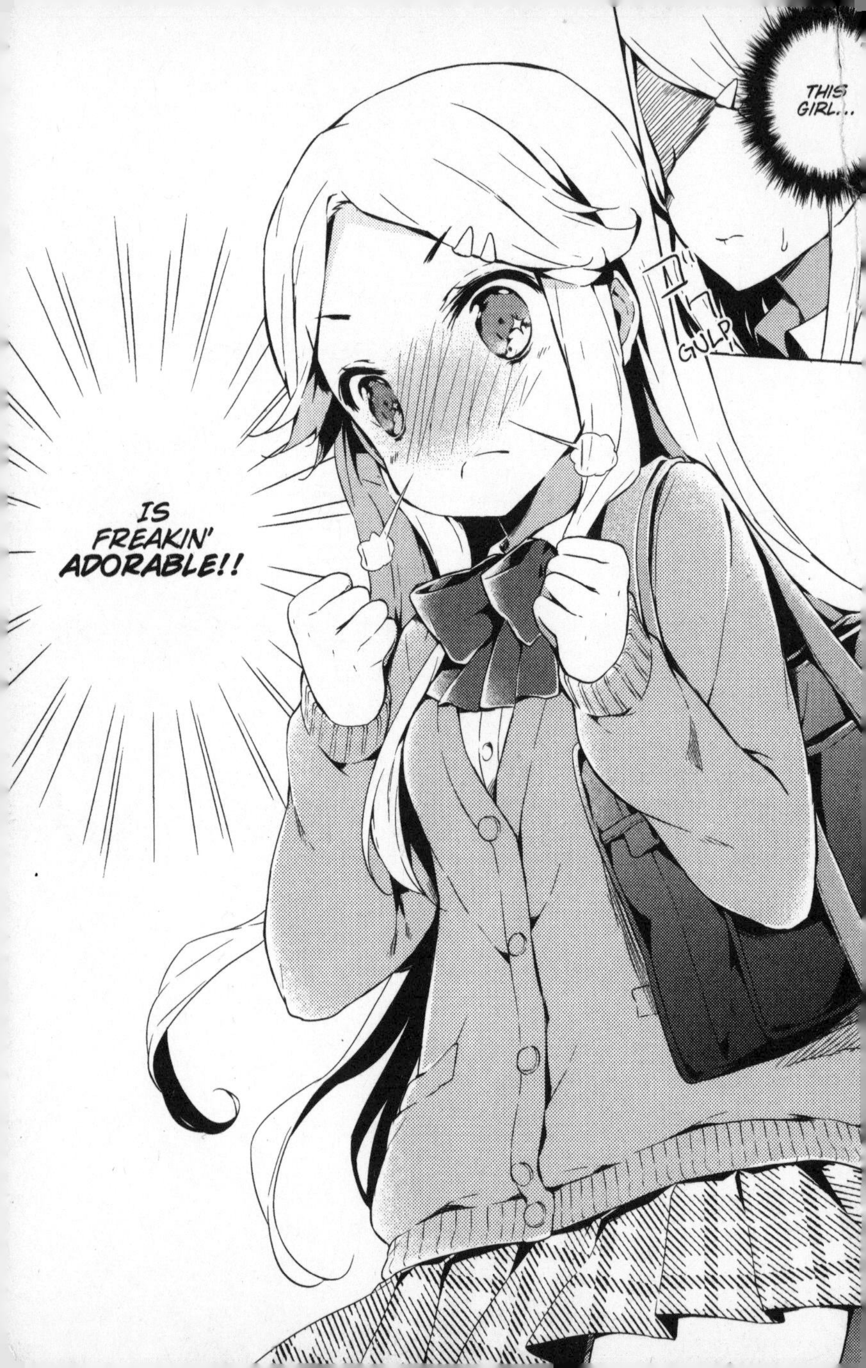
THIS GIRL...
GULP
IS FREAKIN' ADORABLE!!

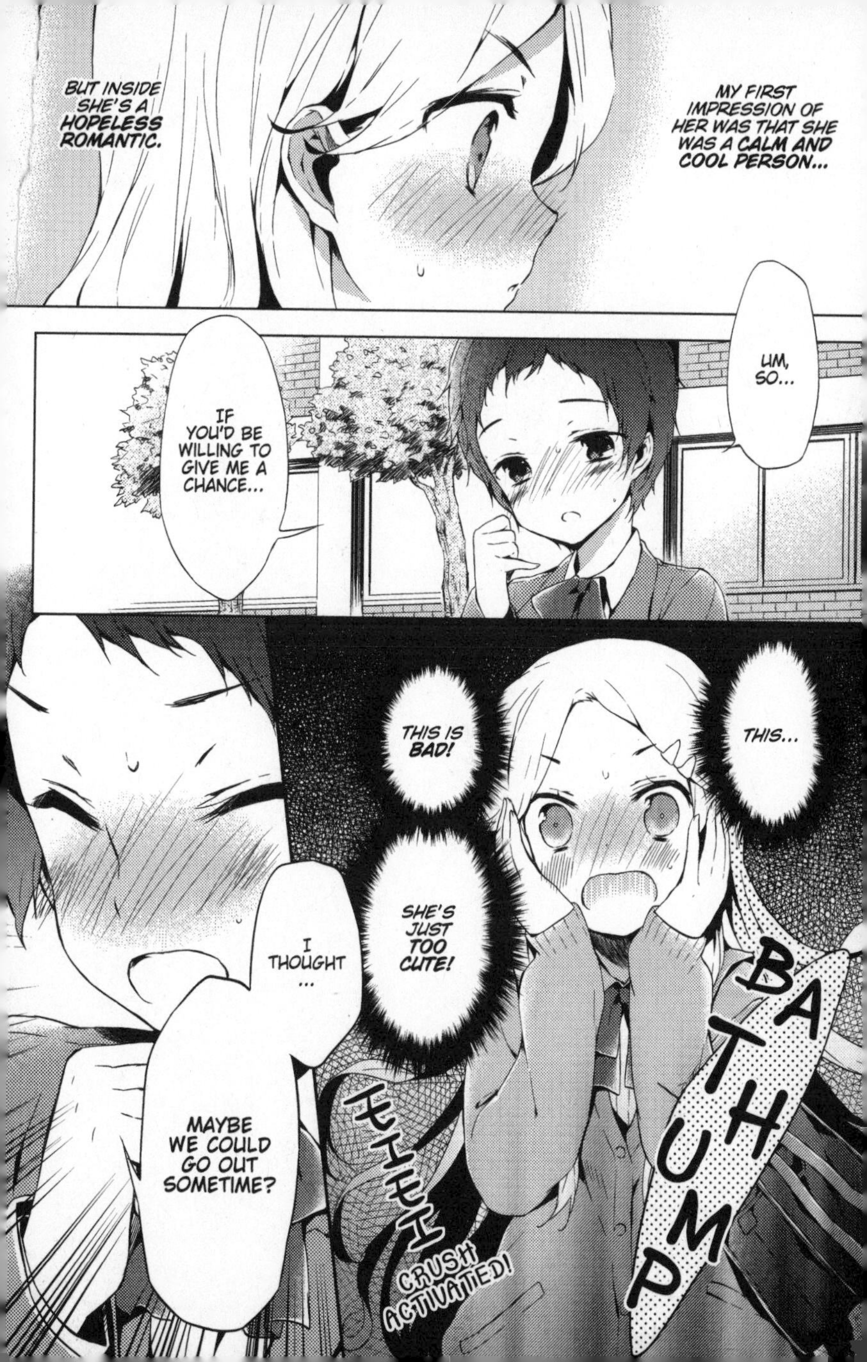
MY FIRST IMPRESSION OF HER WAS THAT SHE WAS A CALM AND COOL PERSON...
BUT INSIDE SHE'S A HOPELESS ROMANTIC.
UM, SO...
IF YOU'D BE WILLING TO GIVE ME A CHANCE...
THIS...
THIS IS BAD!
SHE'S JUST TOO CUTE!
BATHUMP
I THOUGHT...
MAYBE WE COULD GO OUT SOMETIME?
CRUSH ACTIVATED!

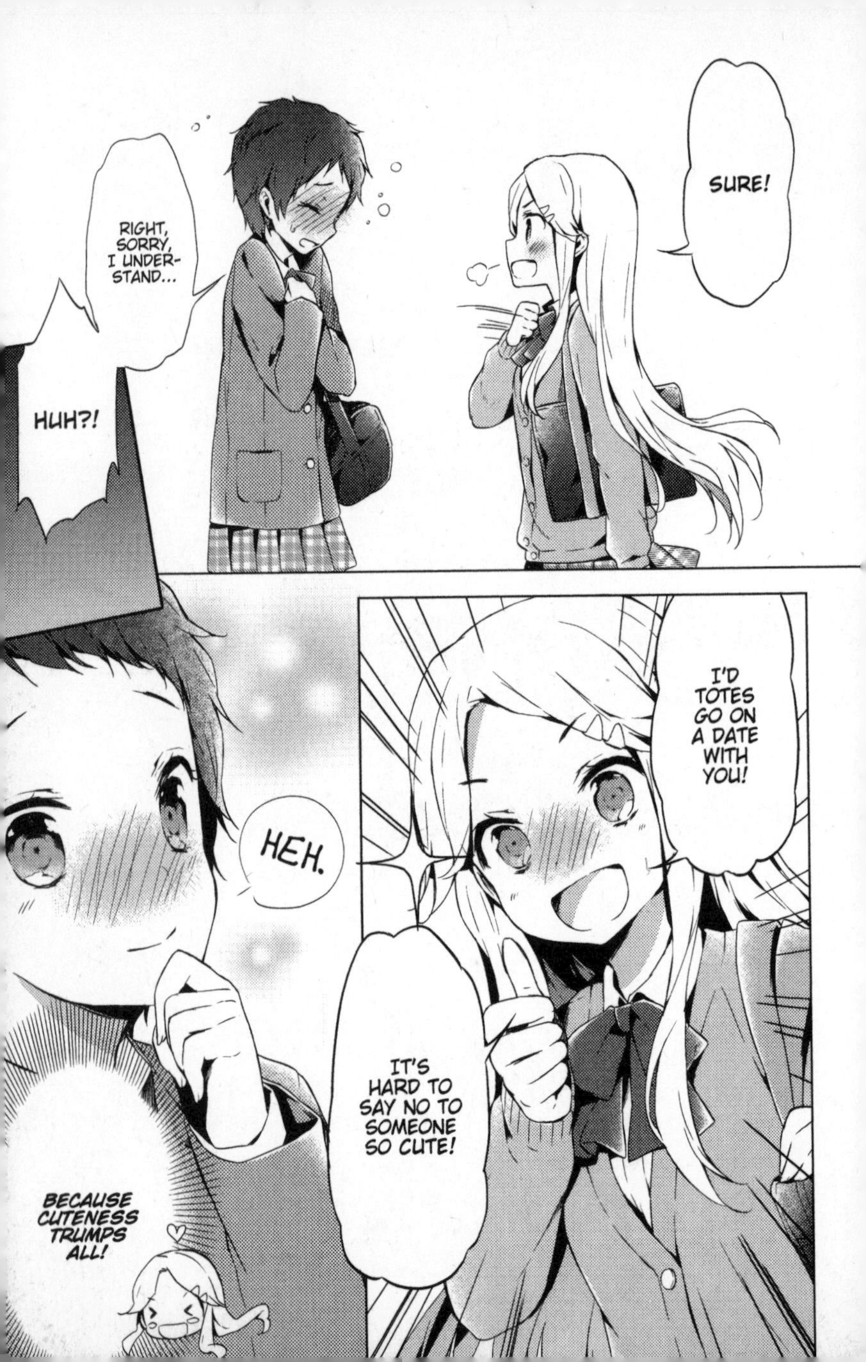
SURE!
RIGHT, SORRY, I UNDER-STAND...
HUH?!
I'D TOTES GO ON A DATE WITH YOU!
IT'S HARD TO SAY NO TO SOMEONE SO CUTE!
HEH.
BECAUSE CUTENESS TRUMPS ALL!

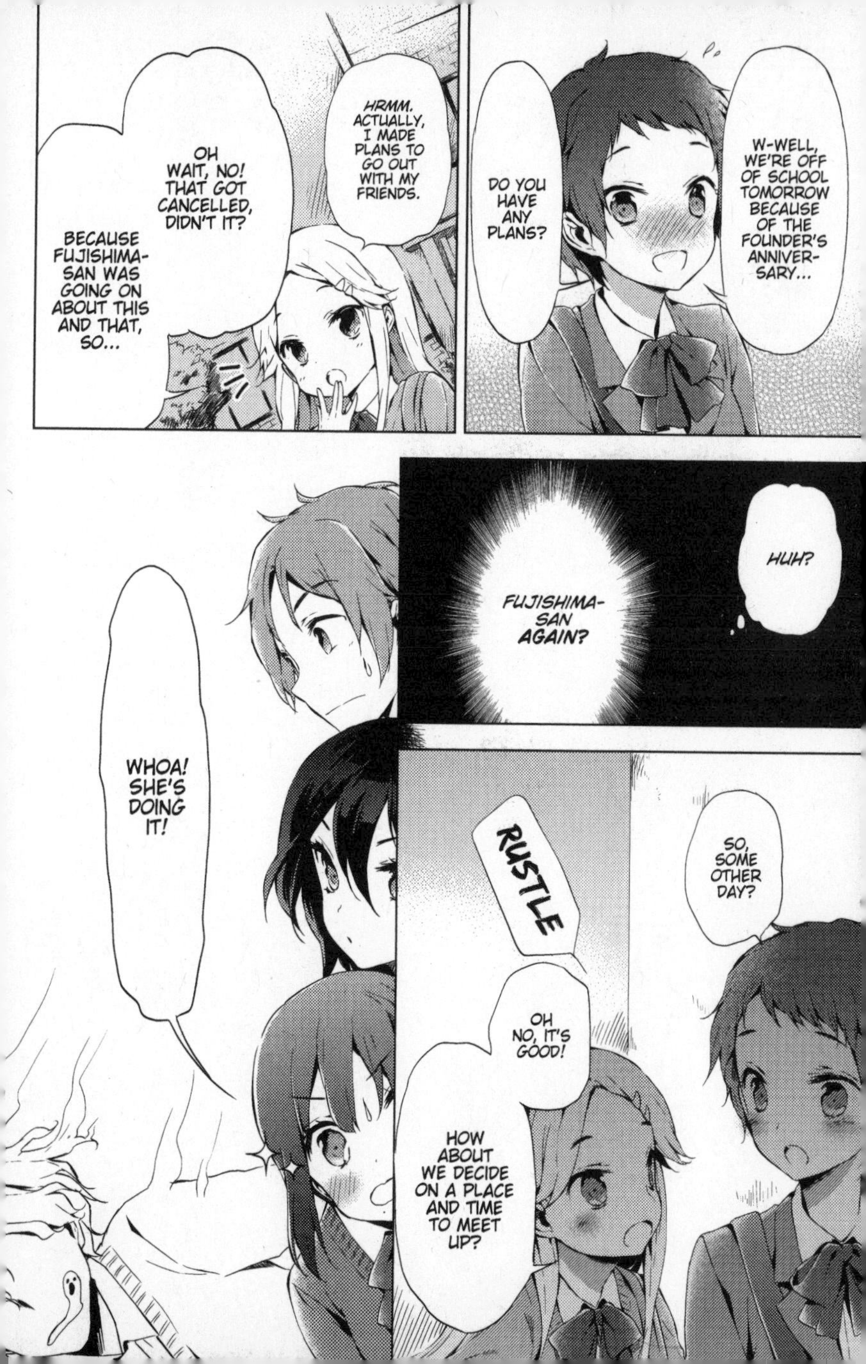
W-WELL, WE'RE OFF OF SCHOOL TOMORROW BECAUSE OF THE FOUNDER'S ANNIVERSARY...
DO YOU HAVE ANY PLANS?
HRMM. ACTUALLY, I MADE PLANS TO GO OUT WITH MY FRIENDS.
OH WAIT, NO! THAT GOT CANCELLED, DIDN'T IT?
BECAUSE FUJISHIMA-SAN WAS GOING ON ABOUT THIS AND THAT, SO...
HUH?
FUJISHIMA-SAN AGAIN?
SO, SOME OTHER DAY?
RUSTLE
OH NO, IT'S GOOD!
HOW ABOUT WE DECIDE ON A PLACE AND TIME TO MEET UP?
WHOA! SHE'S DOING IT!

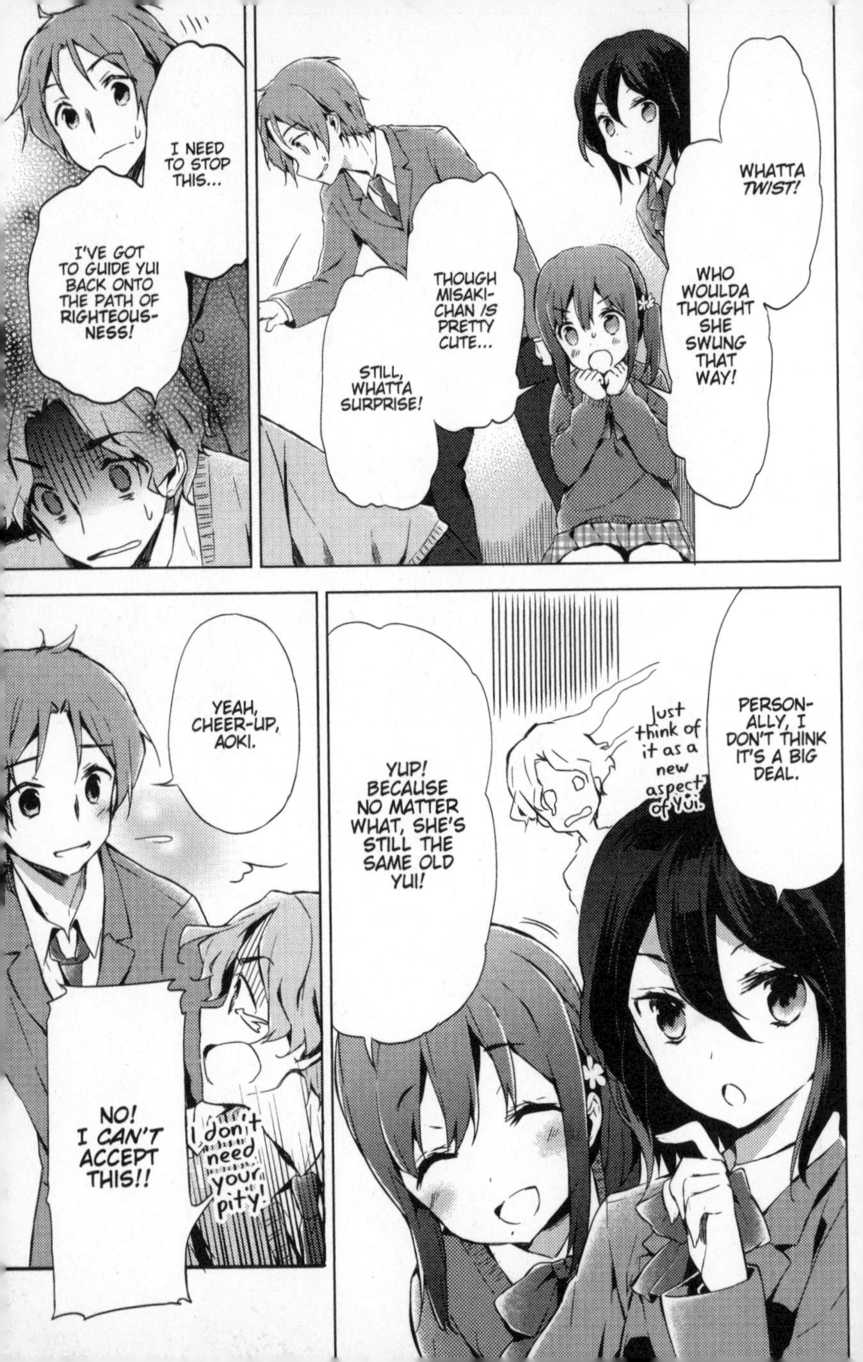
WHATTA *TWIST!*
WHO WOULDA THOUGHT SHE SWUNG THAT WAY!
THOUGH MISAKI-CHAN *IS* PRETTY CUTE...
STILL, WHATTA SURPRISE!
I NEED TO STOP THIS...
I'VE GOT TO GUIDE YUI BACK ONTO THE PATH OF RIGHTEOUSNESS!
PERSONALLY, I DON'T THINK IT'S A BIG DEAL.
Just think of it as a new aspect of Yui.
YUP! BECAUSE NO MATTER WHAT, SHE'S STILL THE SAME OLD YUI!
YEAH, CHEER-UP, AOKI.
NO! I *CAN'T* ACCEPT THIS!!
I don't need your pity!

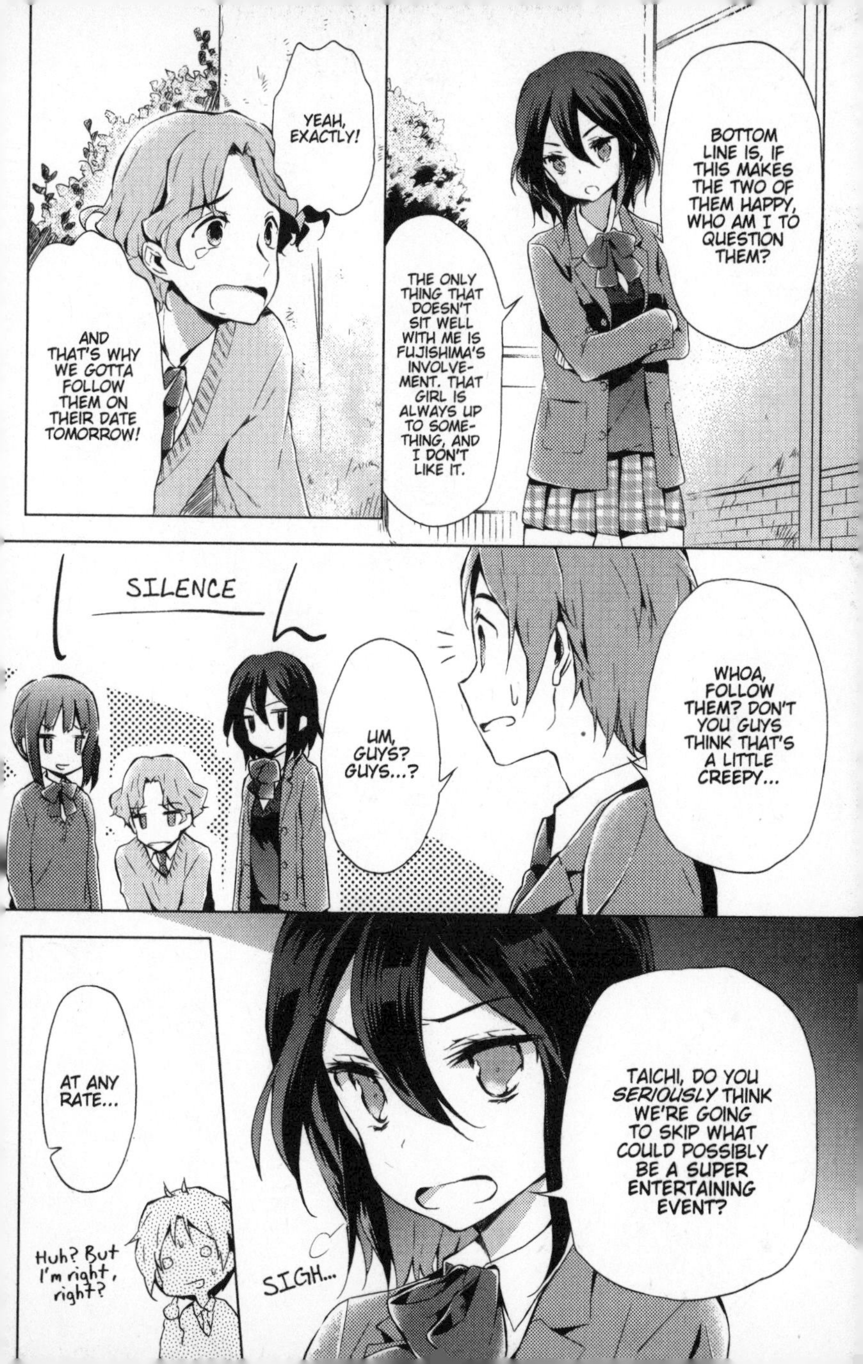
BOTTOM LINE IS, IF THIS MAKES THE TWO OF THEM HAPPY, WHO AM I TO QUESTION THEM?
THE ONLY THING THAT DOESN'T SIT WELL WITH ME IS FUJISHIMA'S INVOLVE-MENT. THAT GIRL IS ALWAYS UP TO SOME-THING, AND I DON'T LIKE IT.
YEAH, EXACTLY!
AND THAT'S WHY WE GOTTA FOLLOW THEM ON THEIR DATE TOMORROW!
WHOA, FOLLOW THEM? DON'T YOU GUYS THINK THAT'S A LITTLE CREEPY...
SILENCE
UM, GUYS? GUYS...?
TAICHI, DO YOU *SERIOUSLY* THINK WE'RE GOING TO SKIP WHAT COULD POSSIBLY BE A SUPER ENTERTAINING EVENT?
Huh? But I'm right, right?
SIGH...
AT ANY RATE...

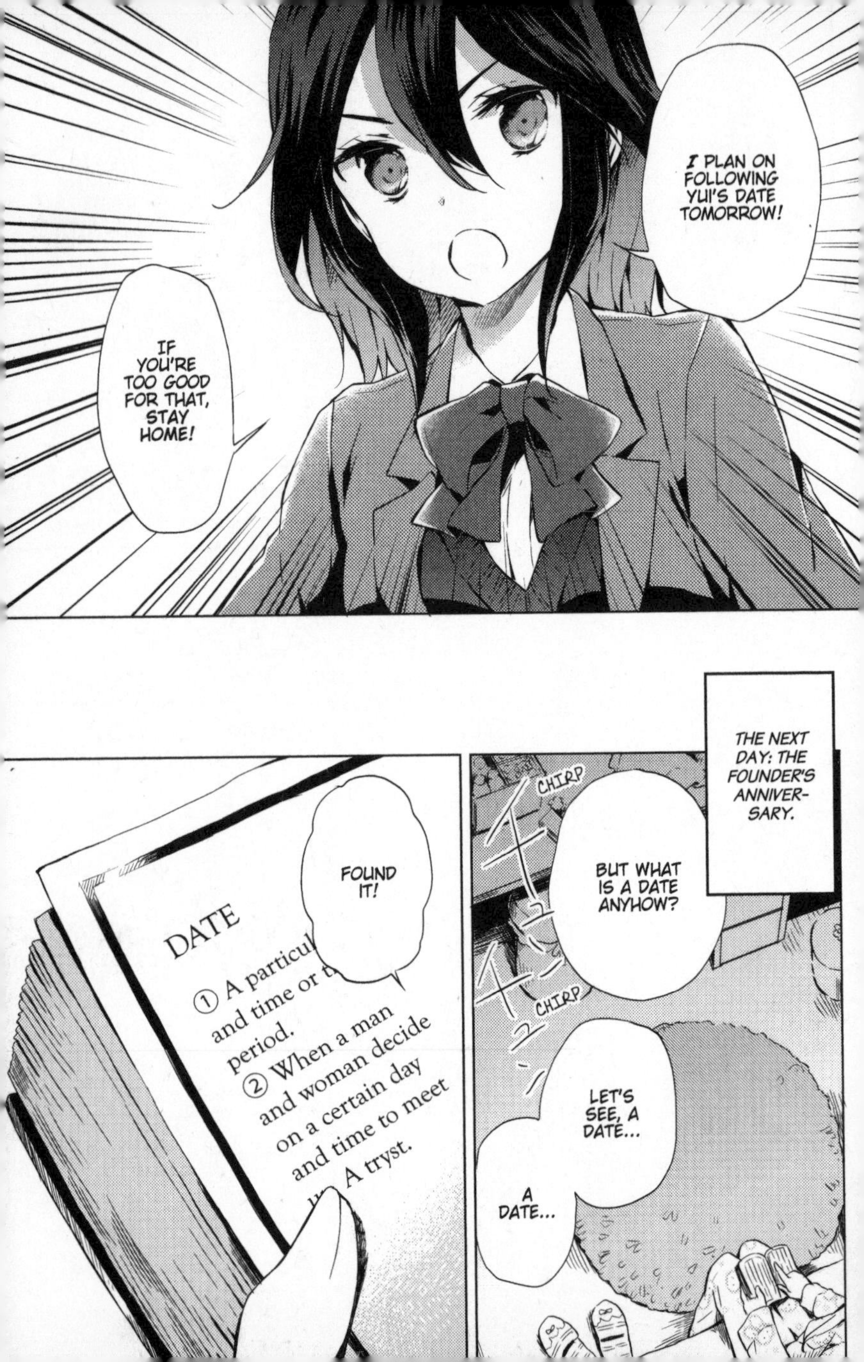
I PLAN ON FOLLOWING YUI'S DATE TOMORROW!
IF YOU'RE TOO GOOD FOR THAT, STAY HOME!
THE NEXT DAY: THE FOUNDER'S ANNIVER-SARY.
CHIRP
BUT WHAT IS A DATE ANYHOW?
CHIRP
LET'S SEE, A DATE...
A DATE...
FOUND IT!
DATE
① A particul
and time or t
period.
② When a man
and woman decide
on a certain day
and time to meet
A tryst.

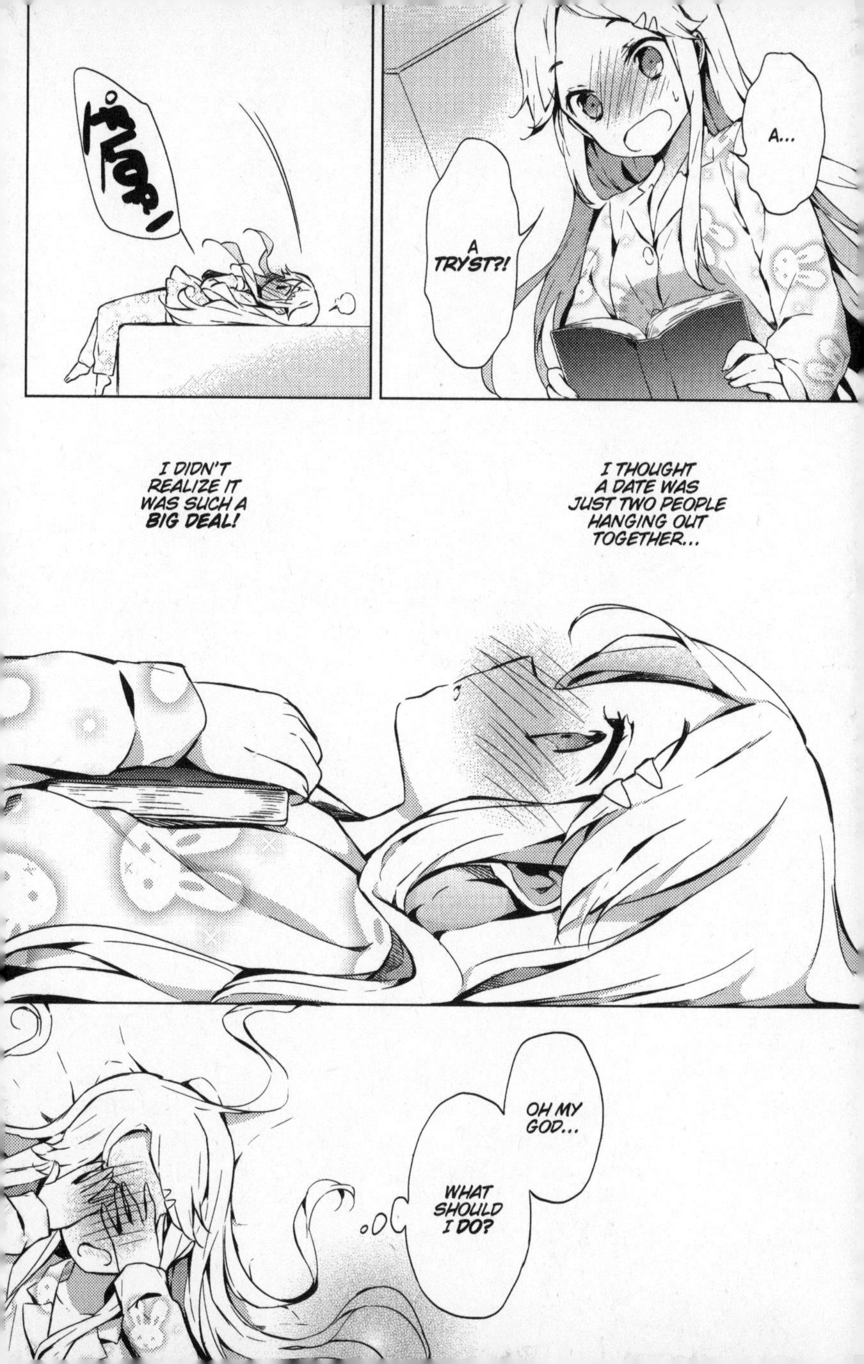
A...
A TRYST?!
PLOP!
I THOUGHT A DATE WAS JUST TWO PEOPLE HANGING OUT TOGETHER...
I DIDN'T REALIZE IT WAS SUCH A BIG DEAL!
OH MY GOD...
WHAT SHOULD I DO?

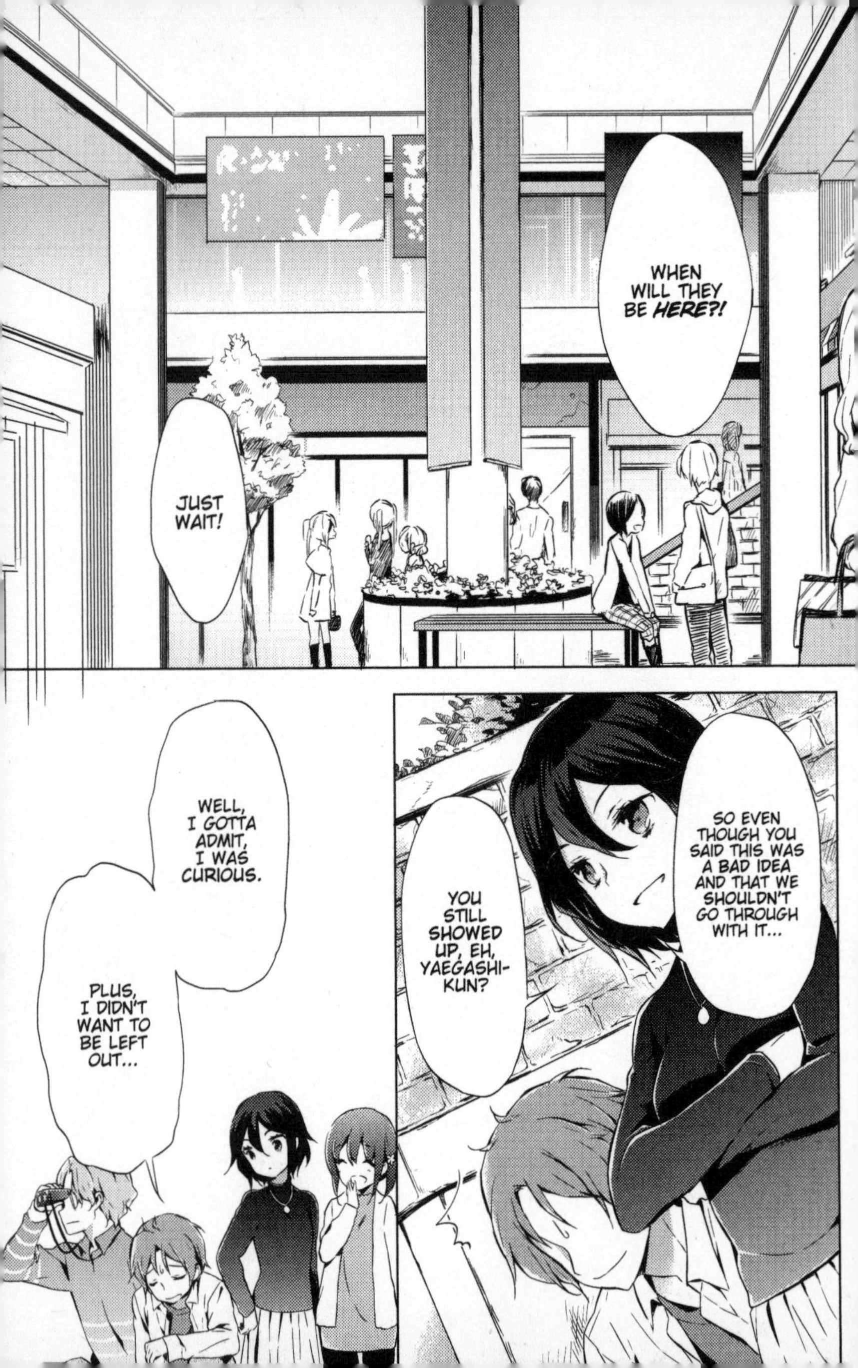
WHEN WILL THEY BE *HERE?!*
JUST WAIT!
SO EVEN THOUGH YOU SAID THIS WAS A BAD IDEA AND THAT WE SHOULDN'T GO THROUGH WITH IT...
YOU STILL SHOWED UP, EH, YAEGASHI-KUN?
WELL, I GOTTA ADMIT, I WAS CURIOUS.
PLUS, I DIDN'T WANT TO BE LEFT OUT...

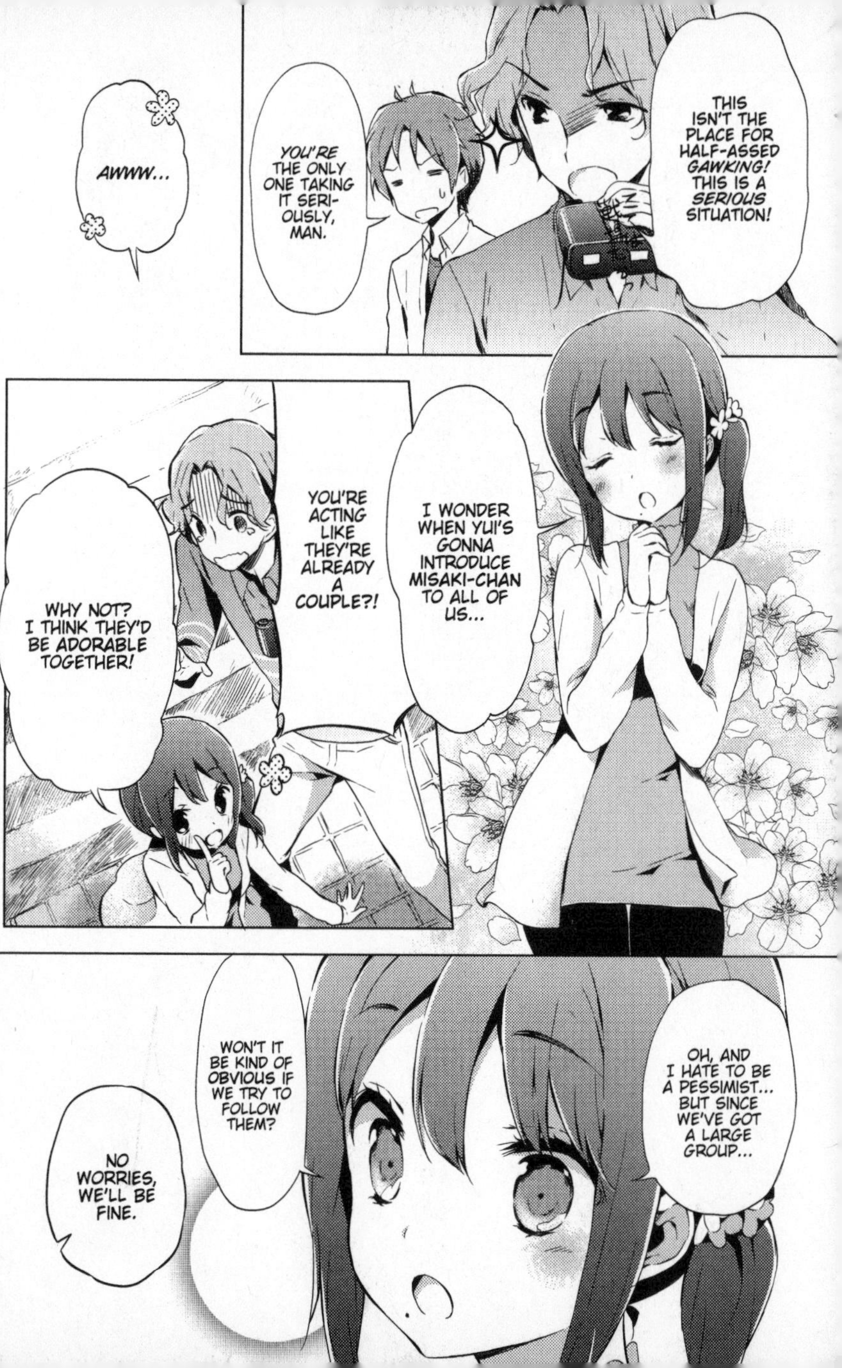
THIS ISN'T THE PLACE FOR HALF-ASSED GAWKING! THIS IS A SERIOUS SITUATION!
YOU'RE THE ONLY ONE TAKING IT SERI-OUSLY, MAN.
AWWW...
I WONDER WHEN YUI'S GONNA INTRODUCE MISAKI-CHAN TO ALL OF US...
YOU'RE ACTING LIKE THEY'RE ALREADY A COUPLE?!
WHY NOT? I THINK THEY'D BE ADORABLE TOGETHER!
OH, AND I HATE TO BE A PESSIMIST... BUT SINCE WE'VE GOT A LARGE GROUP...
WON'T IT BE KIND OF OBVIOUS IF WE TRY TO FOLLOW THEM?
NO WORRIES, WE'LL BE FINE.

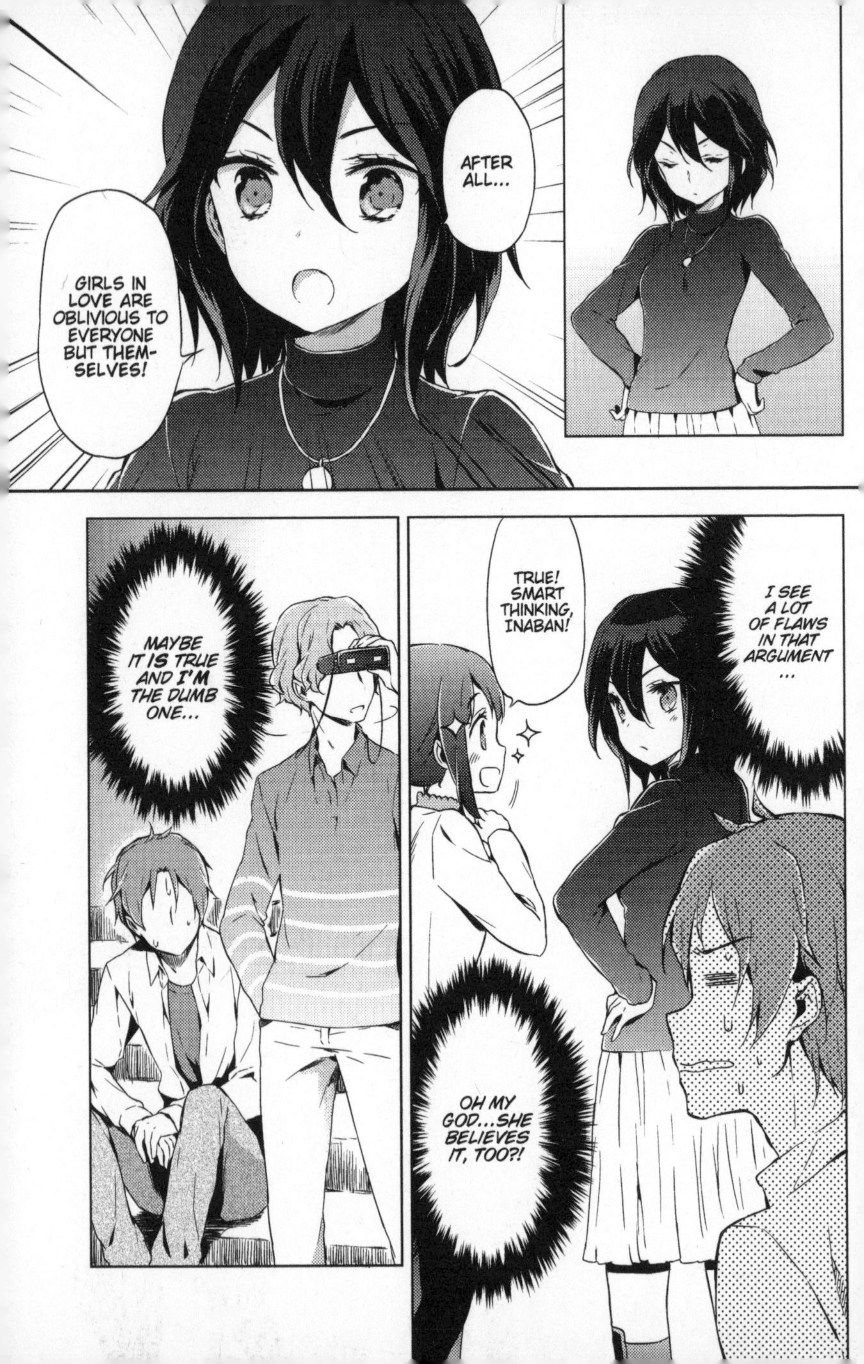
AFTER ALL...
GIRLS IN LOVE ARE OBLIVIOUS TO EVERYONE BUT THEM-SELVES!
TRUE! SMART THINKING, INABAN!
I SEE A LOT OF FLAWS IN THAT ARGUMENT...
OH MY GOD...SHE BELIEVES IT, TOO?!
MAYBE IT IS TRUE AND I'M THE DUMB ONE...

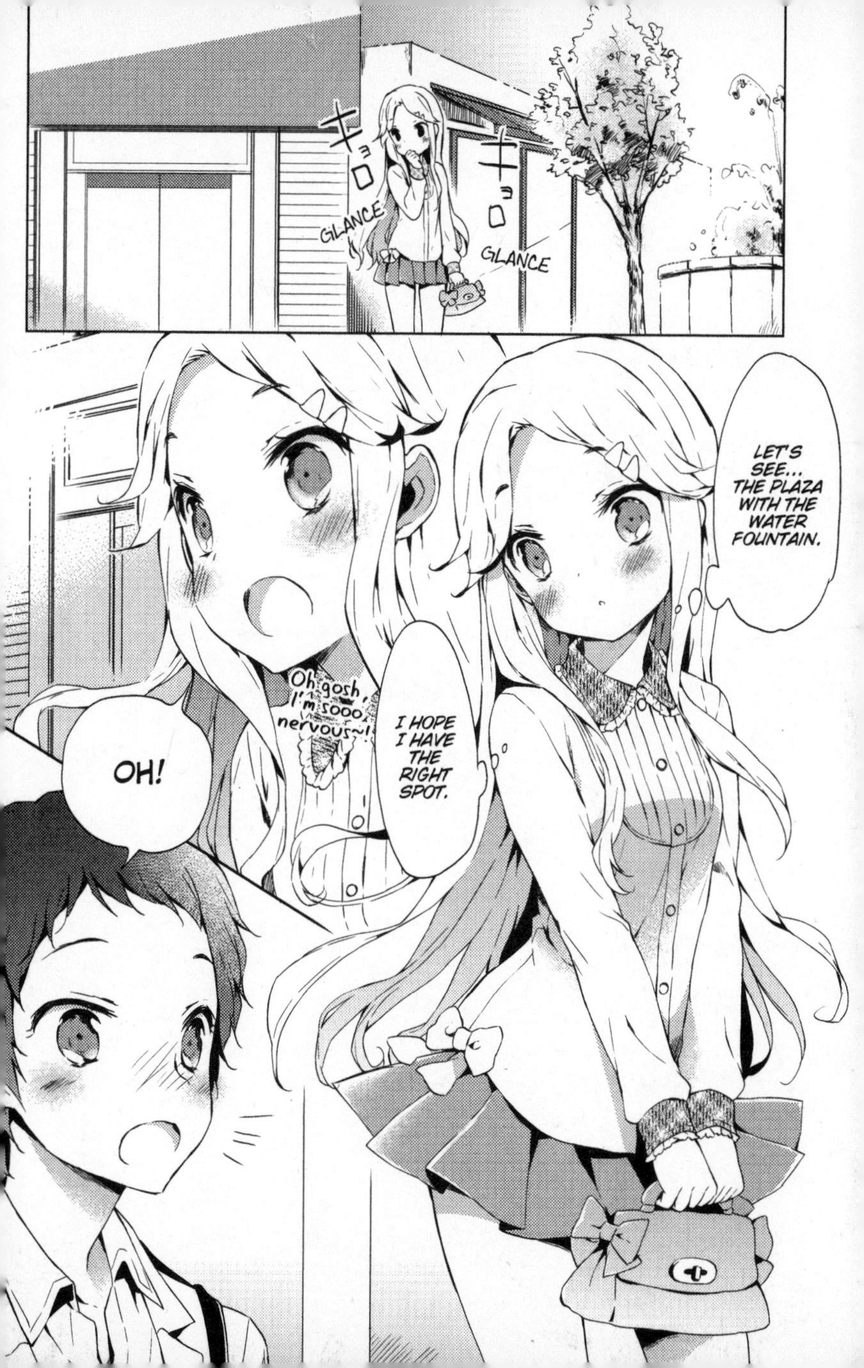
キョロ
GLANCE
キョロ
GLANCE
LET'S SEE... THE PLAZA WITH THE WATER FOUNTAIN.
I HOPE I HAVE THE RIGHT SPOT.
Oh gosh, I'm sooo nervous~!
OH!

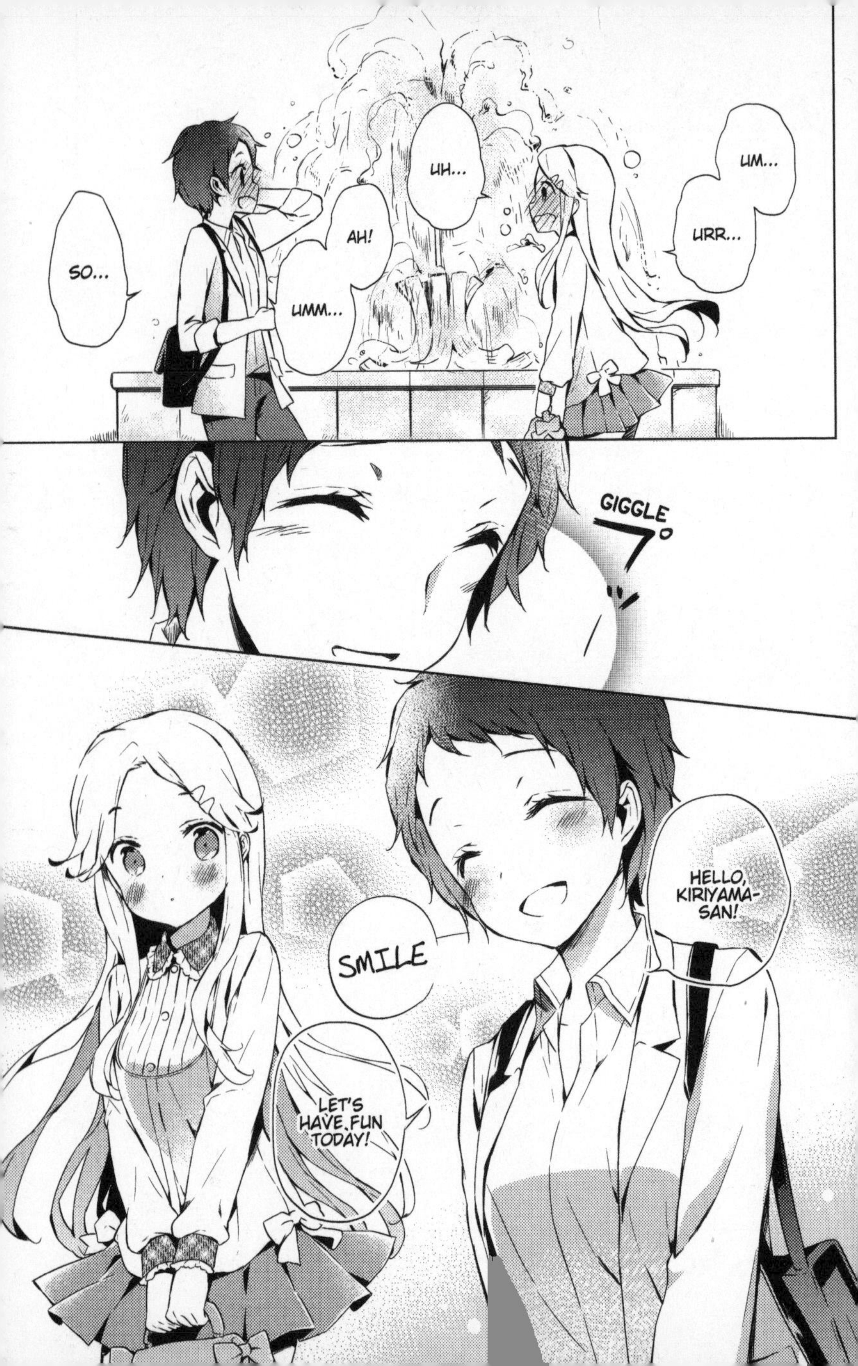
UM... URR...
UH...
AH! UMM...
SO...
GIGGLE
HELLO, KIRIYAMA-SAN!
SMILE
LET'S HAVE FUN TODAY!

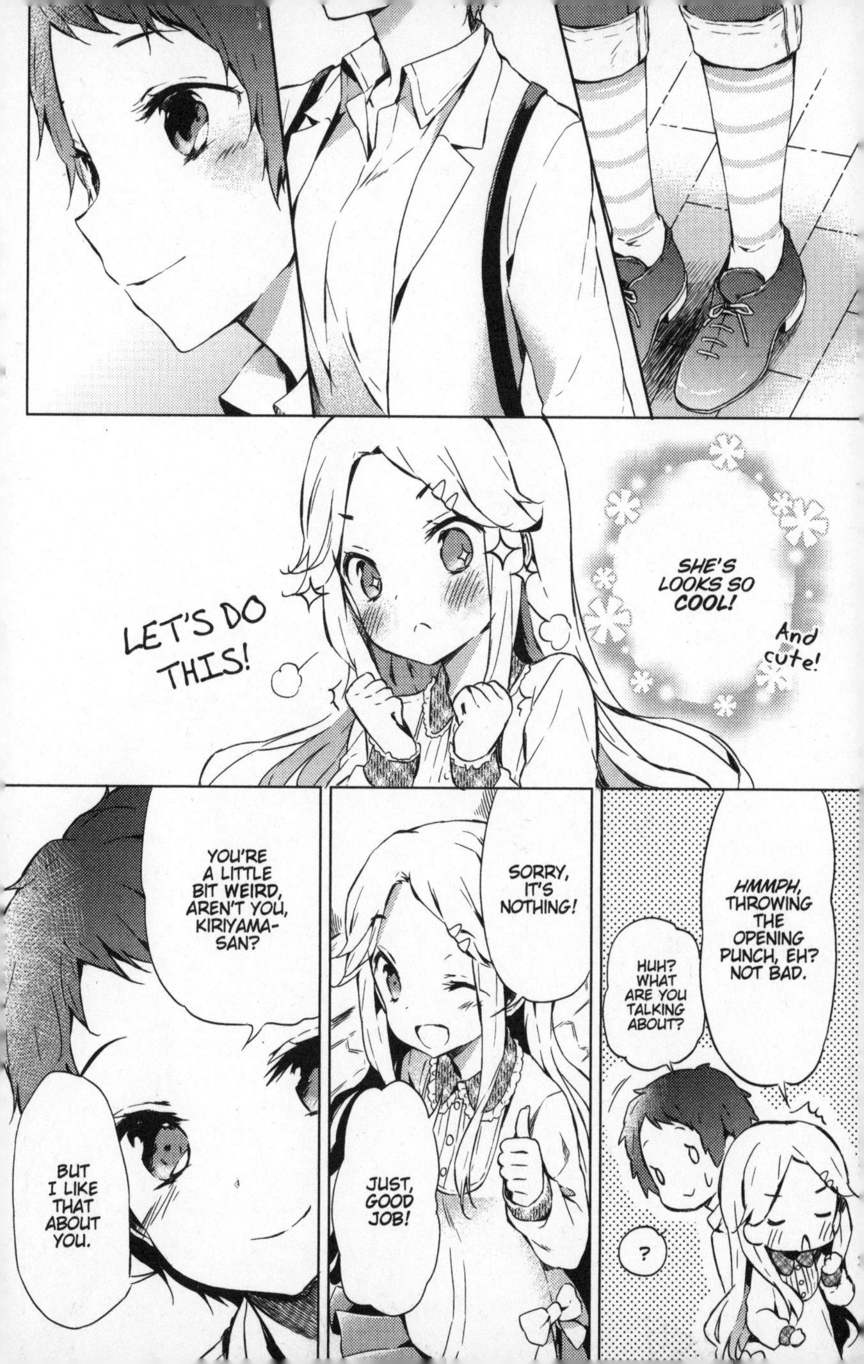
SHE'S LOOKS SO COOL!
And cute!
LET'S DO THIS!
HMMPH, THROWING THE OPENING PUNCH, EH? NOT BAD.
HUH? WHAT ARE YOU TALKING ABOUT?
?
SORRY, IT'S NOTHING!
JUST, GOOD JOB!
YOU'RE A LITTLE BIT WEIRD, AREN'T YOU, KIRIYAMA-SAN?
BUT I LIKE THAT ABOUT YOU.

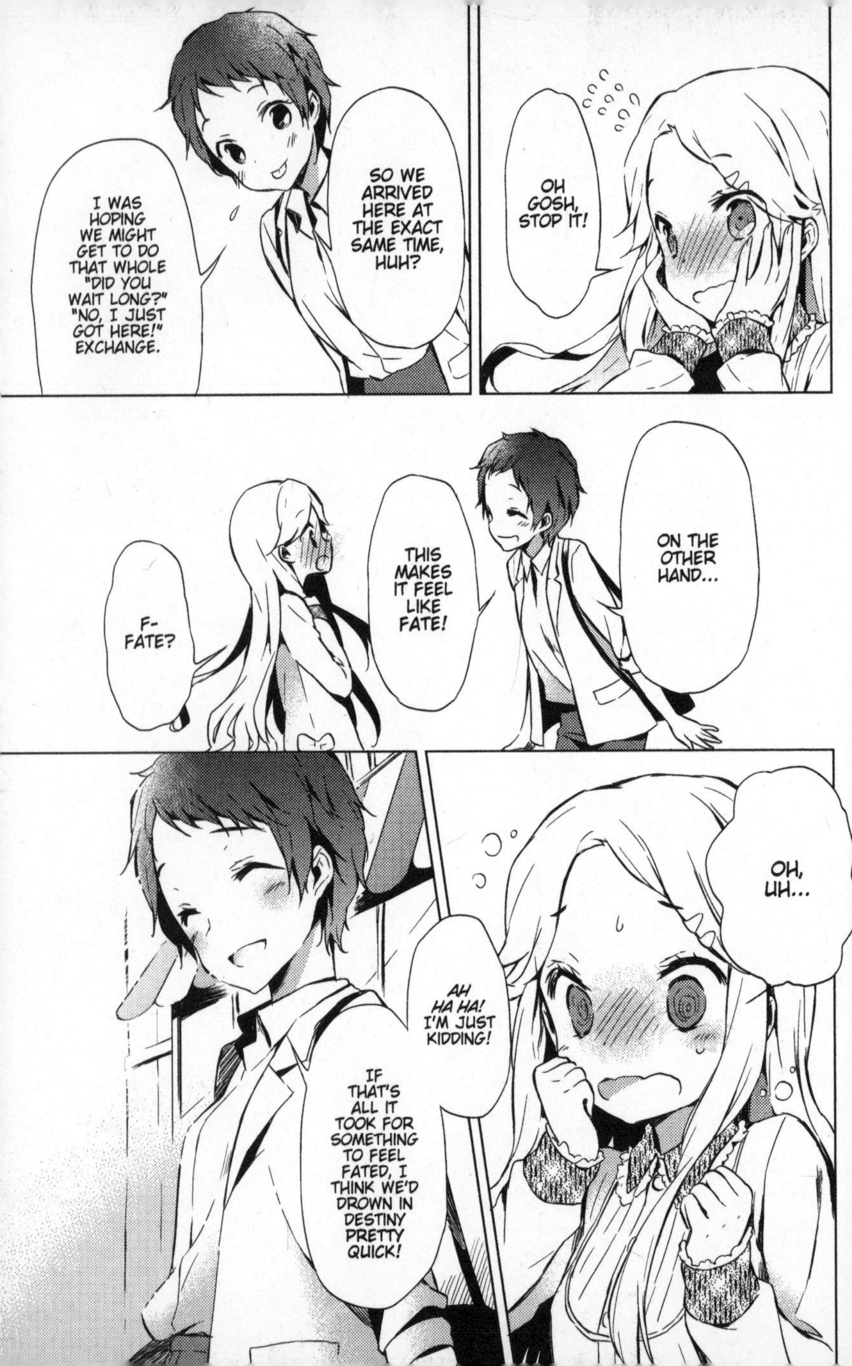
OH GOSH, STOP IT!
SO WE ARRIVED HERE AT THE EXACT SAME TIME, HUH?
I WAS HOPING WE MIGHT GET TO DO THAT WHOLE "DID YOU WAIT LONG?" "NO, I JUST GOT HERE!" EXCHANGE.
ON THE OTHER HAND...
THIS MAKES IT FEEL LIKE FATE!
F-FATE?
OH, UH...
AH HA HA! I'M JUST KIDDING!
IF THAT'S ALL IT TOOK FOR SOMETHING TO FEEL FATED, I THINK WE'D DROWN IN DESTINY PRETTY QUICK!

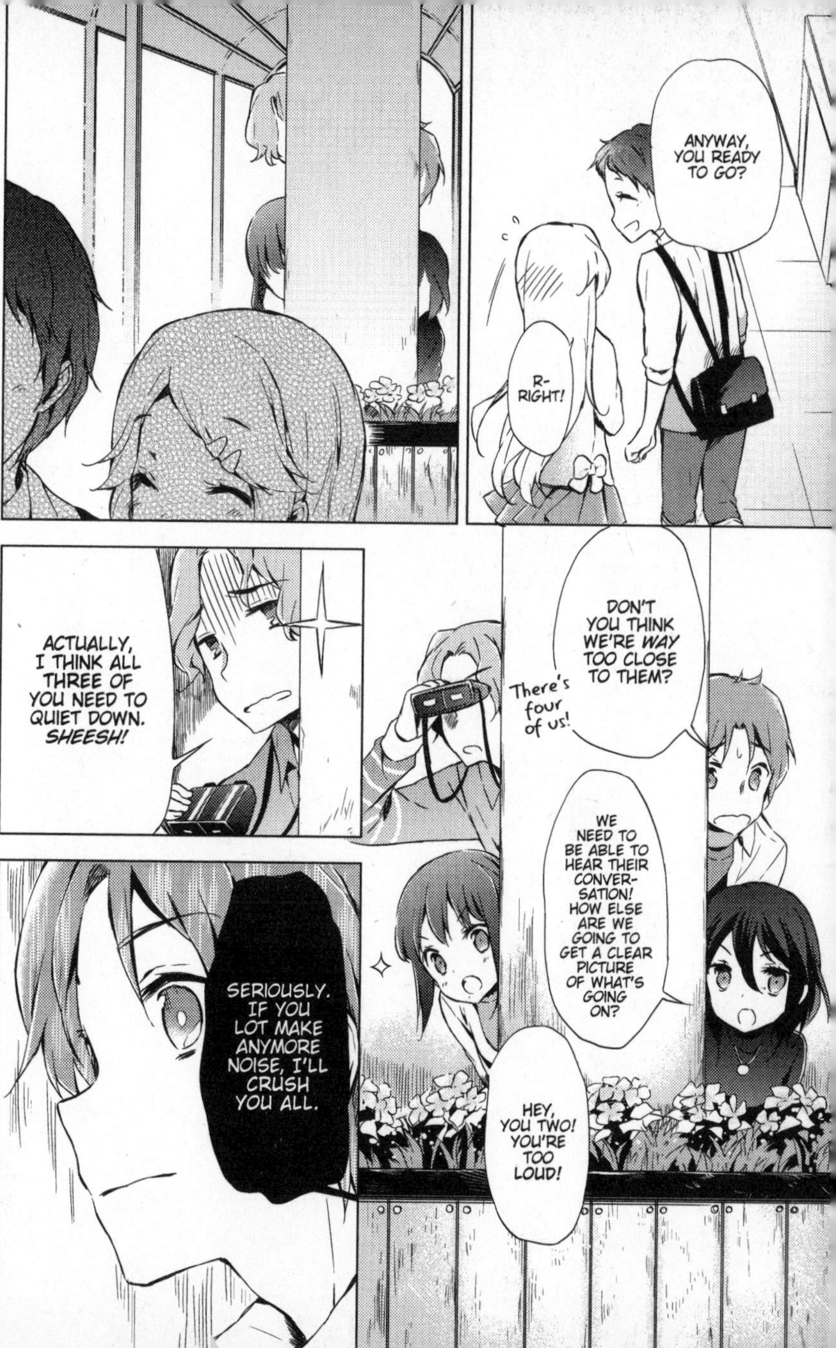
ANYWAY, YOU READY TO GO?
R-RIGHT!
DON'T YOU THINK WE'RE *WAY* TOO CLOSE TO THEM?
There's four of us!
WE NEED TO BE ABLE TO HEAR THEIR CONVER-SATION! HOW ELSE ARE WE GOING TO GET A CLEAR PICTURE OF WHAT'S GOING ON?
HEY, YOU TWO! YOU'RE TOO LOUD!
ACTUALLY, I THINK ALL THREE OF YOU NEED TO QUIET DOWN. *SHEESH!*
SERIOUSLY. IF YOU LOT MAKE ANYMORE NOISE, I'LL CRUSH YOU ALL.

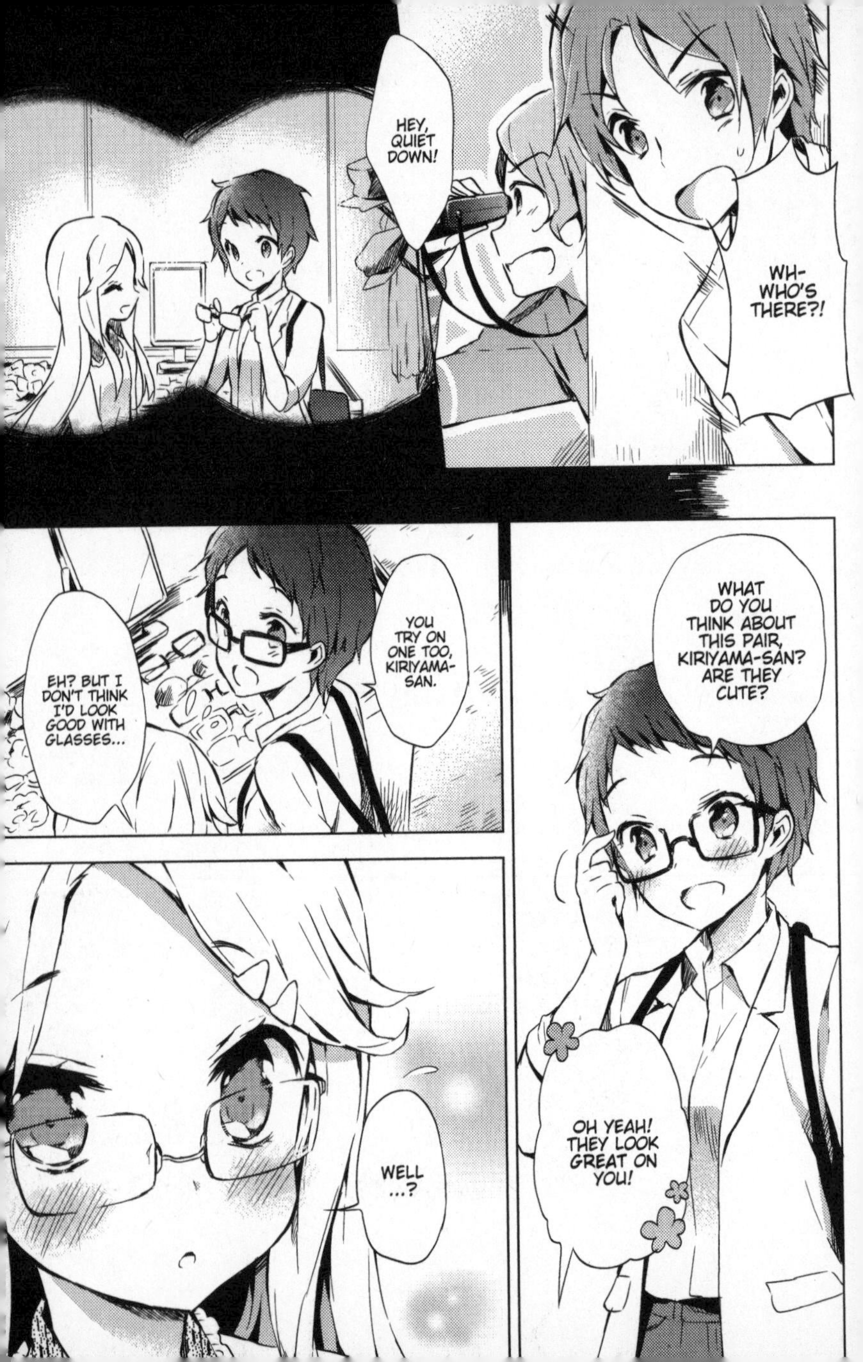
WH- WHO'S THERE?!
HEY, QUIET DOWN!
WHAT DO YOU THINK ABOUT THIS PAIR, KIRIYAMA-SAN? ARE THEY CUTE?
OH YEAH! THEY LOOK GREAT ON YOU!
YOU TRY ON ONE TOO, KIRIYAMA-SAN.
EH? BUT I DON'T THINK I'D LOOK GOOD WITH GLASSES...
WELL ...?

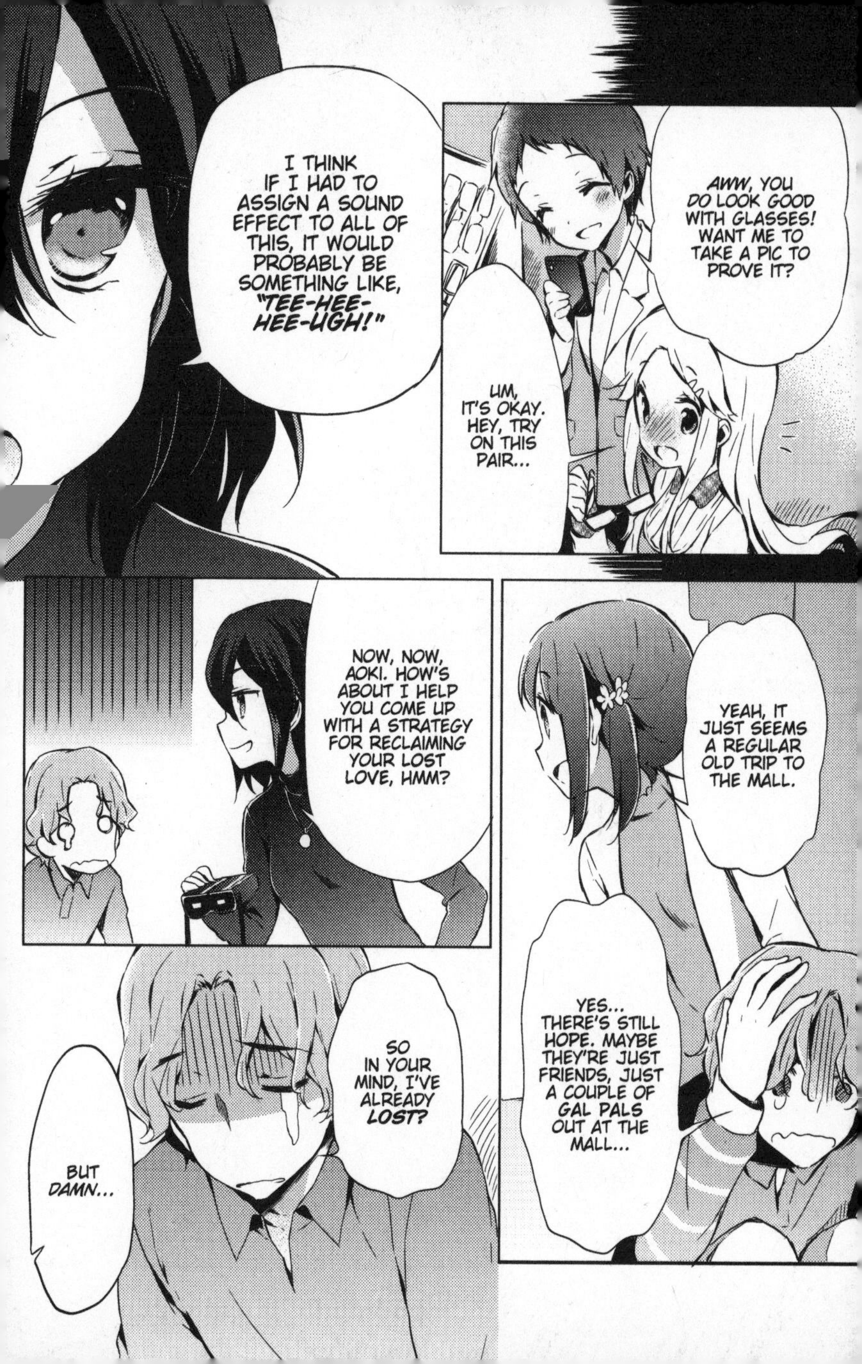
AWW, YOU DO LOOK GOOD WITH GLASSES! WANT ME TO TAKE A PIC TO PROVE IT?
UM, IT'S OKAY. HEY, TRY ON THIS PAIR...
I THINK IF I HAD TO ASSIGN A SOUND EFFECT TO ALL OF THIS, IT WOULD PROBABLY BE SOMETHING LIKE, "TEE-HEE-HEE-UGH!"
YEAH, IT JUST SEEMS A REGULAR OLD TRIP TO THE MALL.
YES... THERE'S STILL HOPE. MAYBE THEY'RE JUST FRIENDS, JUST A COUPLE OF GAL PALS OUT AT THE MALL...
NOW, NOW, AOKI. HOW'S ABOUT I HELP YOU COME UP WITH A STRATEGY FOR RECLAIMING YOUR LOST LOVE, HMM?
SO IN YOUR MIND, I'VE ALREADY LOST?
BUT DAMN...

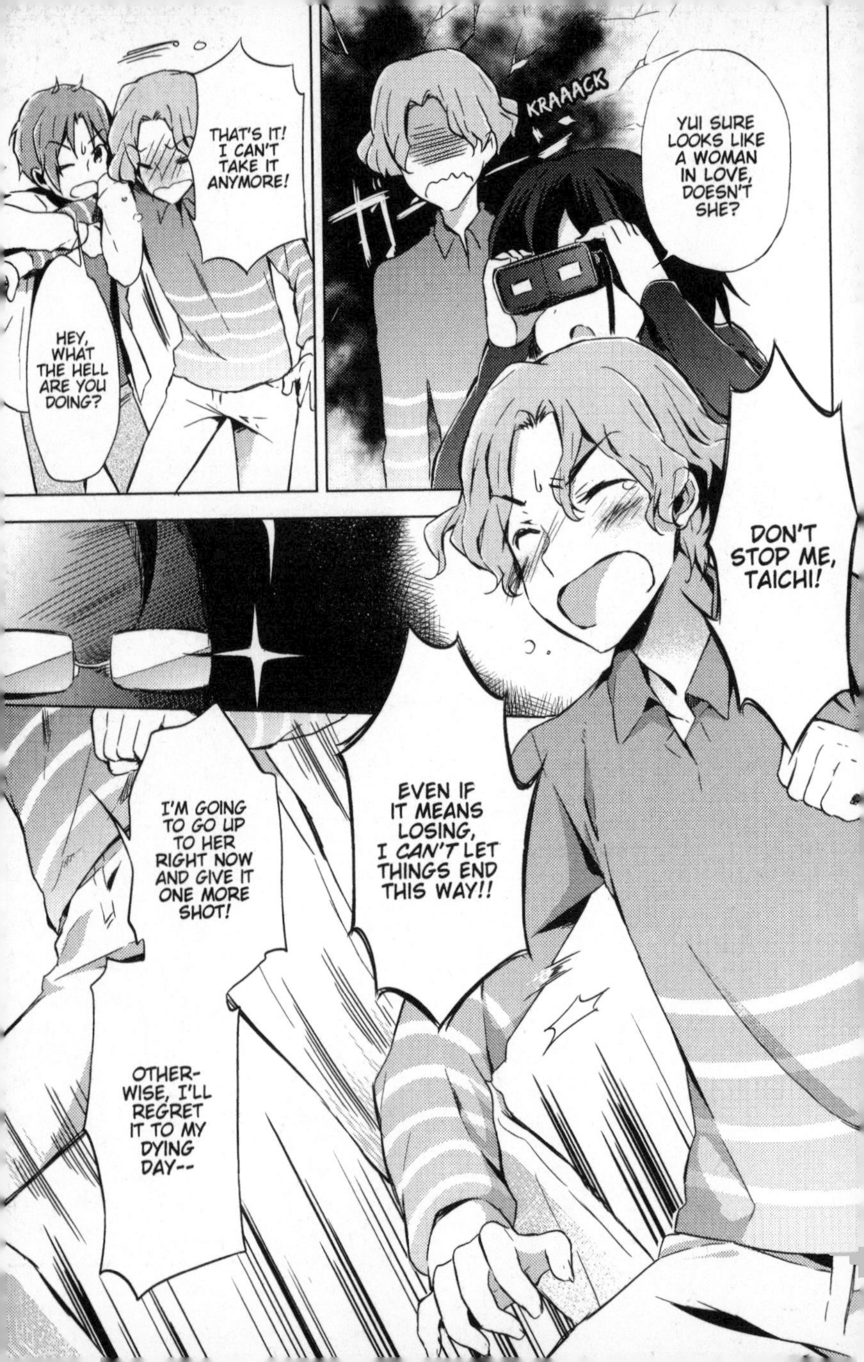
YUI SURE LOOKS LIKE A WOMAN IN LOVE, DOESN'T SHE?
KRAAACK
THAT'S IT! I CAN'T TAKE IT ANYMORE!
HEY, WHAT THE HELL ARE YOU DOING?
DON'T STOP ME, TAICHI!
EVEN IF IT MEANS LOSING, I *CAN'T* LET THINGS END THIS WAY!!
I'M GOING TO GO UP TO HER RIGHT NOW AND GIVE IT ONE MORE SHOT!
OTHER-WISE, I'LL REGRET IT TO MY DYING DAY--

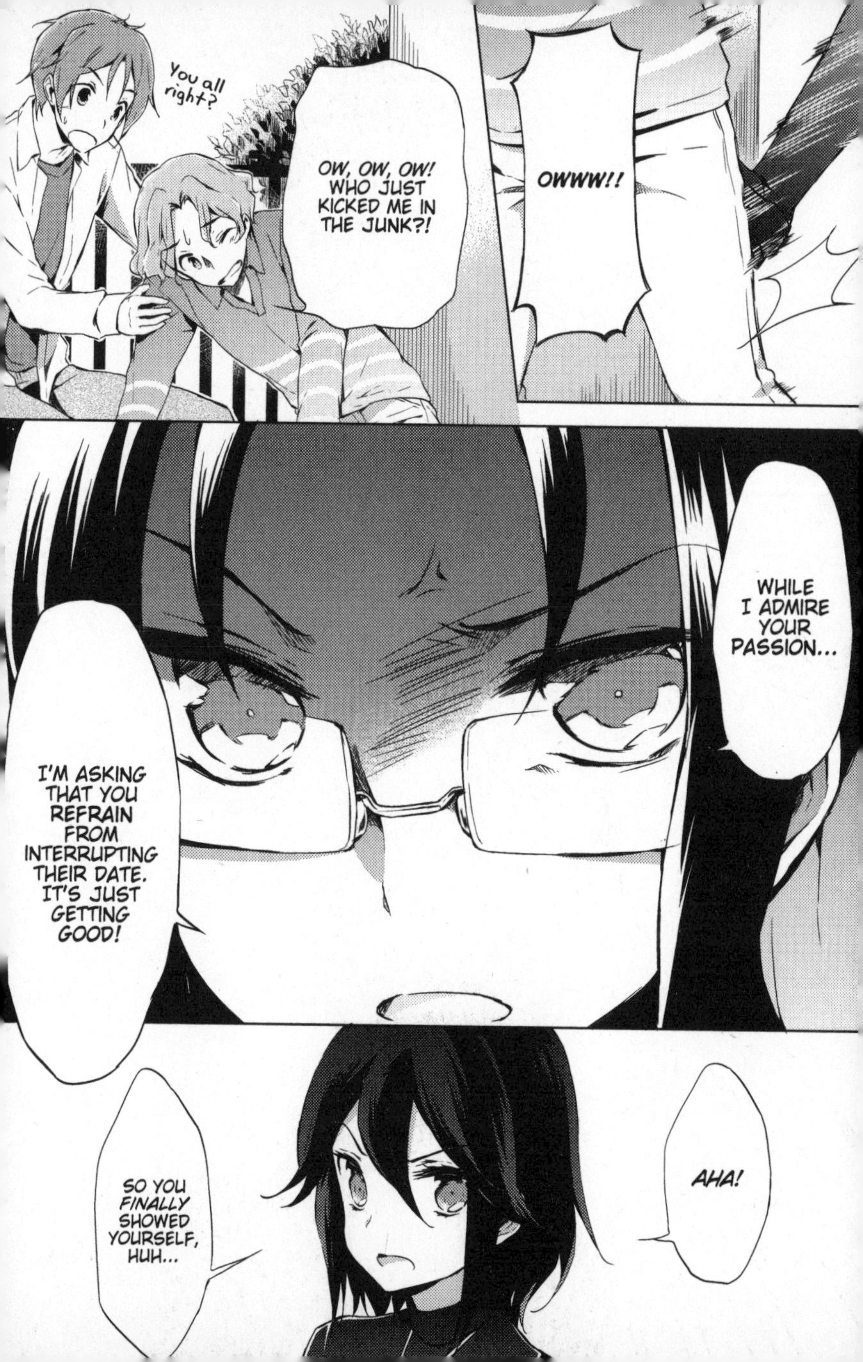
OWWW!!
OW, OW, OW! WHO JUST KICKED ME IN THE JUNK?!
You all right?
WHILE I ADMIRE YOUR PASSION...
I'M ASKING THAT YOU REFRAIN FROM INTERRUPTING THEIR DATE. IT'S JUST GETTING GOOD!
AHA!
SO YOU FINALLY SHOWED YOURSELF, HUH...

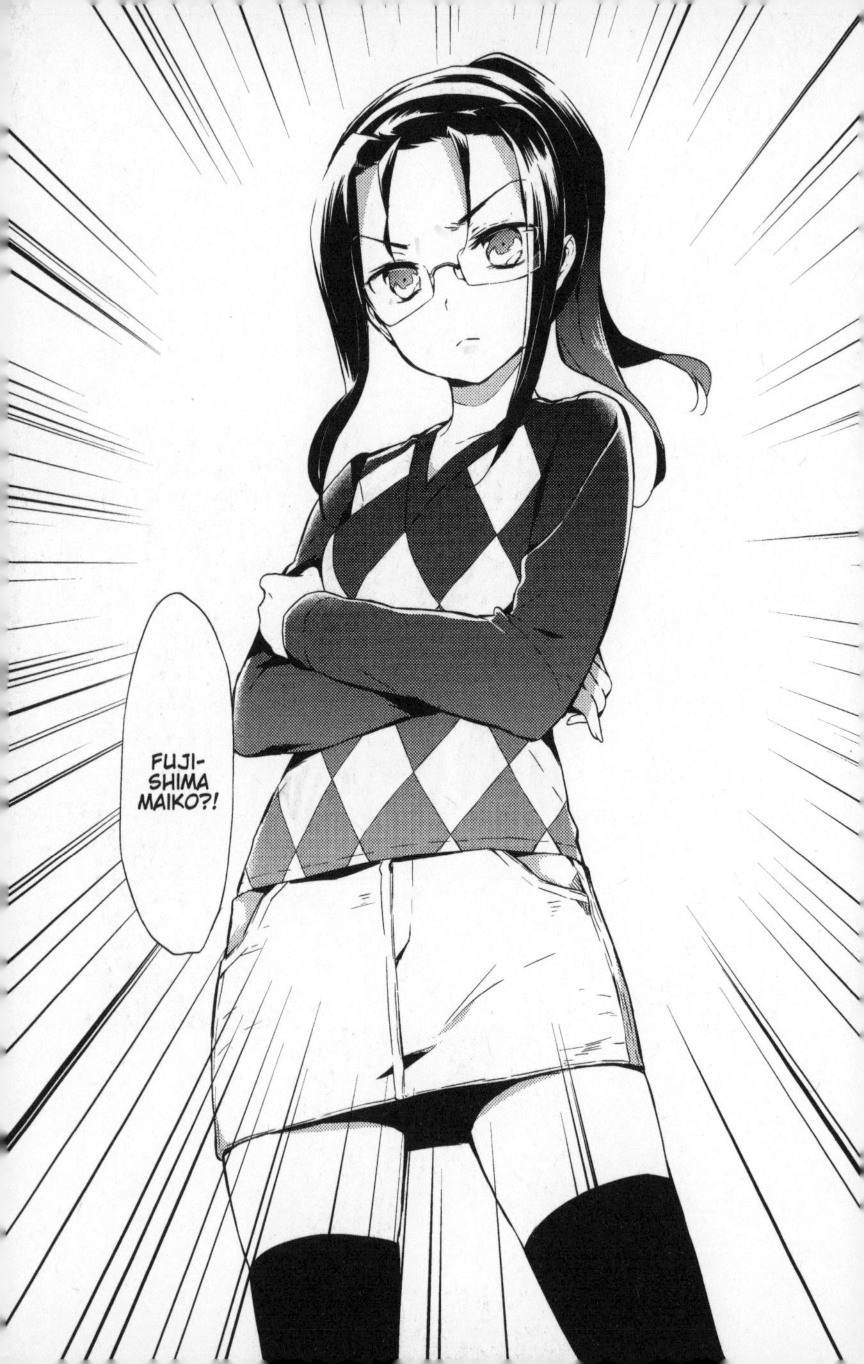
FUJI-SHIMA MAIKO?!

KOKORO CONNECT

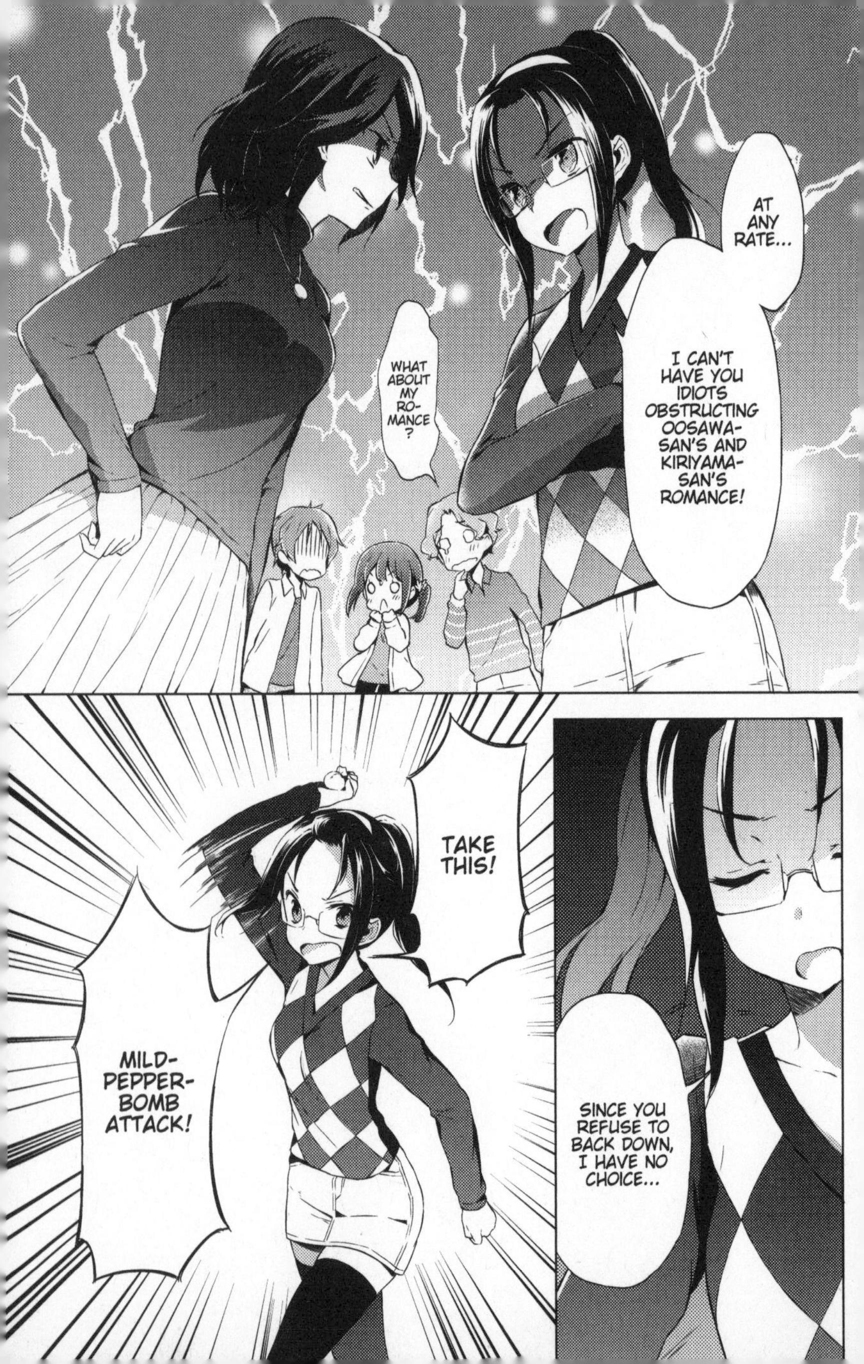
AT ANY RATE...
I CAN'T HAVE YOU IDIOTS OBSTRUCTING OOSAWA-SAN'S AND KIRIYAMA-SAN'S ROMANCE!
WHAT ABOUT MY RO-MANCE?
SINCE YOU REFUSE TO BACK DOWN, I HAVE NO CHOICE...
TAKE THIS!
MILD-PEPPER-BOMB ATTACK!

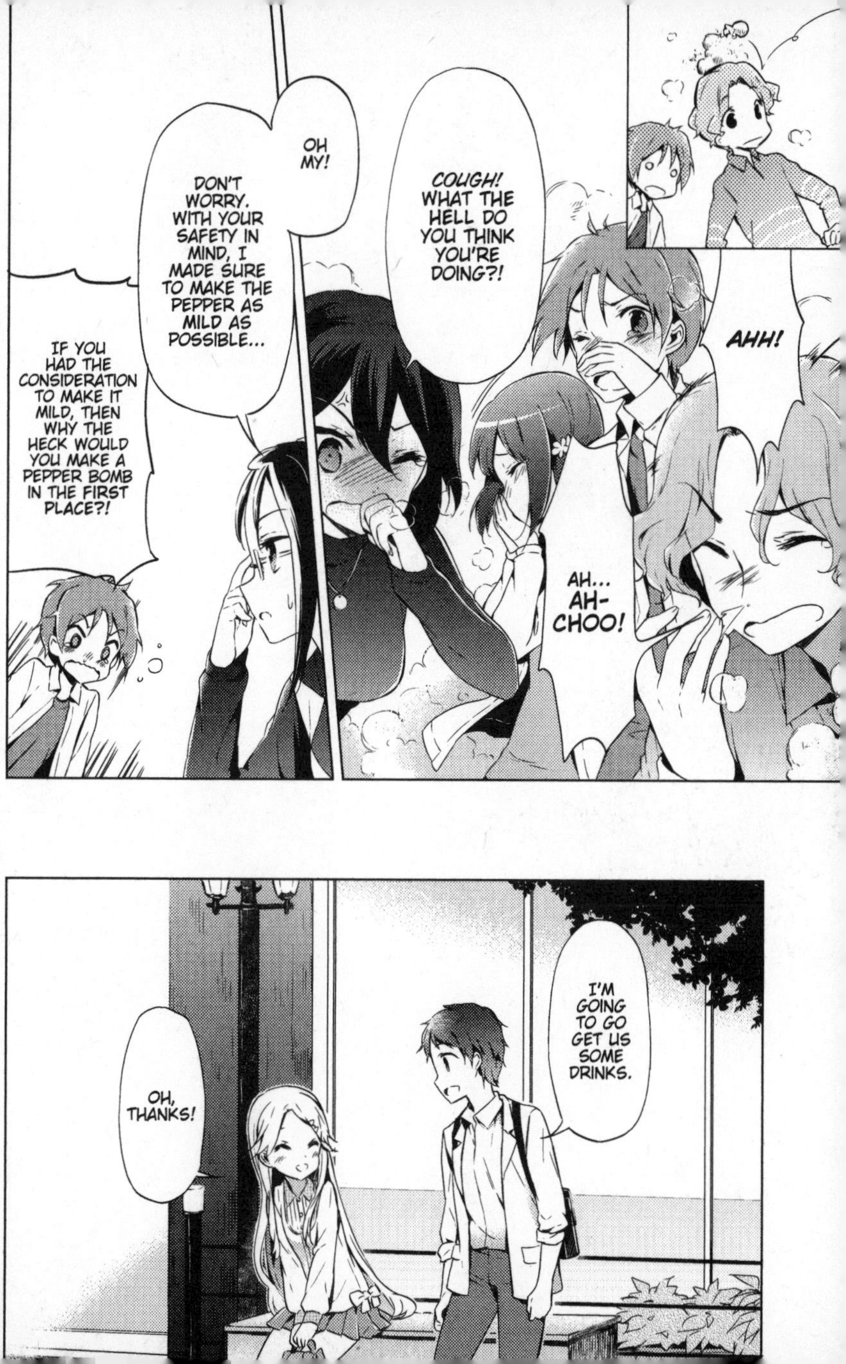
AHH!
COUGH! WHAT THE HELL DO YOU THINK YOU'RE DOING?!
AH... AH-CHOO!
OH MY!
DON'T WORRY. WITH YOUR SAFETY IN MIND, I MADE SURE TO MAKE THE PEPPER AS MILD AS POSSIBLE...
IF YOU HAD THE CONSIDERATION TO MAKE IT MILD, THEN WHY THE HECK WOULD YOU MAKE A PEPPER BOMB IN THE FIRST PLACE?!
I'M GOING TO GO GET US SOME DRINKS.
OH, THANKS!

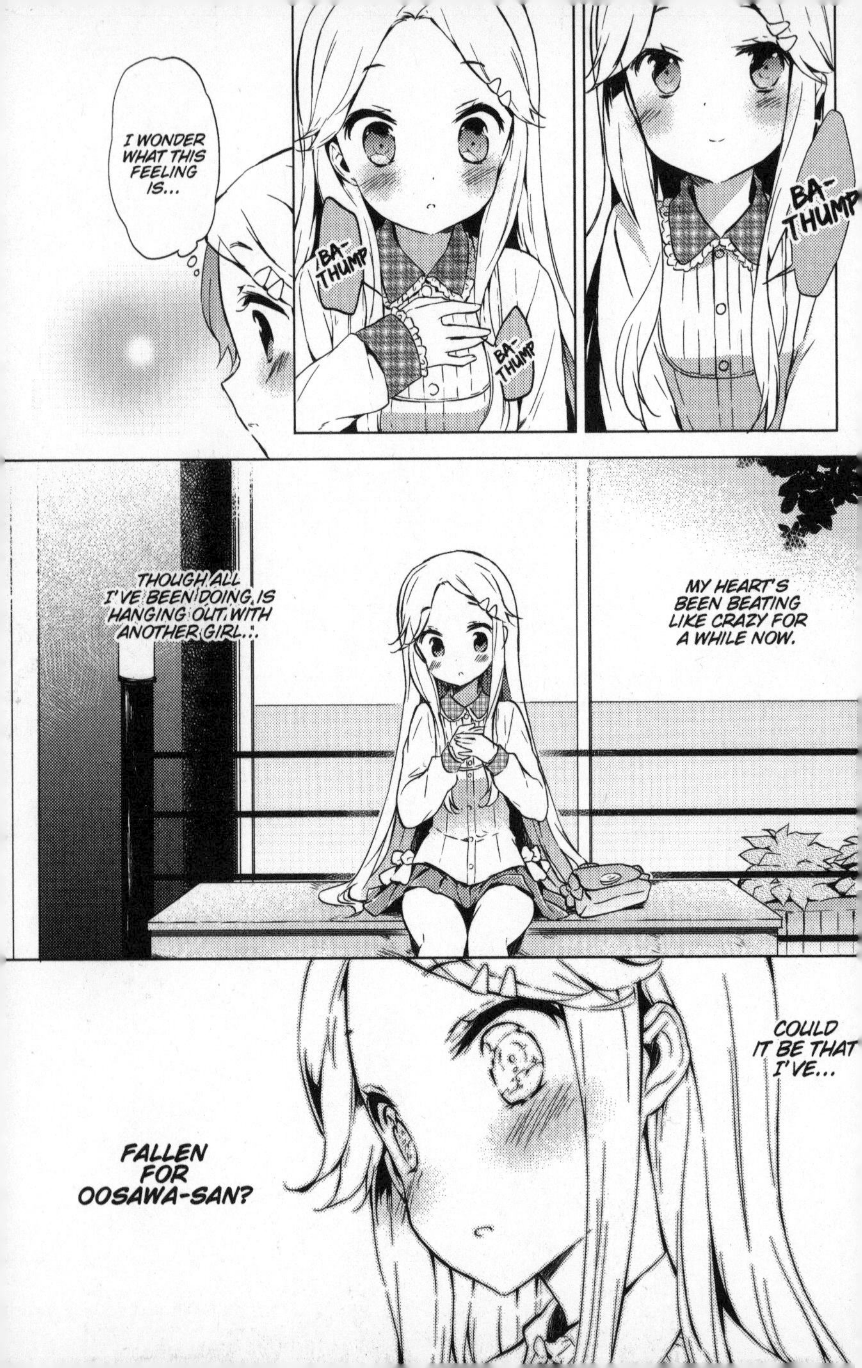
BA-THUMP
BA-THUMP
BA-THUMP
I WONDER WHAT THIS FEELING IS...
MY HEART'S BEEN BEATING LIKE CRAZY FOR A WHILE NOW.
THOUGH ALL I'VE BEEN DOING IS HANGING OUT WITH ANOTHER GIRL...
COULD IT BE THAT I'VE...
FALLEN FOR OOSAWA-SAN?

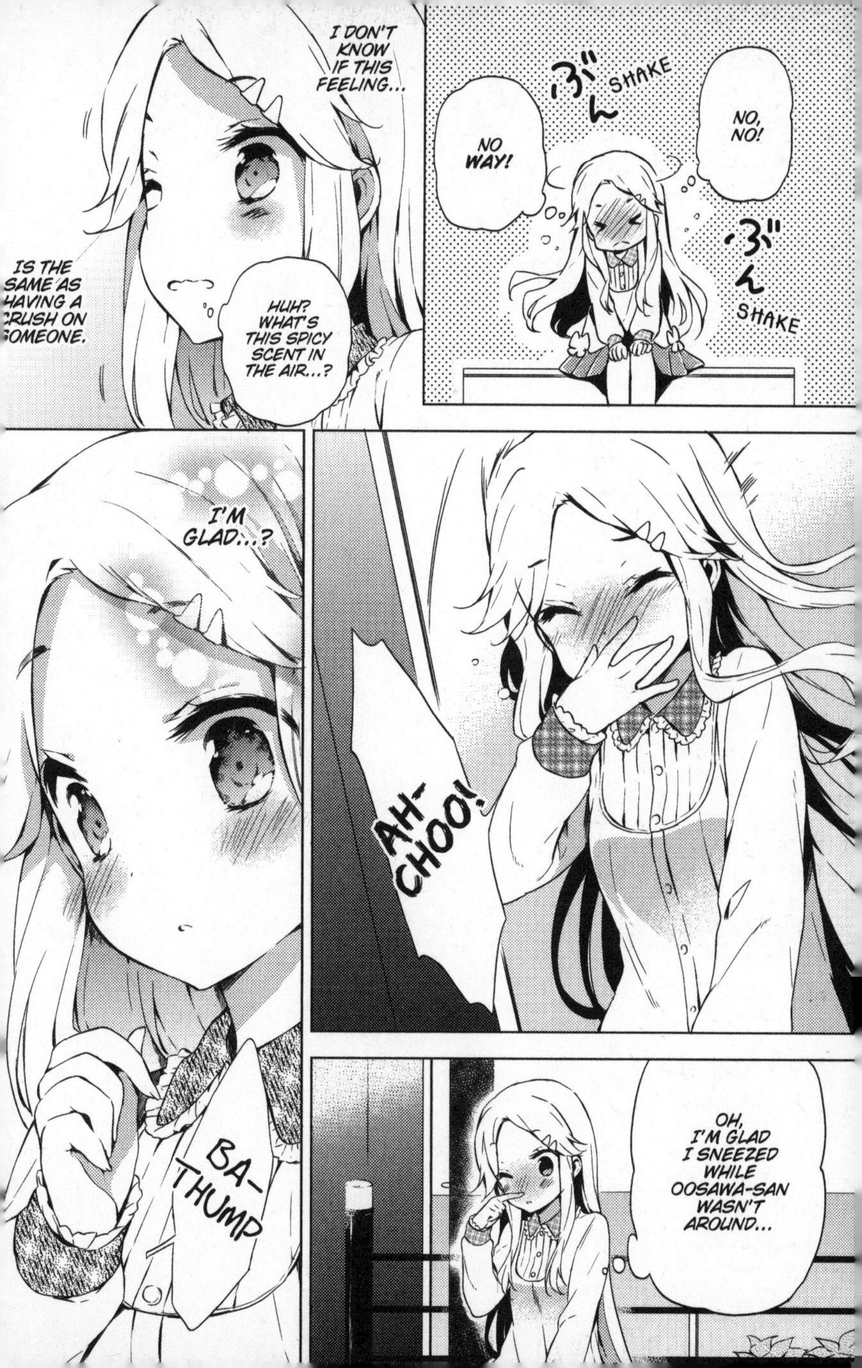
NO, NO!
ぶん SHAKE
NO WAY!
ぶん SHAKE
I DON'T KNOW IF THIS FEELING...
IS THE SAME AS HAVING A CRUSH ON SOMEONE.
HUH? WHAT'S THIS SPICY SCENT IN THE AIR...?
AH-CHOO!
OH, I'M GLAD I SNEEZED WHILE OOSAWA-SAN WASN'T AROUND...
I'M GLAD...?
BA-THUMP

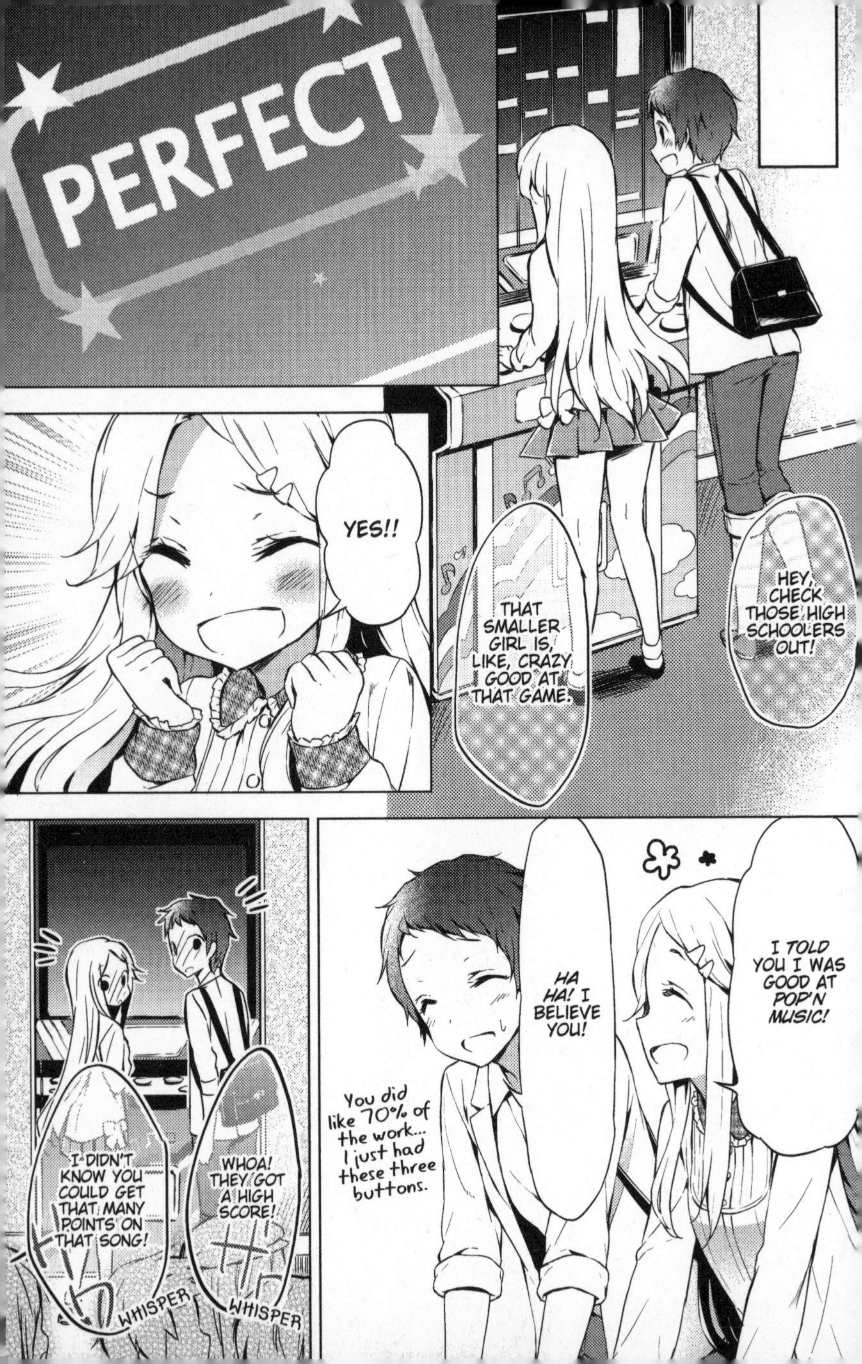
HEY, CHECK THOSE HIGH SCHOOLERS OUT!
THAT SMALLER GIRL IS, LIKE, CRAZY GOOD AT THAT GAME.
PERFECT
YES!!
I *TOLD* YOU I WAS GOOD AT POP'N MUSIC!
HA HA! I BELIEVE YOU!
You did like 70% of the work... I just had these three buttons.
WHOA! THEY GOT A HIGH SCORE!
I DIDN'T KNOW YOU COULD GET THAT MANY POINTS ON THAT SONG!
WHISPER
WHISPER

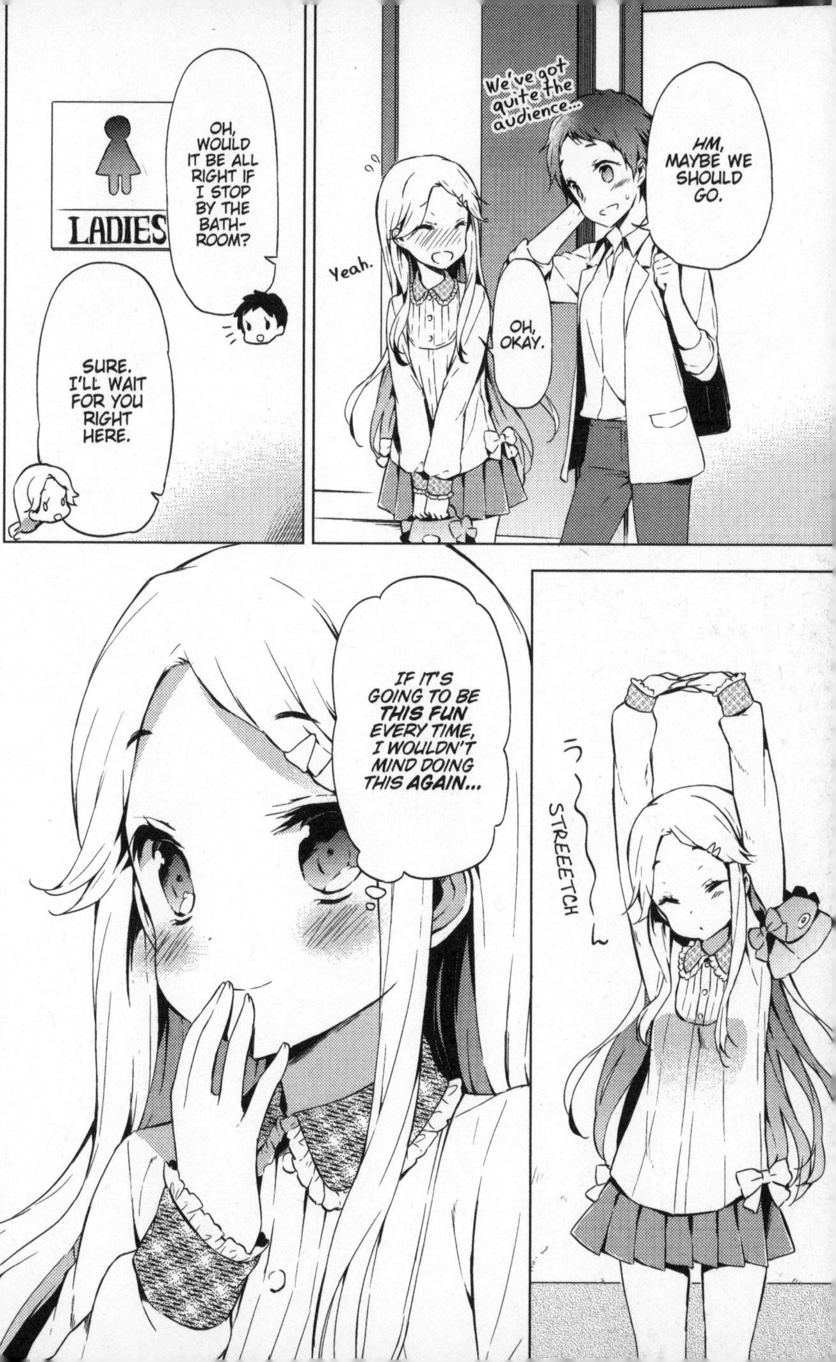
HM, MAYBE WE SHOULD GO.
We've got quite the audience...
OH, OKAY.
Yeah.
OH, WOULD IT BE ALL RIGHT IF I STOP BY THE BATH-ROOM?
LADIES
SURE. I'LL WAIT FOR YOU RIGHT HERE.
STREEETCH
IF IT'S GOING TO BE THIS FUN EVERY TIME, I WOULDN'T MIND DOING THIS AGAIN...

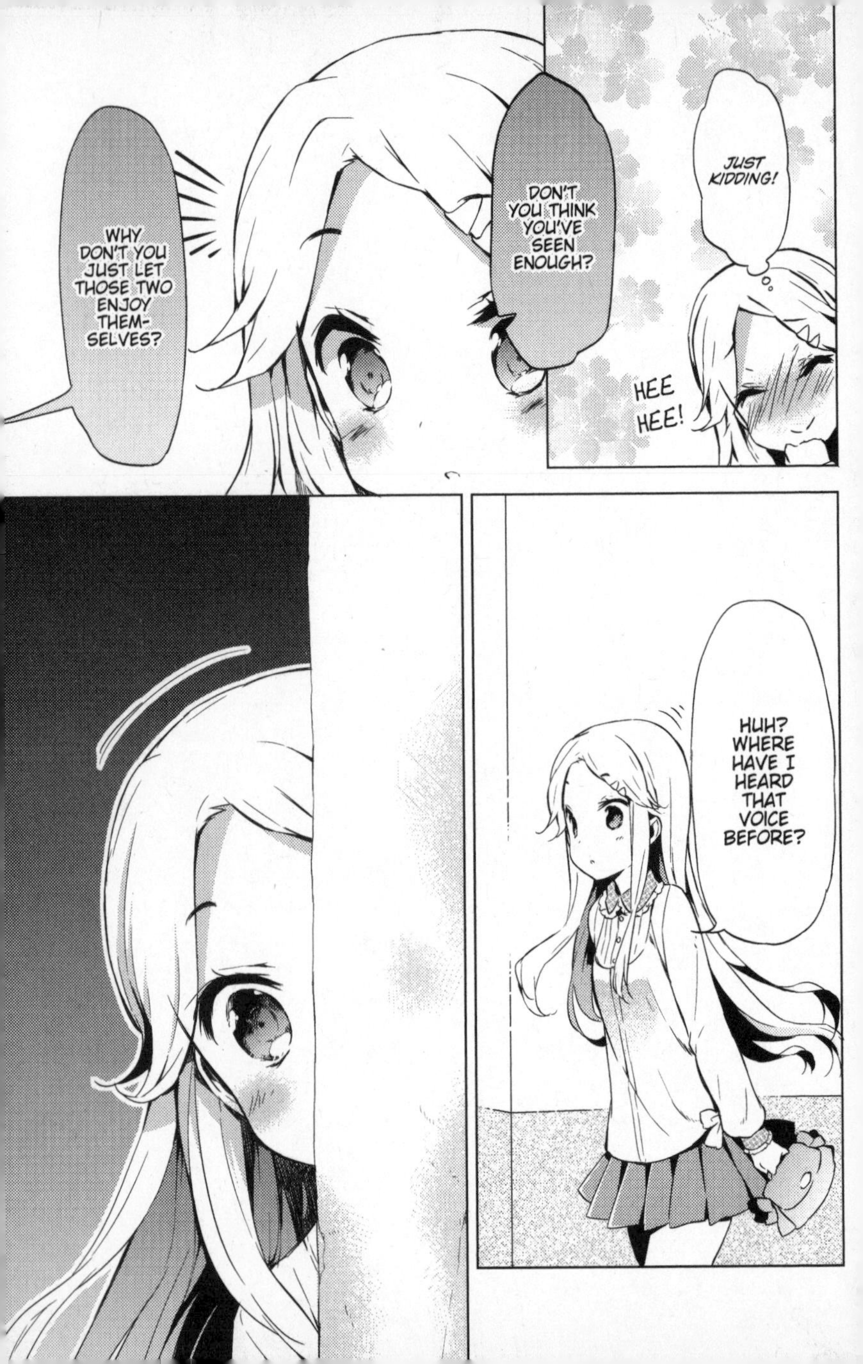
JUST KIDDING!
HEE HEE!
DON'T YOU THINK YOU'VE SEEN ENOUGH?
WHY DON'T YOU JUST LET THOSE TWO ENJOY THEM-SELVES?
HUH? WHERE HAVE I HEARD THAT VOICE BEFORE?

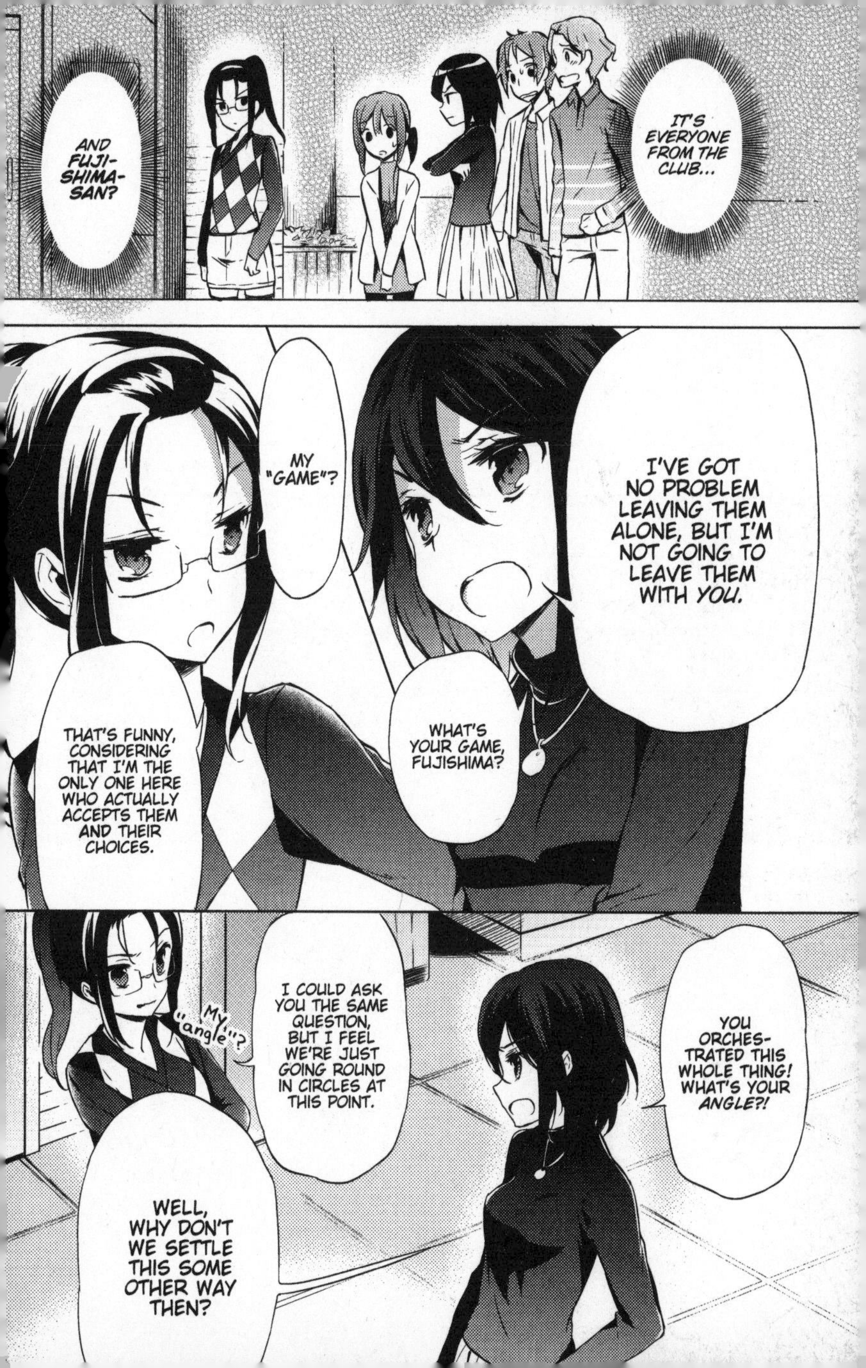
IT'S EVERYONE FROM THE CLUB...
AND FUJI-SHIMA-SAN?
I'VE GOT NO PROBLEM LEAVING THEM ALONE, BUT I'M NOT GOING TO LEAVE THEM WITH *YOU*.
MY "GAME"?
WHAT'S YOUR GAME, FUJISHIMA?
THAT'S FUNNY, CONSIDERING THAT I'M THE ONLY ONE HERE WHO ACTUALLY ACCEPTS THEM AND THEIR CHOICES.
YOU ORCHES-TRATED THIS WHOLE THING! WHAT'S YOUR *ANGLE*?!
My "angle"?
I COULD ASK YOU THE SAME QUESTION, BUT I FEEL WE'RE JUST GOING ROUND IN CIRCLES AT THIS POINT.
WELL, WHY DON'T WE SETTLE THIS SOME OTHER WAY THEN?

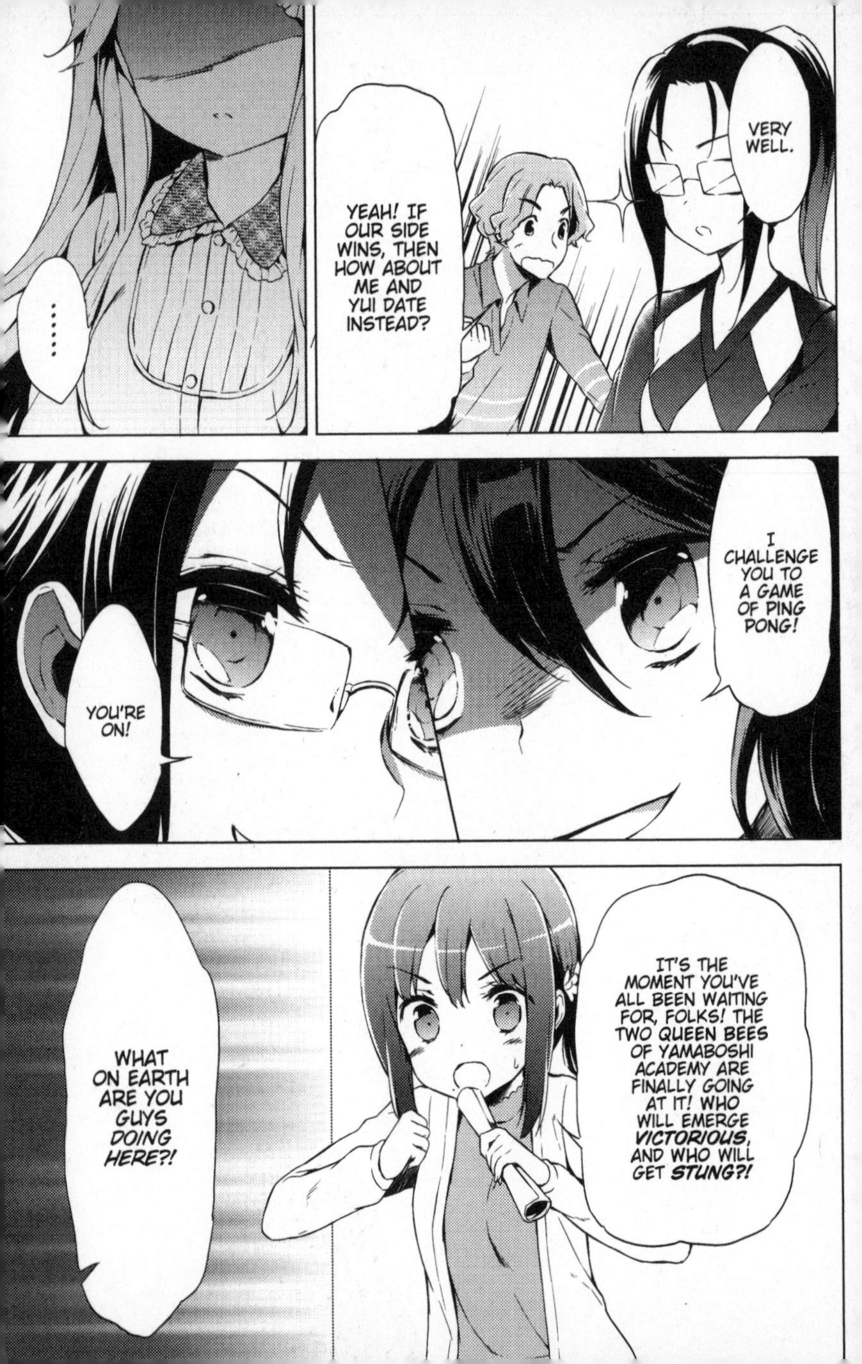
VERY WELL.
YEAH! IF OUR SIDE WINS, THEN HOW ABOUT ME AND YUI DATE INSTEAD?
......
I CHALLENGE YOU TO A GAME OF PING PONG!
YOU'RE ON!
IT'S THE MOMENT YOU'VE ALL BEEN WAITING FOR, FOLKS! THE TWO QUEEN BEES OF YAMABOSHI ACADEMY ARE FINALLY GOING AT IT! WHO WILL EMERGE *VICTORIOUS*, AND WHO WILL GET *STUNG*?!
WHAT ON EARTH ARE YOU GUYS *DOING HERE?!*

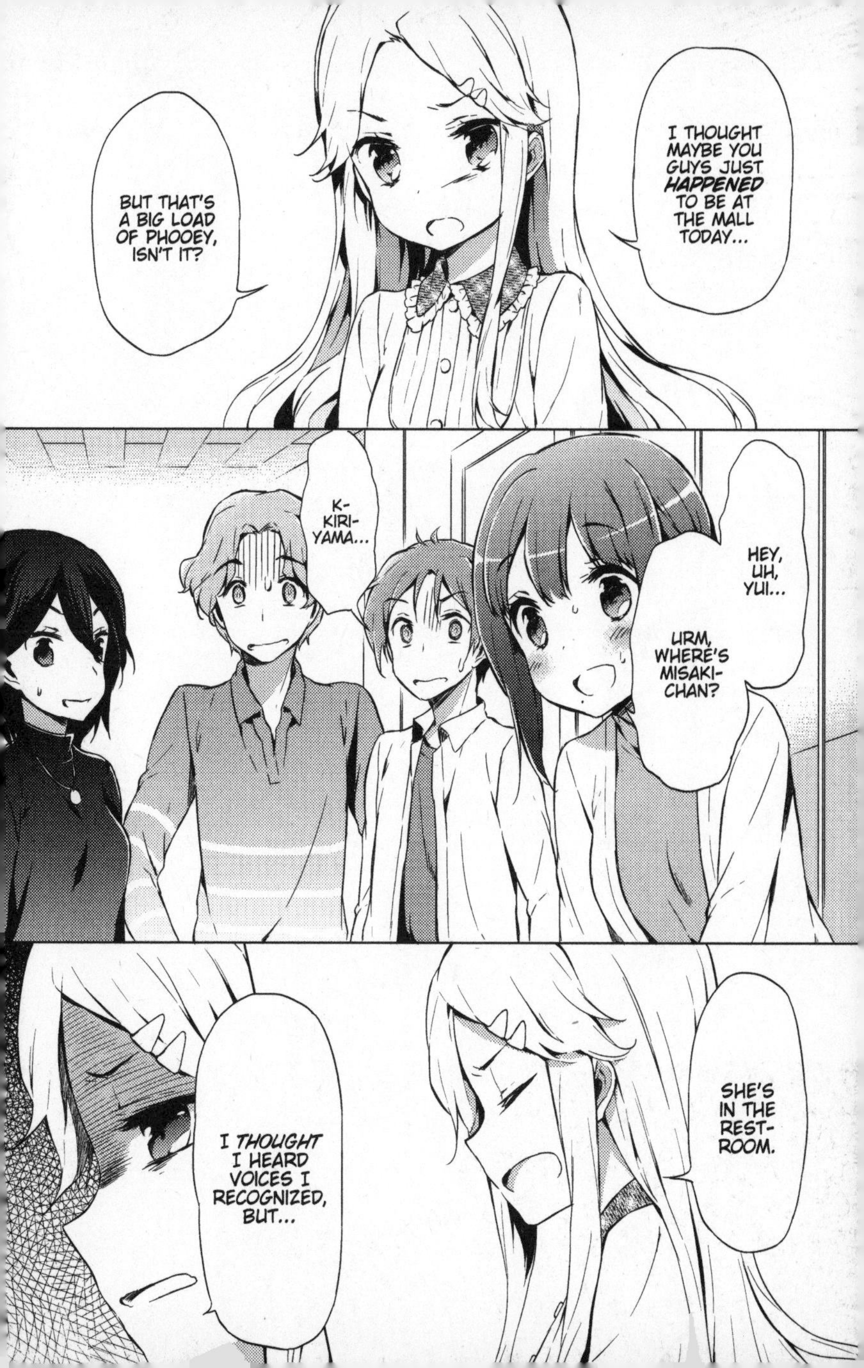
I THOUGHT MAYBE YOU GUYS JUST ***HAPPENED*** TO BE AT THE MALL TODAY...
BUT THAT'S A BIG LOAD OF PHOOEY, ISN'T IT?
HEY, UH, YUI...
URM, WHERE'S MISAKI-CHAN?
K-KIRI-YAMA...
SHE'S IN THE REST-ROOM.
I *THOUGHT* I HEARD VOICES I RECOGNIZED, BUT...

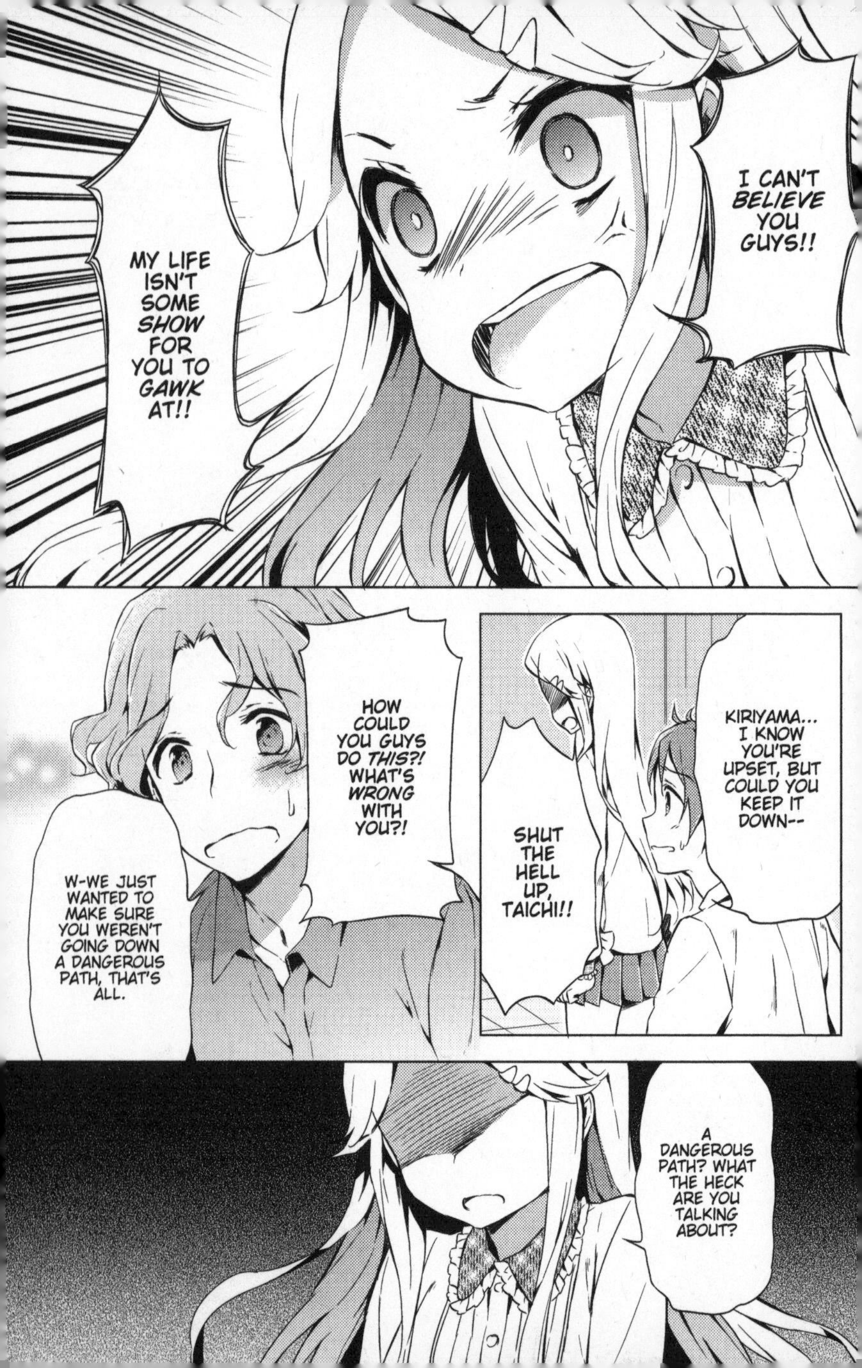
I CAN'T BELIEVE YOU GUYS!!
MY LIFE ISN'T SOME SHOW FOR YOU TO GAWK AT!!
KIRIYAMA... I KNOW YOU'RE UPSET, BUT COULD YOU KEEP IT DOWN--
SHUT THE HELL UP, TAICHI!!
HOW COULD YOU GUYS DO THIS?! WHAT'S WRONG WITH YOU?!
W-WE JUST WANTED TO MAKE SURE YOU WEREN'T GOING DOWN A DANGEROUS PATH, THAT'S ALL.
A DANGEROUS PATH? WHAT THE HECK ARE YOU TALKING ABOUT?

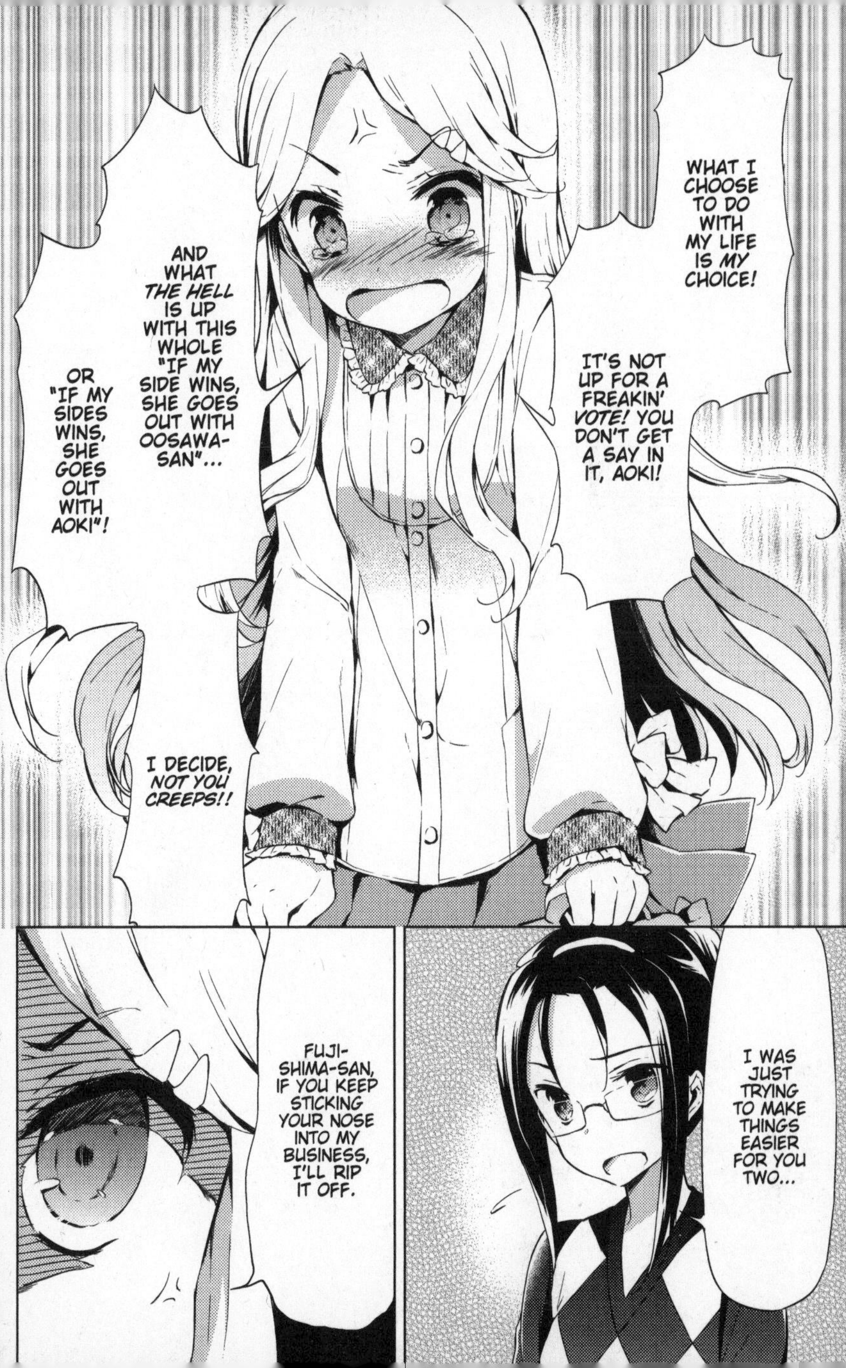
WHAT I CHOOSE TO DO WITH MY LIFE IS *MY* CHOICE!
IT'S NOT UP FOR A FREAKIN' *VOTE!* YOU DON'T GET A SAY IN IT, AOKI!
AND WHAT *THE HELL* IS UP WITH THIS WHOLE "IF MY SIDE WINS, SHE GOES OUT WITH OOSAWA-SAN"...
OR "IF MY SIDES WINS, SHE GOES OUT WITH AOKI"!
I DECIDE, *NOT YOU CREEPS!!*
I WAS JUST TRYING TO MAKE THINGS EASIER FOR YOU TWO...
FUJI-SHIMA-SAN, IF YOU KEEP STICKING YOUR NOSE INTO MY BUSINESS, I'LL RIP IT OFF.

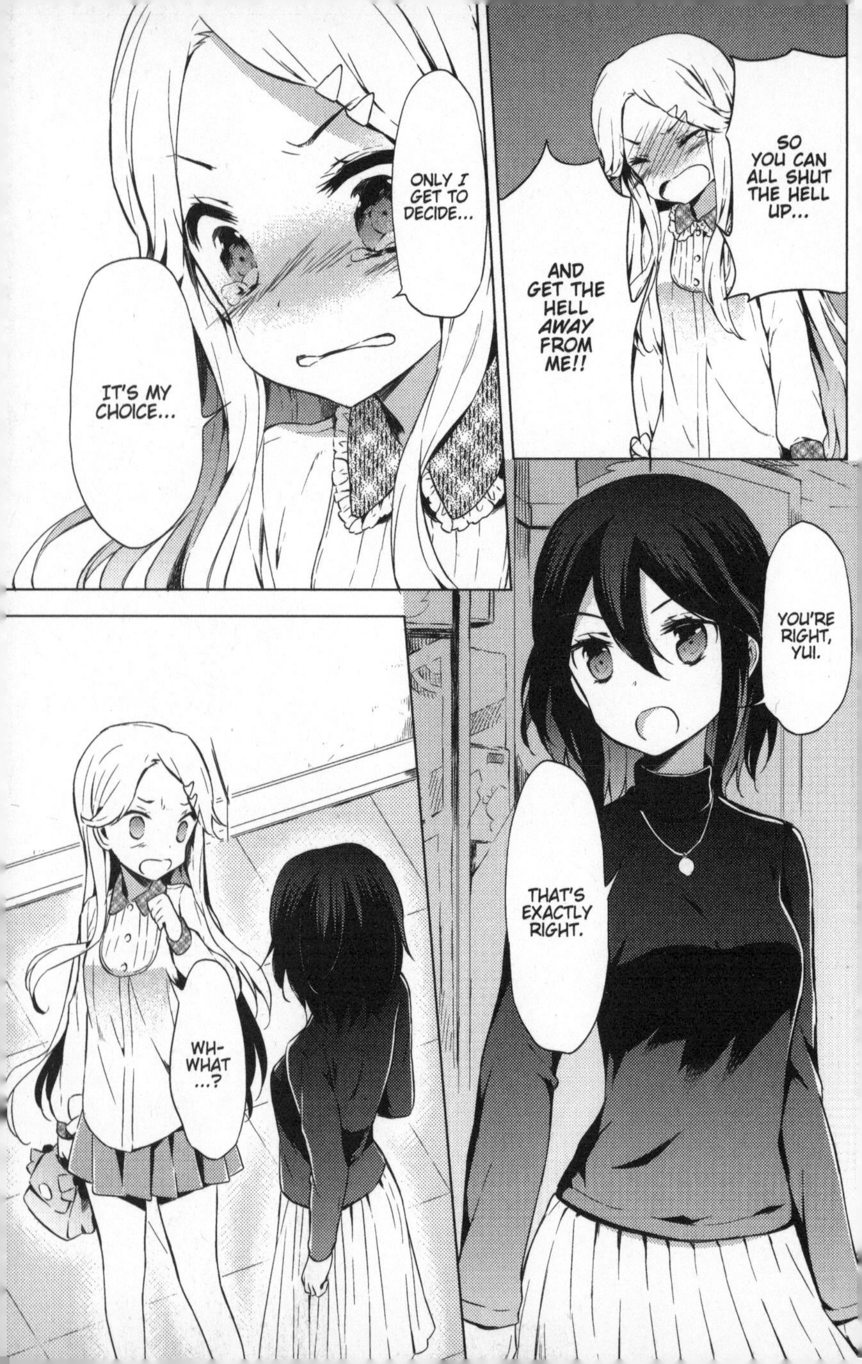
ONLY I GET TO DECIDE...
IT'S MY CHOICE...
SO YOU CAN ALL SHUT THE HELL UP...
AND GET THE HELL *AWAY* FROM ME!!
YOU'RE RIGHT, YUI.
THAT'S EXACTLY RIGHT.
WH-WHAT ...?

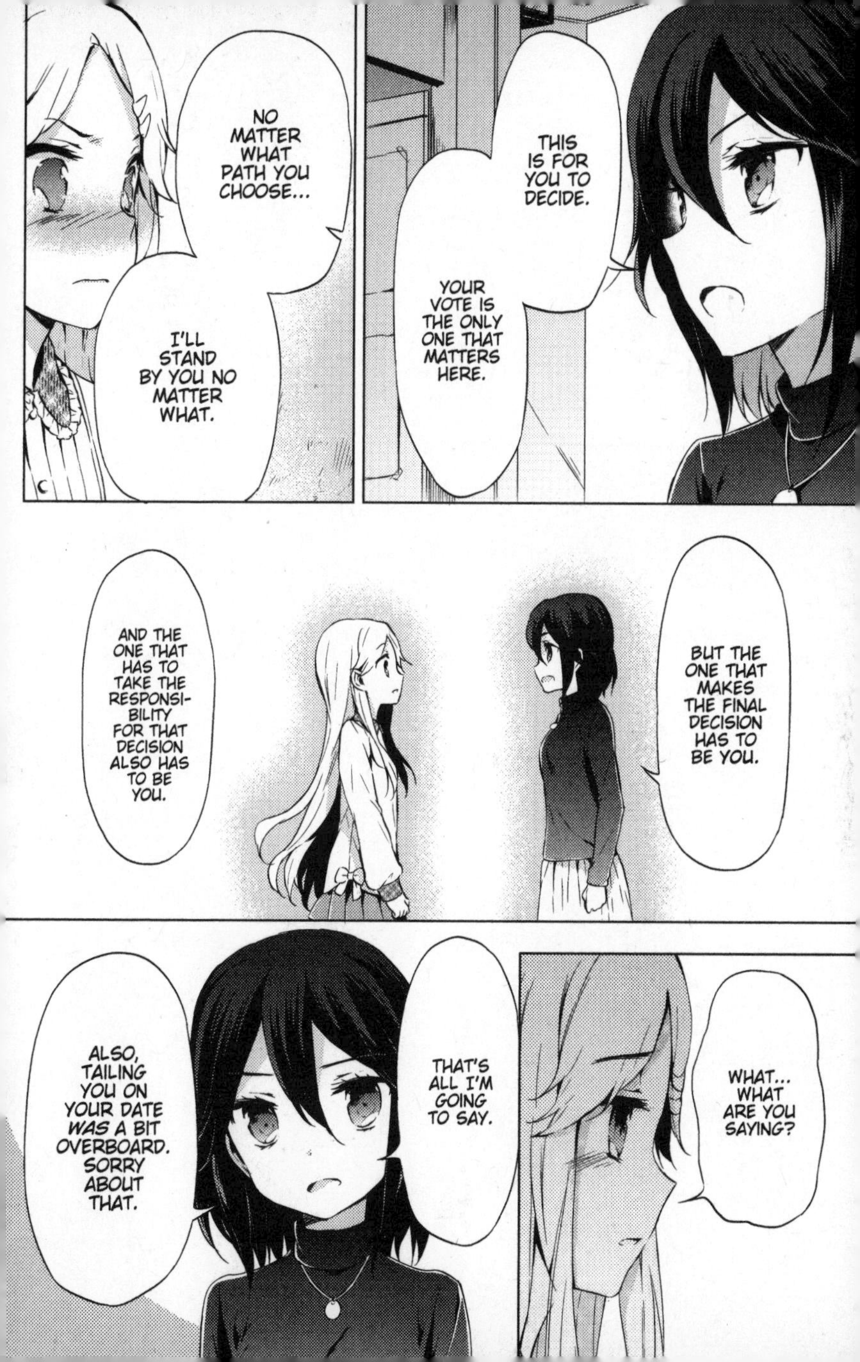
THIS IS FOR YOU TO DECIDE.
YOUR VOTE IS THE ONLY ONE THAT MATTERS HERE.
NO MATTER WHAT PATH YOU CHOOSE...
I'LL STAND BY YOU NO MATTER WHAT.
BUT THE ONE THAT MAKES THE FINAL DECISION HAS TO BE YOU.
AND THE ONE THAT HAS TO TAKE THE RESPONSIBILITY FOR THAT DECISION ALSO HAS TO BE YOU.
WHAT... WHAT ARE YOU SAYING?
THAT'S ALL I'M GOING TO SAY.
ALSO, TAILING YOU ON YOUR DATE *WAS* A BIT OVERBOARD. SORRY ABOUT THAT.

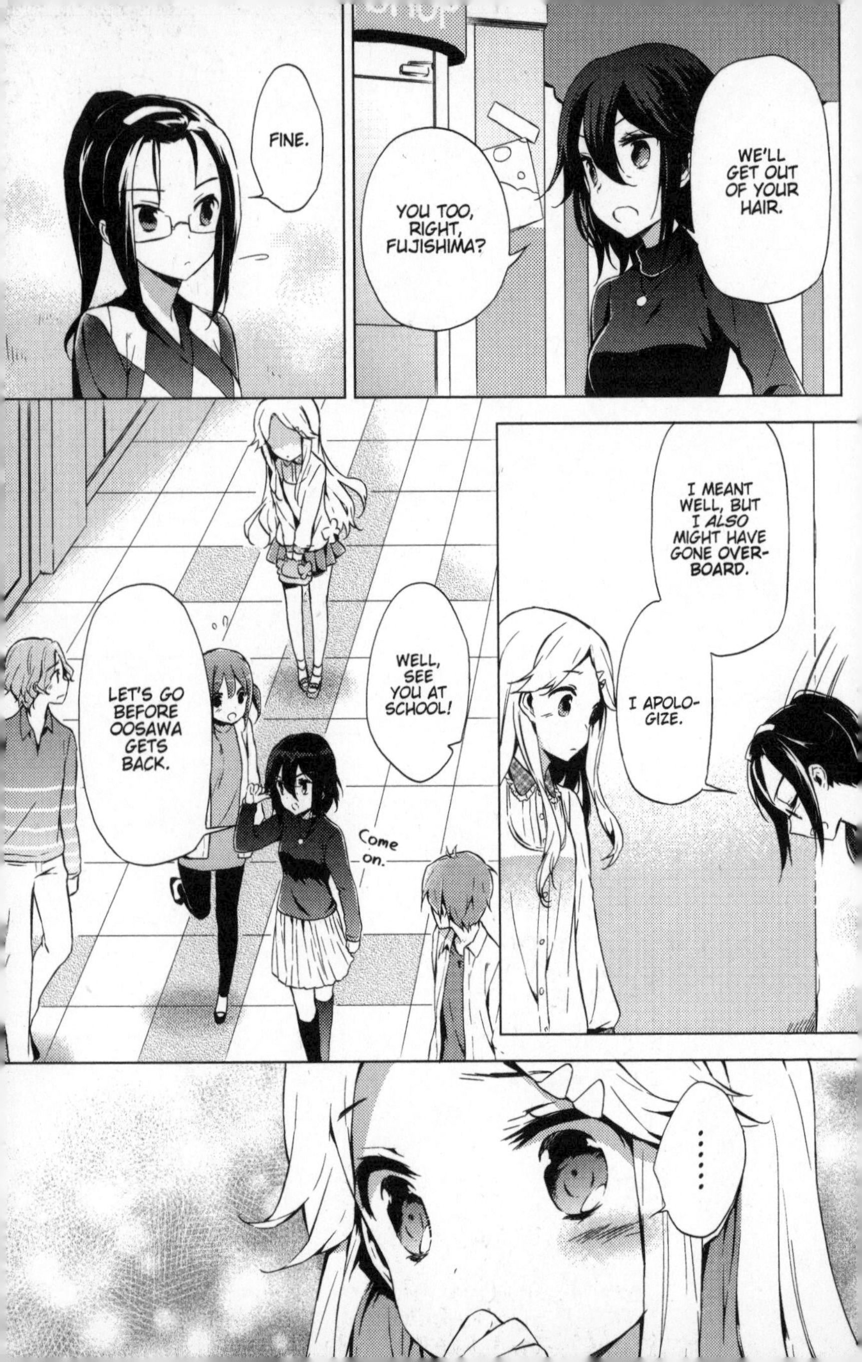
WE'LL GET OUT OF YOUR HAIR.
YOU TOO, RIGHT, FUJISHIMA?
FINE.
I MEANT WELL, BUT I *ALSO* MIGHT HAVE GONE OVER-BOARD.
I APOLO-GIZE.
WELL, SEE YOU AT SCHOOL!
LET'S GO BEFORE OOSAWA GETS BACK.
Come on.
......

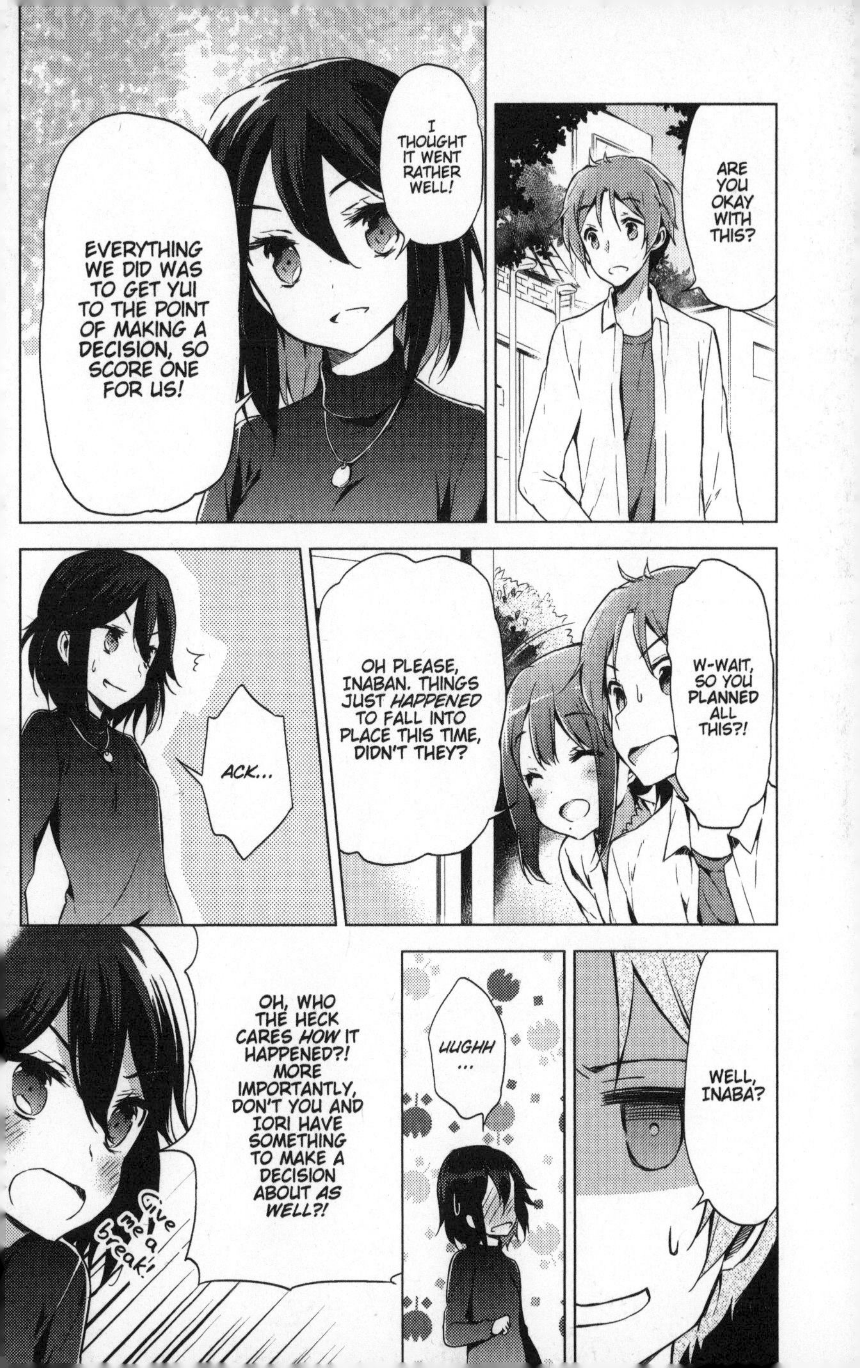
ARE YOU OKAY WITH THIS?
I THOUGHT IT WENT RATHER WELL!
EVERYTHING WE DID WAS TO GET YUI TO THE POINT OF MAKING A DECISION, SO SCORE ONE FOR US!
W-WAIT, SO YOU PLANNED ALL THIS?!
OH PLEASE, INABAN. THINGS JUST *HAPPENED* TO FALL INTO PLACE THIS TIME, DIDN'T THEY?
ACK...
WELL, INABA?
UUGHH ...
OH, WHO THE HECK CARES *HOW* IT HAPPENED?! MORE IMPORTANTLY, DON'T YOU AND IORI HAVE SOMETHING TO MAKE A DECISION ABOUT AS *WELL?!*
Give me a break!

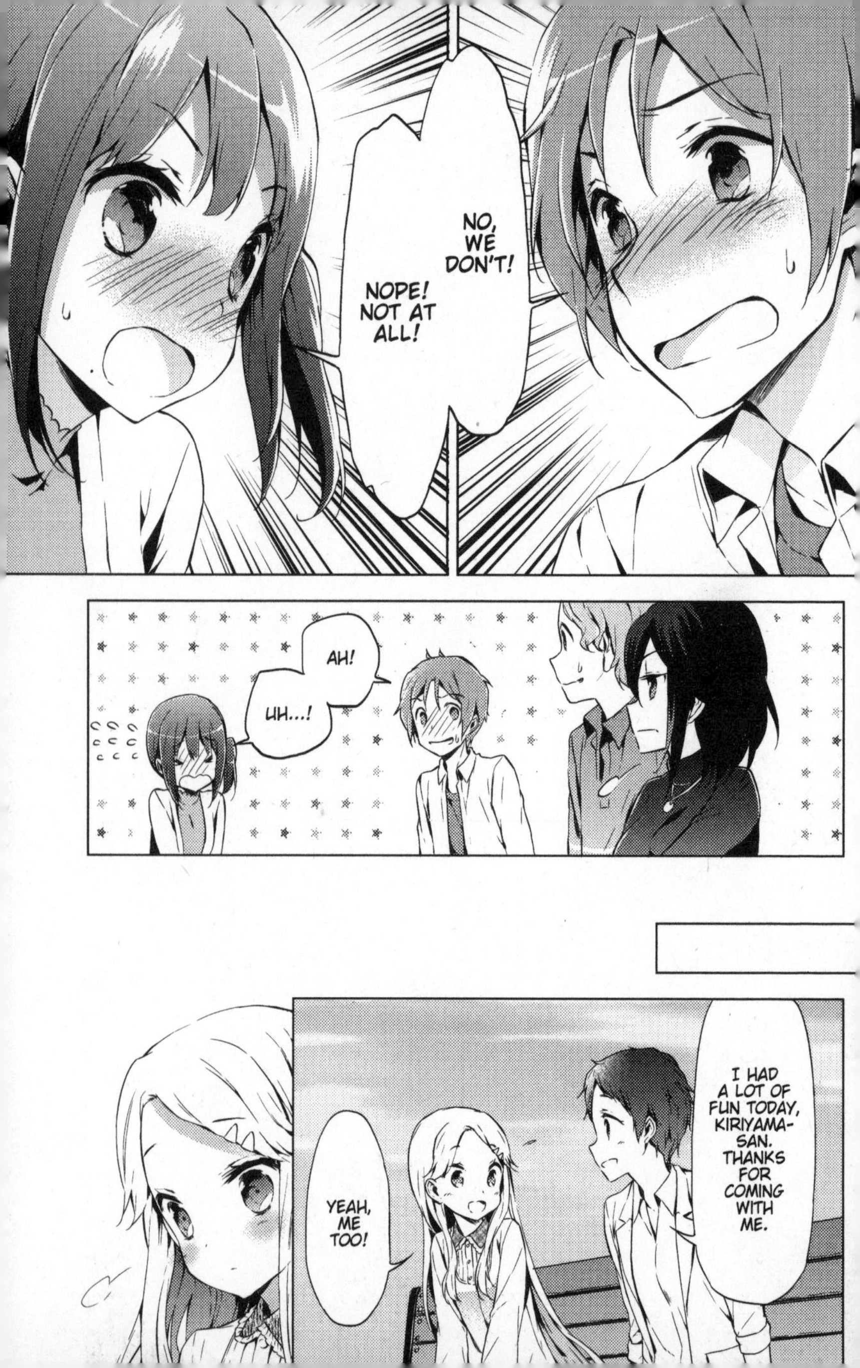
NO, WE DON'T!
NOPE! NOT AT ALL!
AH!
UH...!
I HAD A LOT OF FUN TODAY, KIRIYAMA-SAN. THANKS FOR COMING WITH ME.
YEAH, ME TOO!

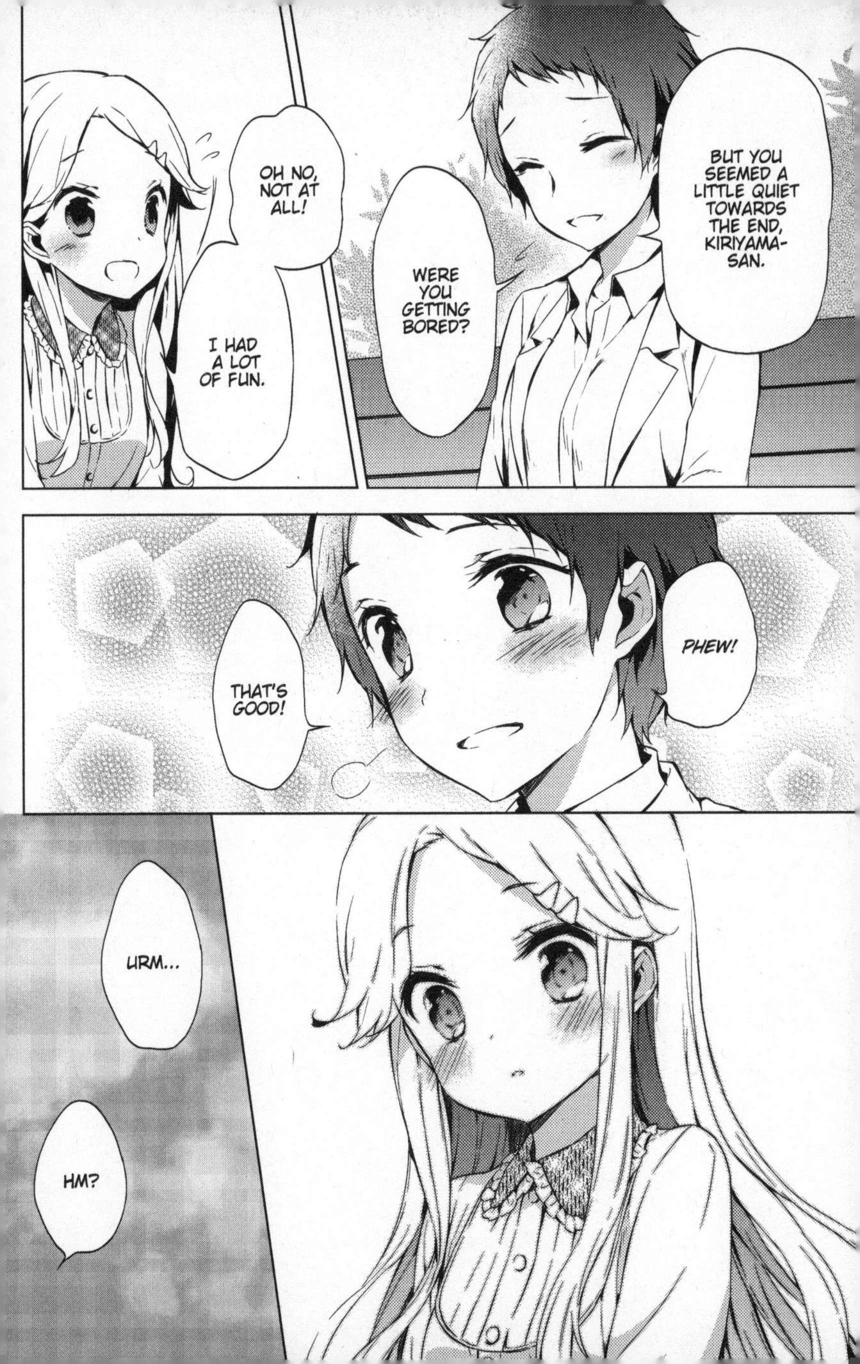
BUT YOU SEEMED A LITTLE QUIET TOWARDS THE END, KIRIYAMA-SAN.
WERE YOU GETTING BORED?
OH NO, NOT AT ALL!
I HAD A LOT OF FUN.
PHEW!
THAT'S GOOD!
URM...
HM?

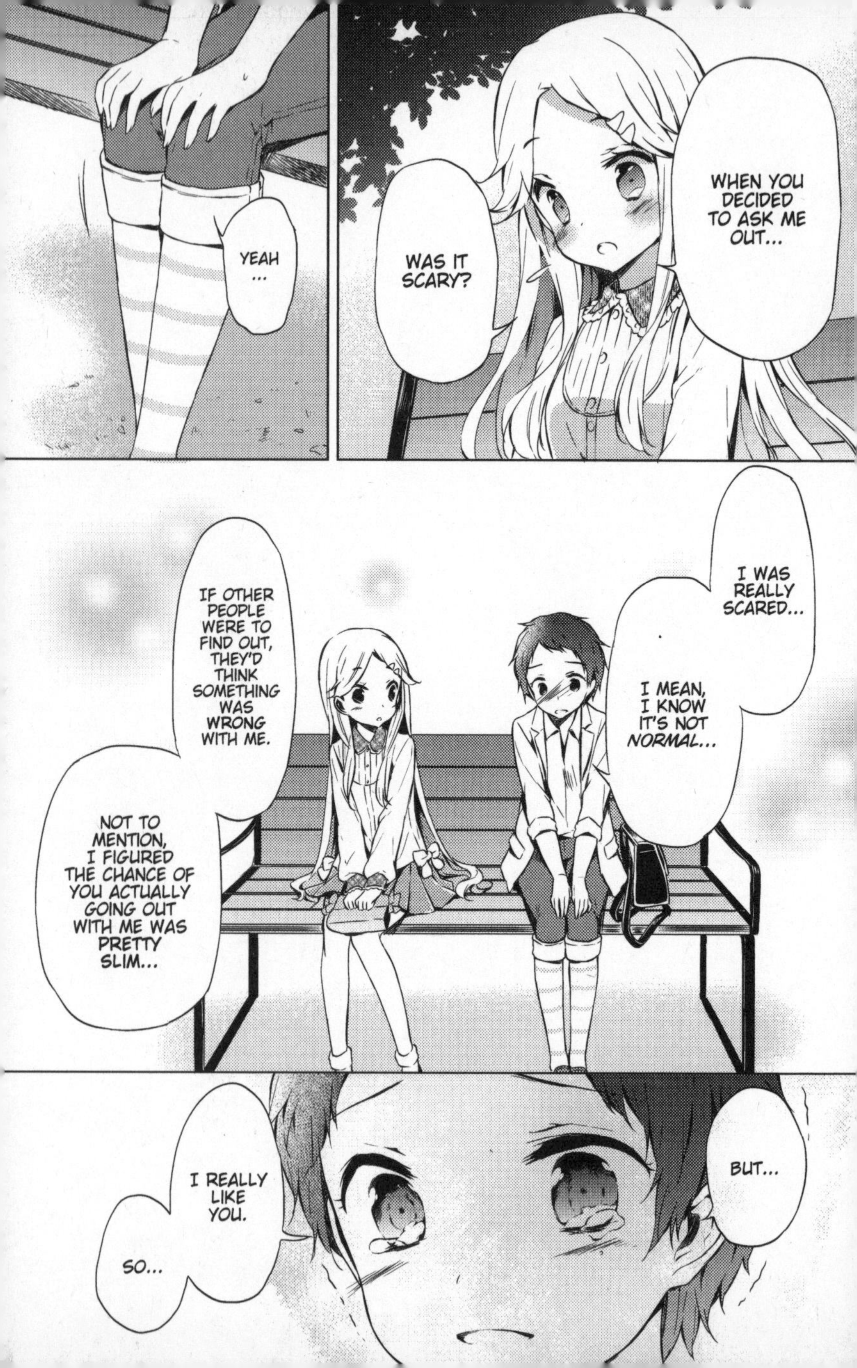

WHEN YOU DECIDED TO ASK ME OUT...
WAS IT SCARY?
YEAH ...
I WAS REALLY SCARED...
I MEAN, I KNOW IT'S NOT *NORMAL*...
IF OTHER PEOPLE WERE TO FIND OUT, THEY'D THINK SOMETHING WAS WRONG WITH ME.
NOT TO MENTION, I FIGURED THE CHANCE OF YOU ACTUALLY GOING OUT WITH ME WAS PRETTY SLIM...
BUT...
I REALLY LIKE YOU.
SO...

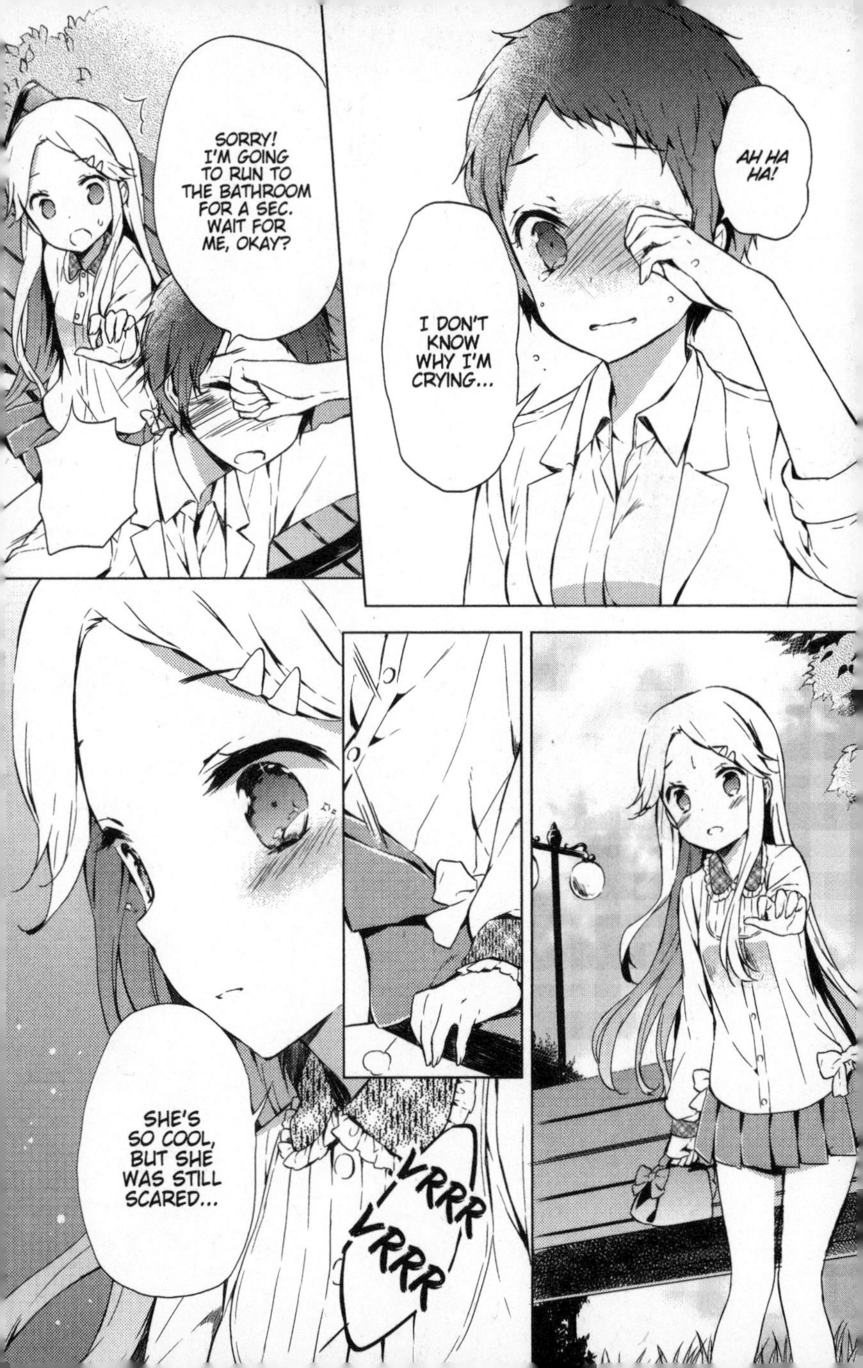
AH HA HA!
I DON'T KNOW WHY I'M CRYING...
SORRY! I'M GOING TO RUN TO THE BATHROOM FOR A SEC. WAIT FOR ME, OKAY?
SHE'S SO COOL, BUT SHE WAS STILL SCARED...
VRRR
VRRR

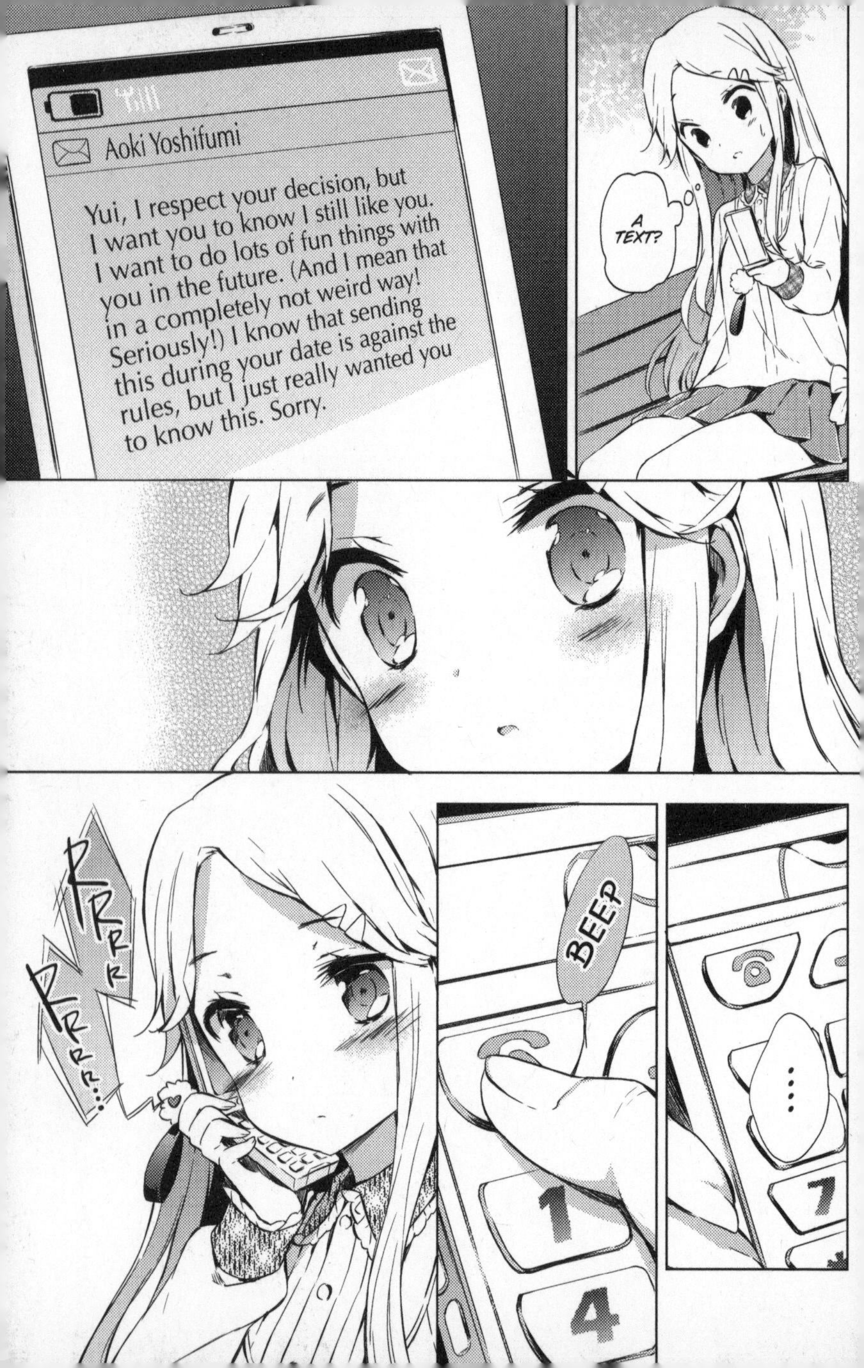
A TEXT?
Aoki Yoshifumi
Yui, I respect your decision, but I want you to know I still like you. I want to do lots of fun things with you in the future. (And I mean that in a completely not weird way! Seriously!) I know that sending this during your date is against the rules, but I just really wanted you to know this. Sorry.
...
BEEP
PRRR
PRRRR...

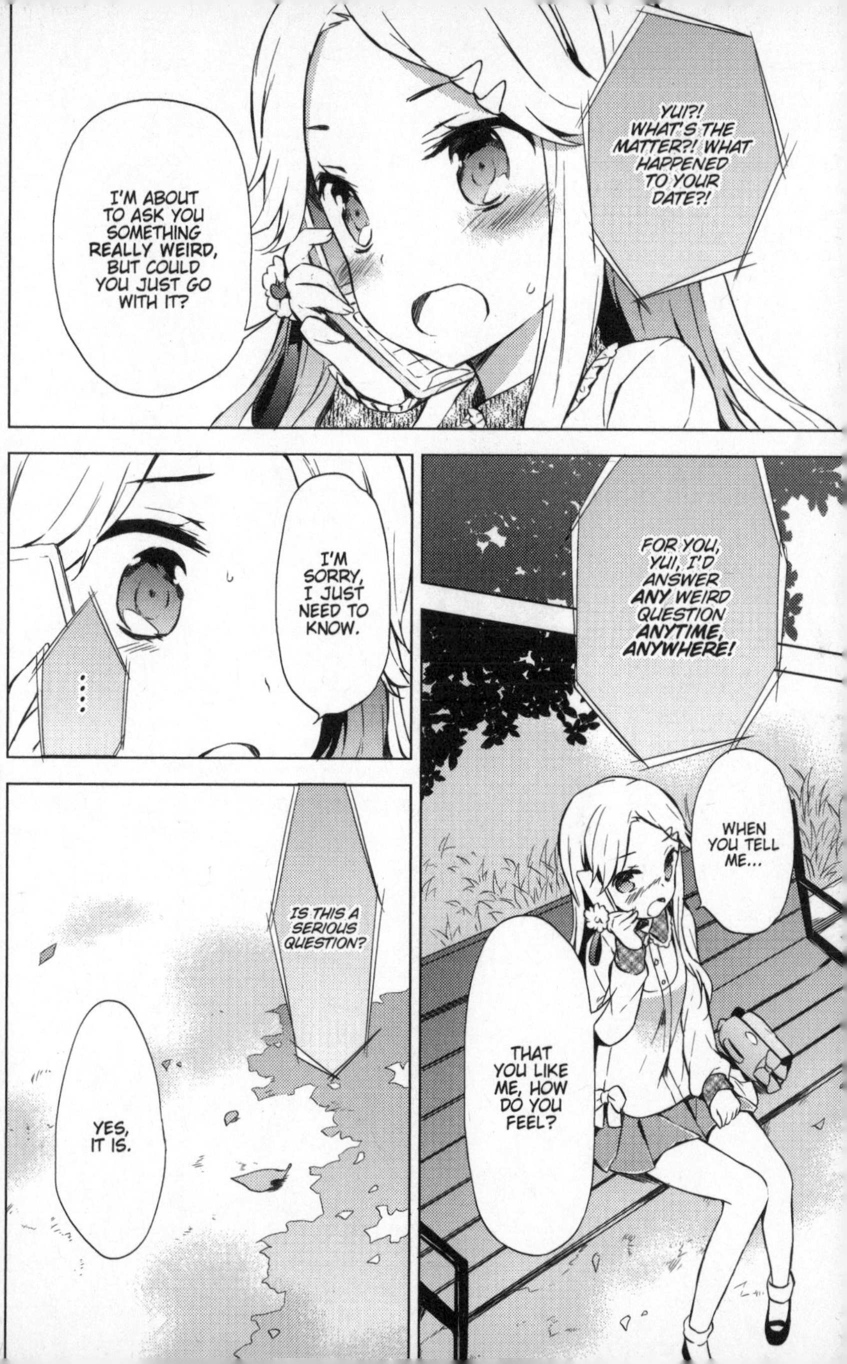
YUI?! WHAT'S THE MATTER?! WHAT HAPPENED TO YOUR DATE?!
I'M ABOUT TO ASK YOU SOMETHING REALLY WEIRD, BUT COULD YOU JUST GO WITH IT?
FOR YOU, YUI, I'D ANSWER **ANY** WEIRD QUESTION **ANYTIME, ANYWHERE!**
WHEN YOU TELL ME...
THAT YOU LIKE ME, HOW DO YOU FEEL?
I'M SORRY, I JUST NEED TO KNOW.
....
IS THIS A SERIOUS QUESTION?
YES, IT IS.

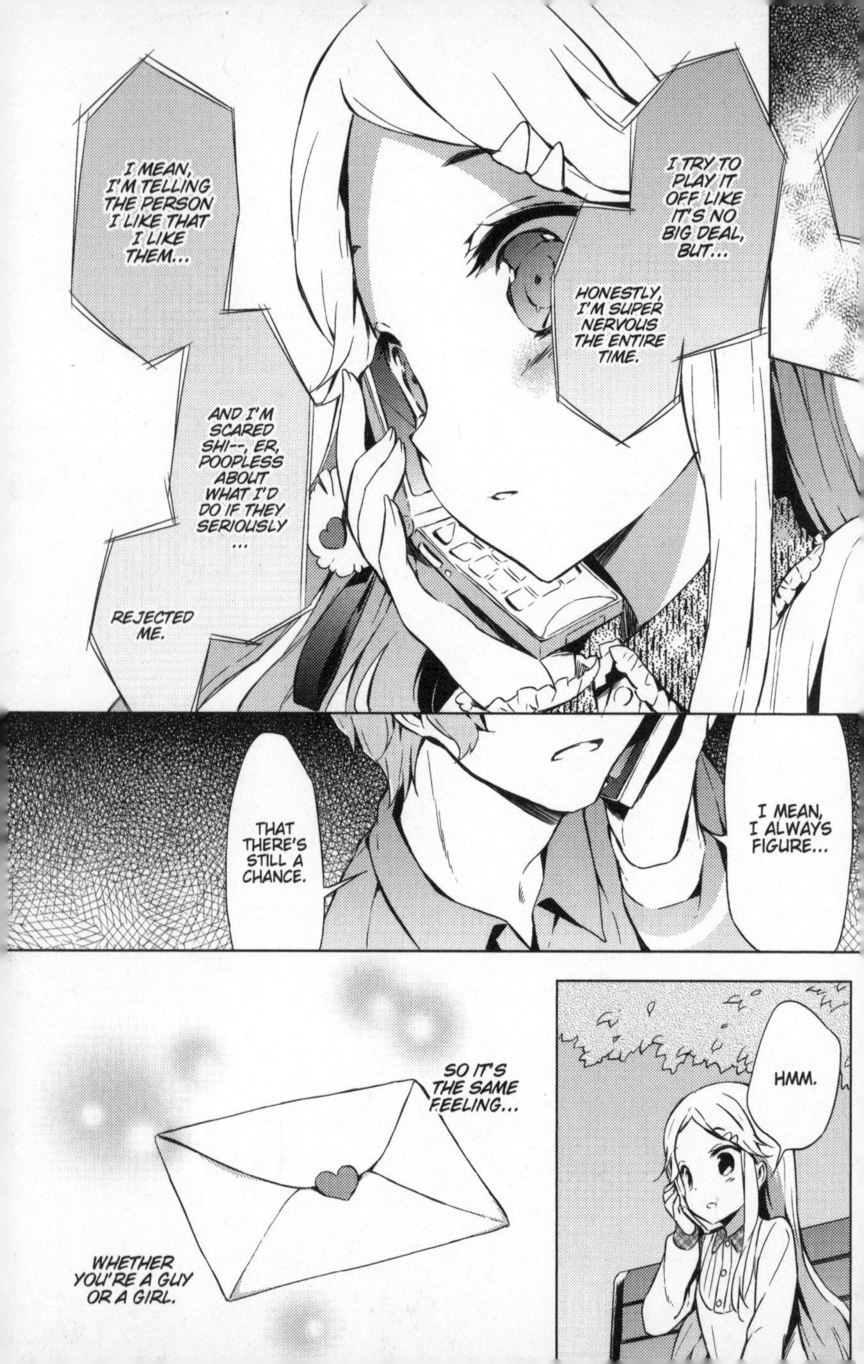
I TRY TO PLAY IT OFF LIKE IT'S NO BIG DEAL, BUT...
HONESTLY, I'M SUPER NERVOUS THE ENTIRE TIME.
I MEAN, I'M TELLING THE PERSON I LIKE THAT I LIKE THEM...
AND I'M SCARED SHI--, ER, POOPLESS ABOUT WHAT I'D DO IF THEY SERIOUSLY ...
REJECTED ME.
I MEAN, I ALWAYS FIGURE...
THAT THERE'S STILL A CHANCE.
HMM.
SO IT'S THE SAME FEELING...
WHETHER YOU'RE A GUY OR A GIRL.

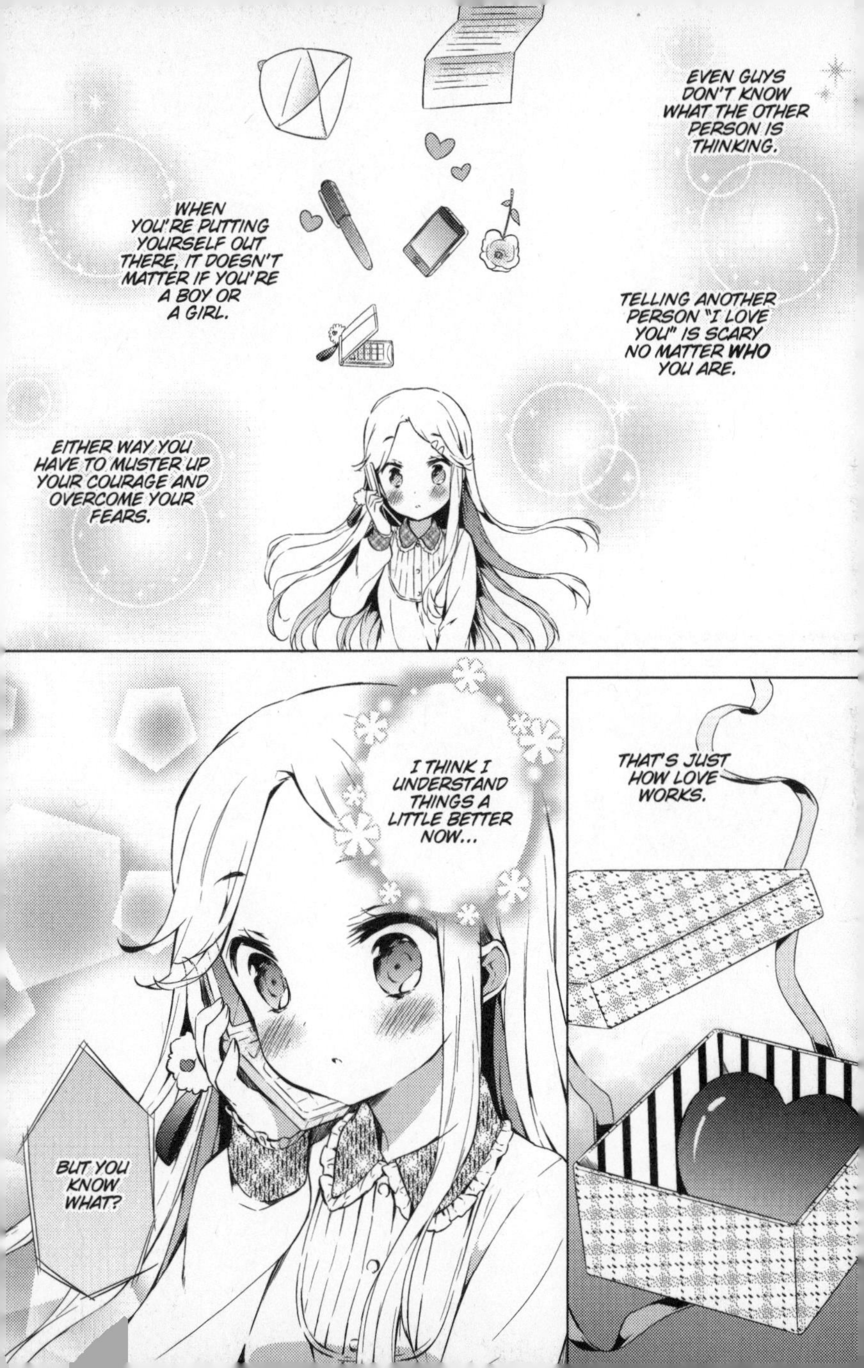
EVEN GUYS DON'T KNOW WHAT THE OTHER PERSON IS THINKING.
WHEN YOU'RE PUTTING YOURSELF OUT THERE, IT DOESN'T MATTER IF YOU'RE A BOY OR A GIRL.
TELLING ANOTHER PERSON "I LOVE YOU" IS SCARY NO MATTER **WHO** YOU ARE.
EITHER WAY YOU HAVE TO MUSTER UP YOUR COURAGE AND OVERCOME YOUR FEARS.
THAT'S JUST HOW LOVE WORKS.
I THINK I UNDERSTAND THINGS A LITTLE BETTER NOW...
BUT YOU KNOW WHAT?

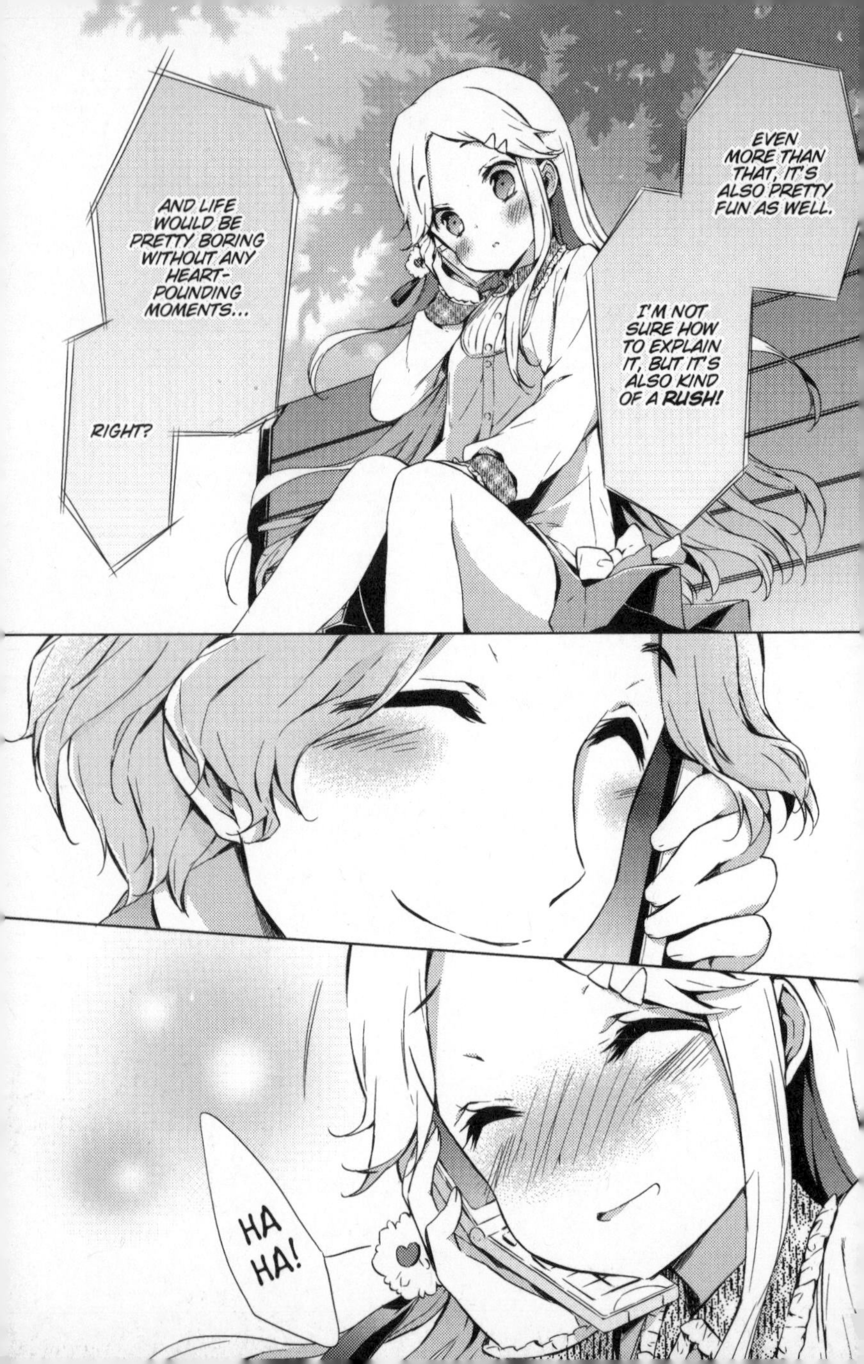
EVEN MORE THAN THAT, IT'S ALSO PRETTY FUN AS WELL.
I'M NOT SURE HOW TO EXPLAIN IT, BUT IT'S ALSO KIND OF A **RUSH!**
AND LIFE WOULD BE PRETTY BORING WITHOUT ANY HEART-POUNDING MOMENTS...
RIGHT?
HA HA!

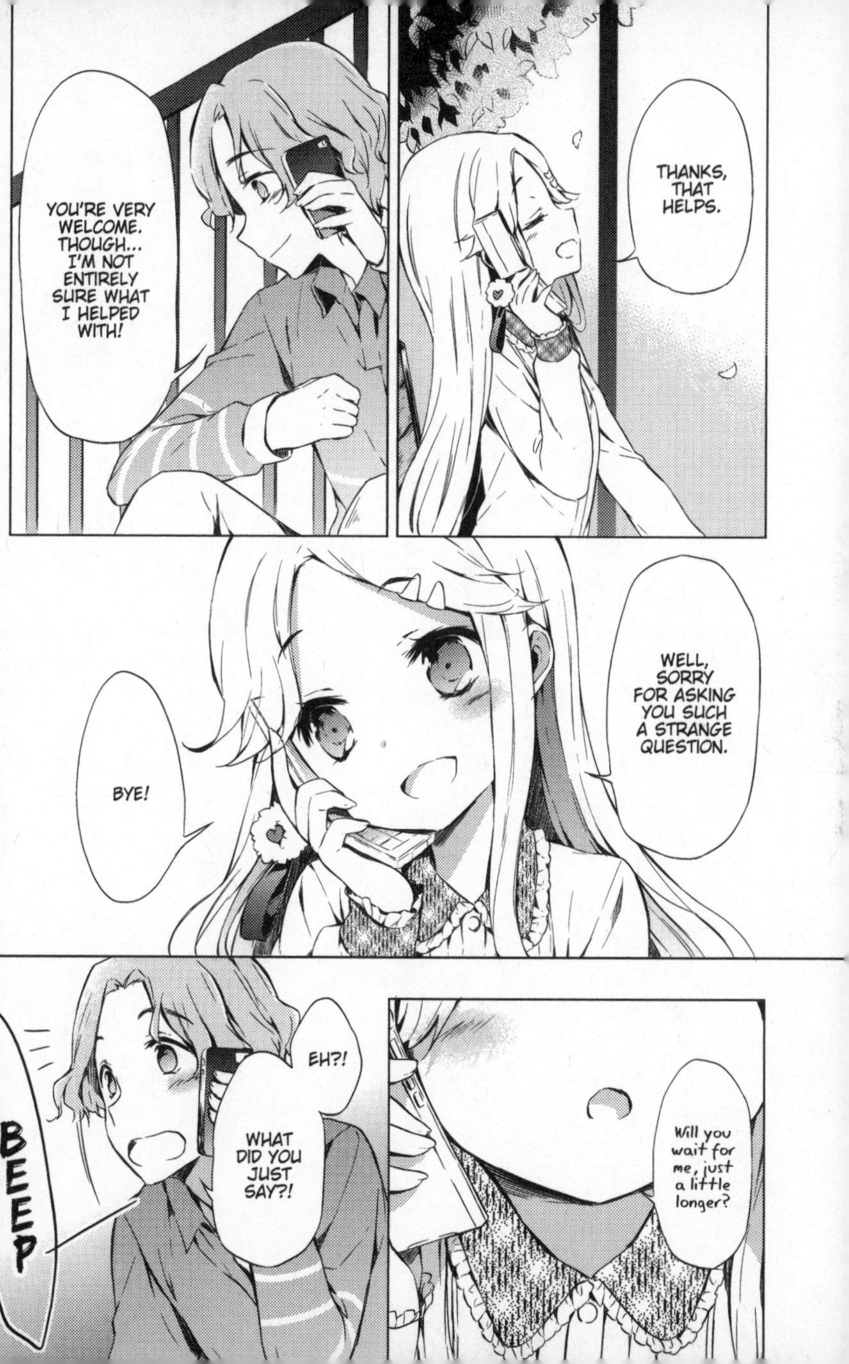
THANKS, THAT HELPS.
YOU'RE VERY WELCOME. THOUGH... I'M NOT ENTIRELY SURE WHAT I HELPED WITH!
WELL, SORRY FOR ASKING YOU SUCH A STRANGE QUESTION.
BYE!
Will you wait for me, just a little longer?
EH?!
WHAT DID YOU JUST SAY?!
BEEP

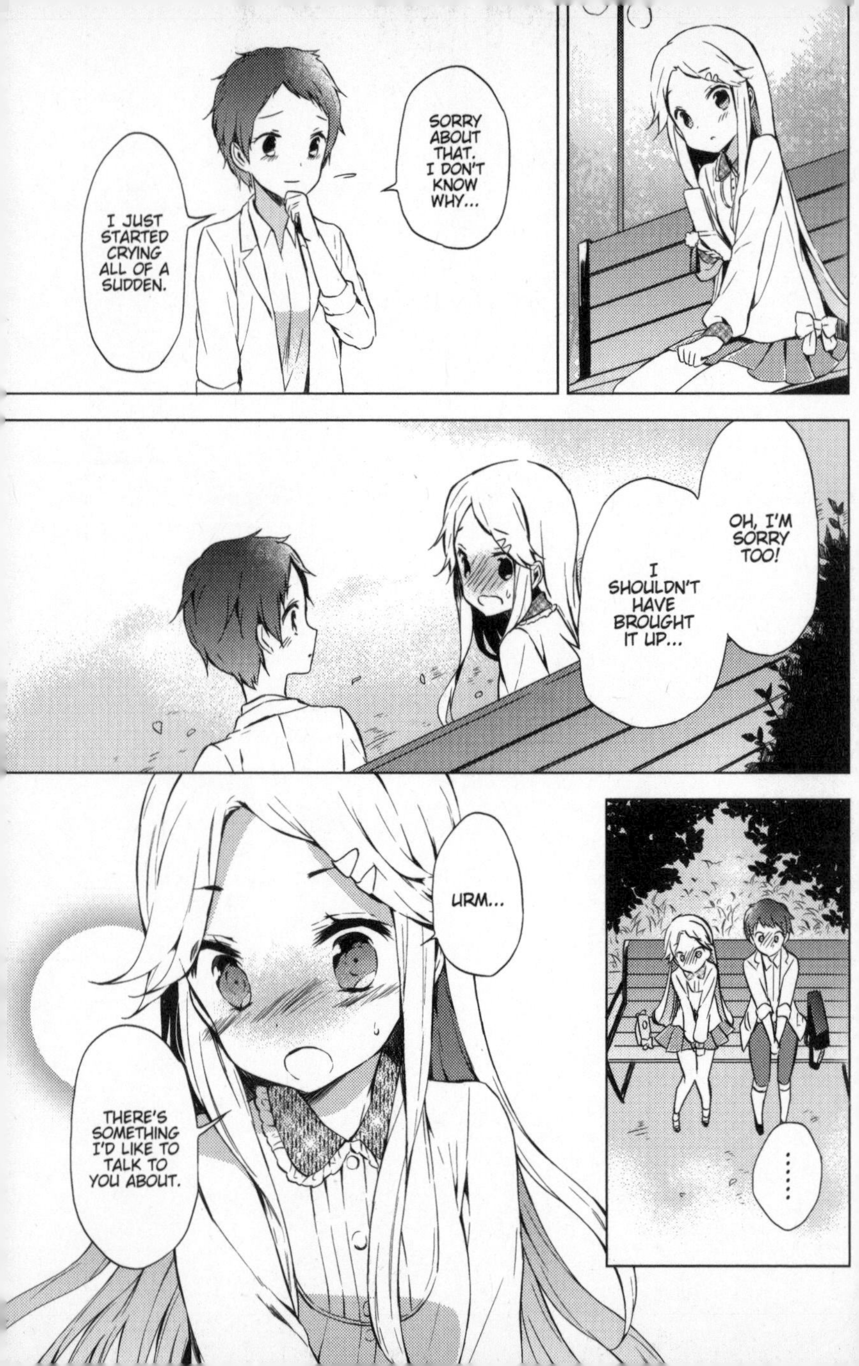
SORRY ABOUT THAT. I DON'T KNOW WHY...
I JUST STARTED CRYING ALL OF A SUDDEN.
OH, I'M SORRY TOO!
I SHOULDN'T HAVE BROUGHT IT UP...
......
URM...
THERE'S SOMETHING I'D LIKE TO TALK TO YOU ABOUT.

KOKORO CONNECT

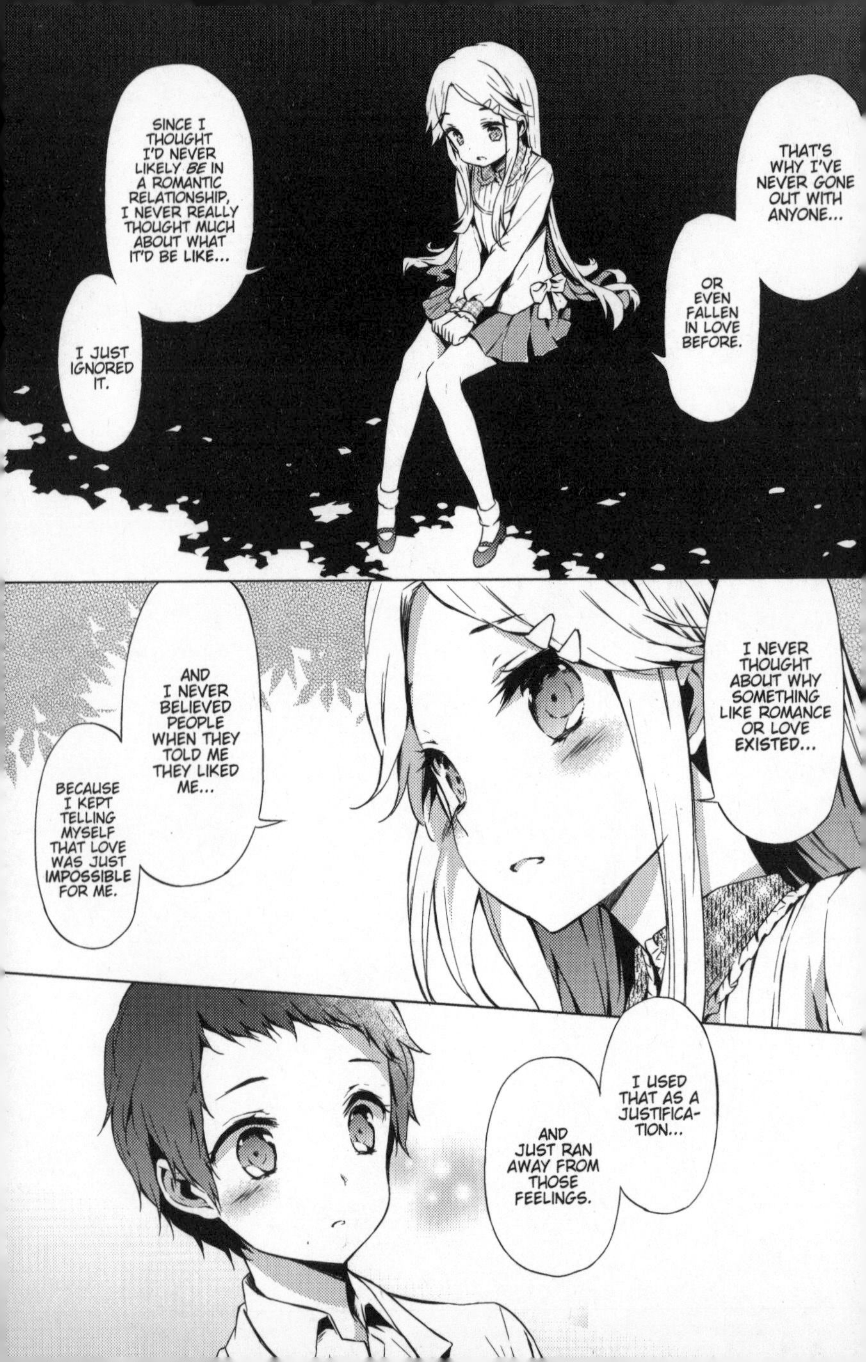
THAT'S WHY I'VE NEVER GONE OUT WITH ANYONE...
OR EVEN FALLEN IN LOVE BEFORE.
SINCE I THOUGHT I'D NEVER LIKELY *BE* IN A ROMANTIC RELATIONSHIP, I NEVER REALLY THOUGHT MUCH ABOUT WHAT IT'D BE LIKE...
I JUST IGNORED IT.
I NEVER THOUGHT ABOUT WHY SOMETHING LIKE ROMANCE OR LOVE EXISTED...
AND I NEVER BELIEVED PEOPLE WHEN THEY TOLD ME THEY LIKED ME...
BECAUSE I KEPT TELLING MYSELF THAT LOVE WAS JUST IMPOSSIBLE FOR ME.
I USED THAT AS A JUSTIFICA-TION...
AND JUST RAN AWAY FROM THOSE FEELINGS.

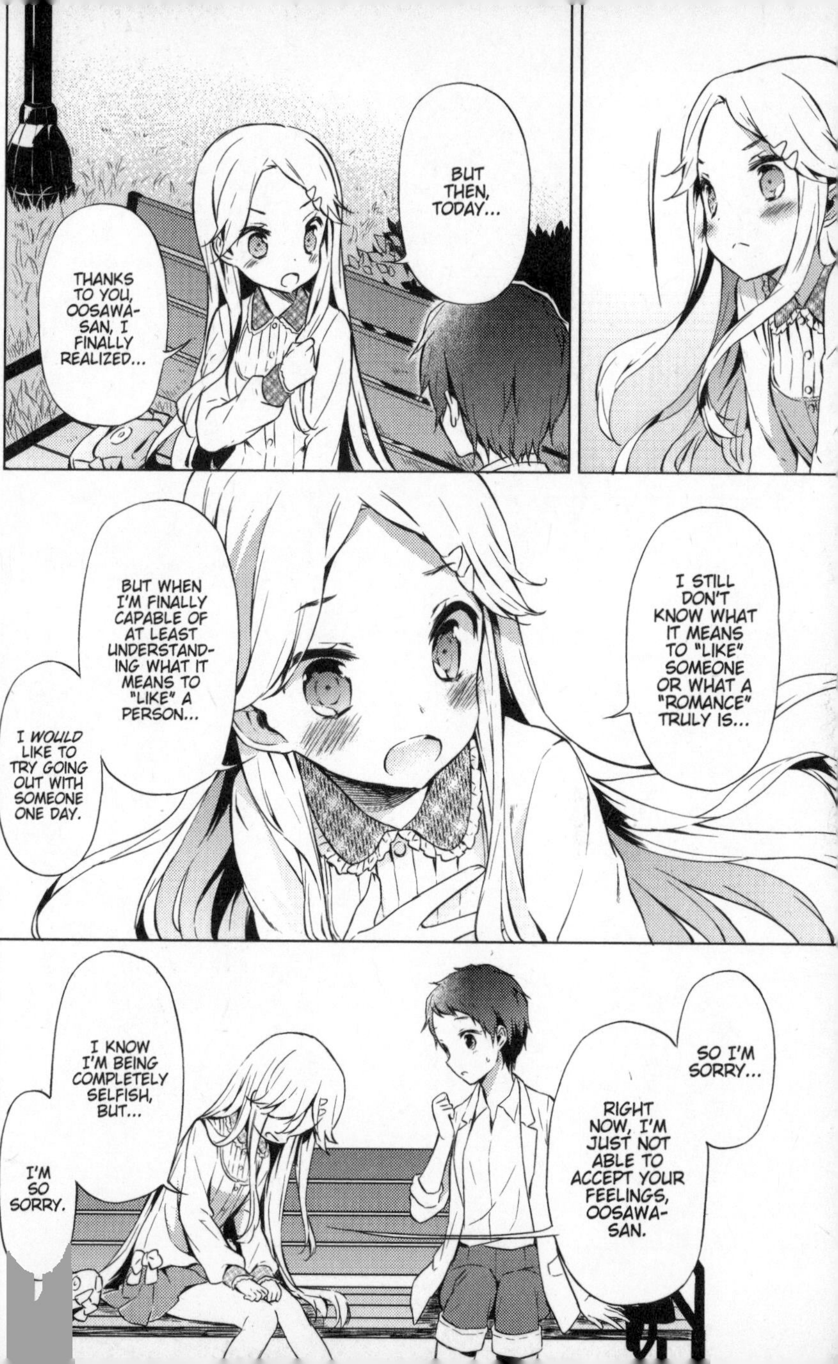
BUT THEN, TODAY...
THANKS TO YOU, OOSAWA-SAN, I FINALLY REALIZED...
I STILL DON'T KNOW WHAT IT MEANS TO "LIKE" SOMEONE OR WHAT A "ROMANCE" TRULY IS...
BUT WHEN I'M FINALLY CAPABLE OF AT LEAST UNDERSTANDING WHAT IT MEANS TO "LIKE" A PERSON...
I *WOULD* LIKE TO TRY GOING OUT WITH SOMEONE ONE DAY.
SO I'M SORRY...
RIGHT NOW, I'M JUST NOT ABLE TO ACCEPT YOUR FEELINGS, OOSAWA-SAN.
I KNOW I'M BEING COMPLETELY SELFISH, BUT...
I'M SO SORRY.

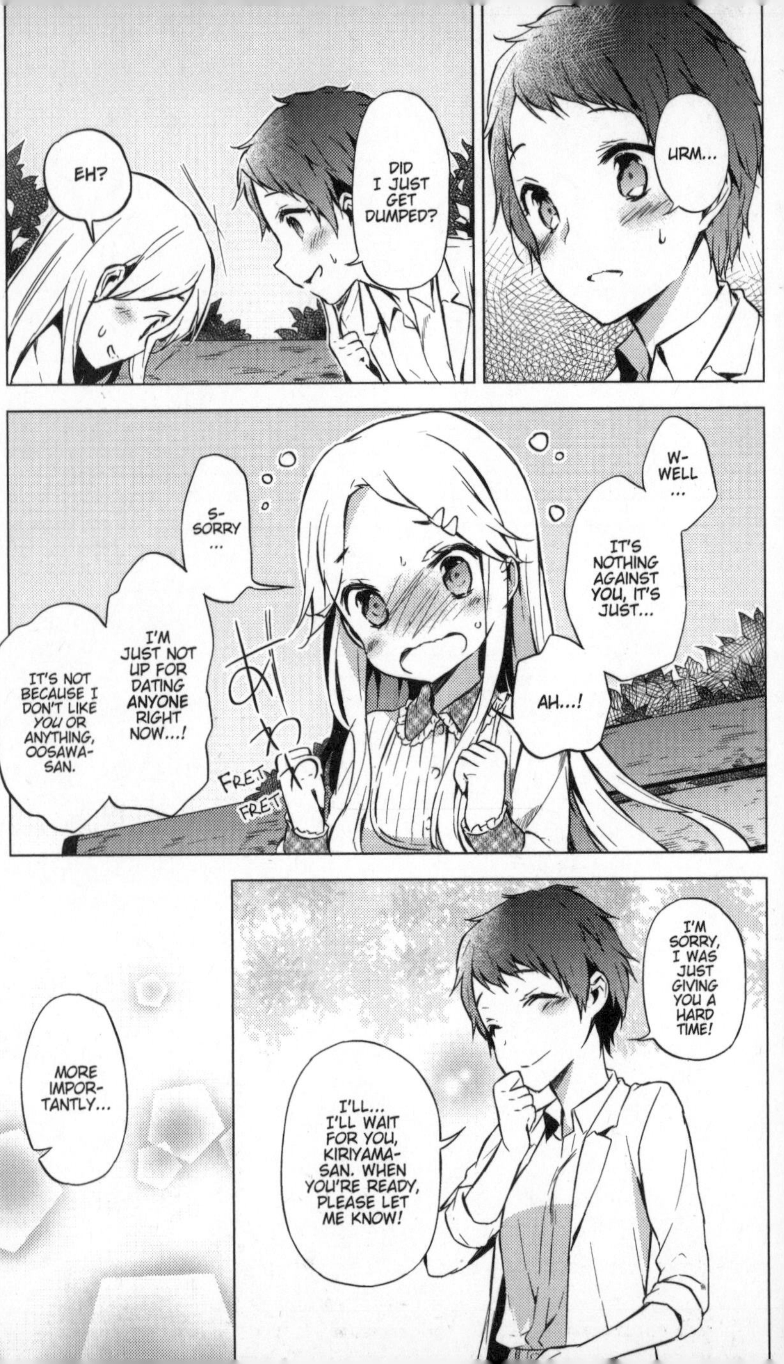
URM...
DID I JUST GET DUMPED?
EH?
W-WELL...
IT'S NOTHING AGAINST YOU, IT'S JUST...
AH...!
S-SORRY...
I'M JUST NOT UP FOR DATING ANYONE RIGHT NOW...!
IT'S NOT BECAUSE I DON'T LIKE *YOU* OR ANYTHING, OOSAWA-SAN.
FRET
FRET
I'M SORRY, I WAS JUST GIVING YOU A HARD TIME!
I'LL... I'LL WAIT FOR YOU, KIRIYAMA-SAN. WHEN YOU'RE READY, PLEASE LET ME KNOW!
MORE IMPORTANTLY...

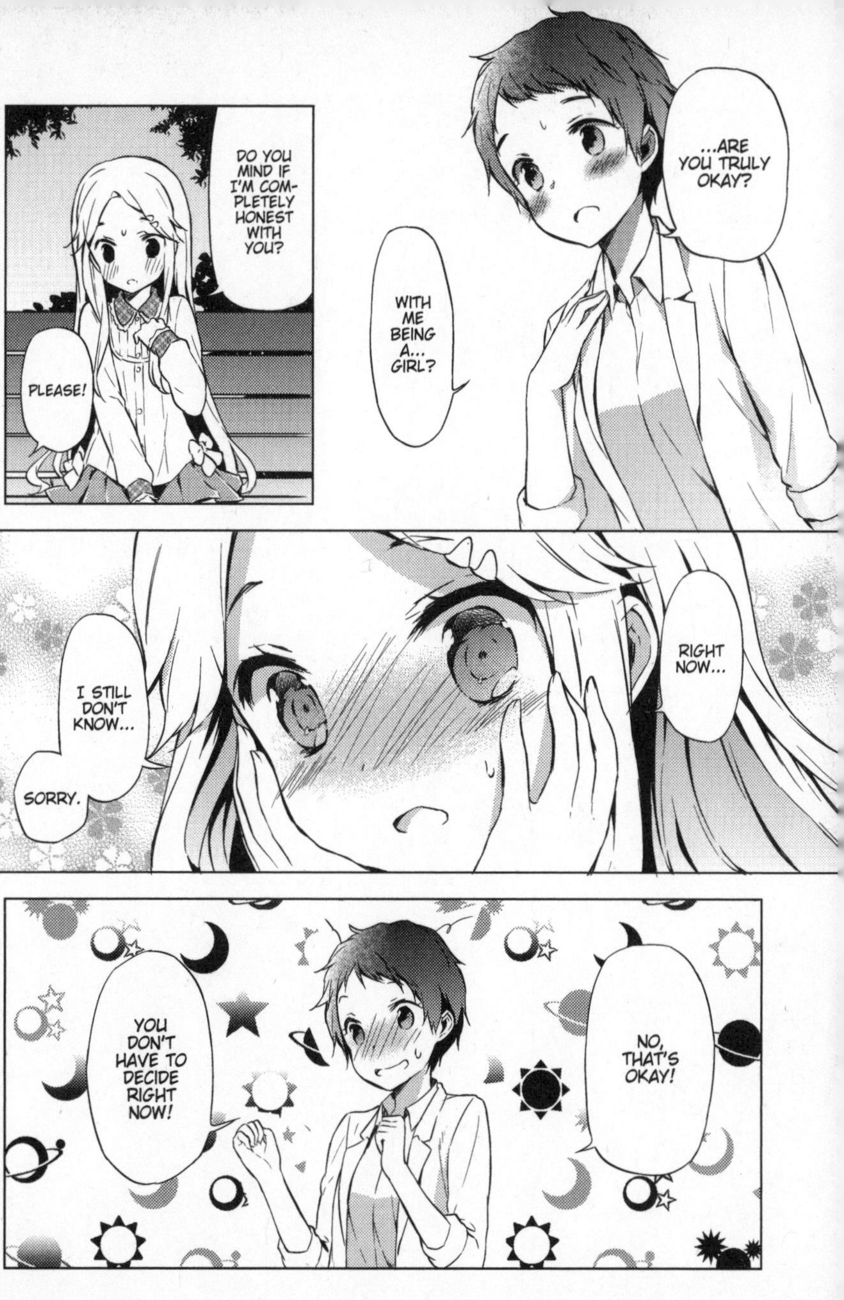
...ARE YOU TRULY OKAY?
WITH ME BEING A... GIRL?
DO YOU MIND IF I'M COM-PLETELY HONEST WITH YOU?
PLEASE!
RIGHT NOW...
I STILL DON'T KNOW...
SORRY.
NO, THAT'S OKAY!
YOU DON'T HAVE TO DECIDE RIGHT NOW!

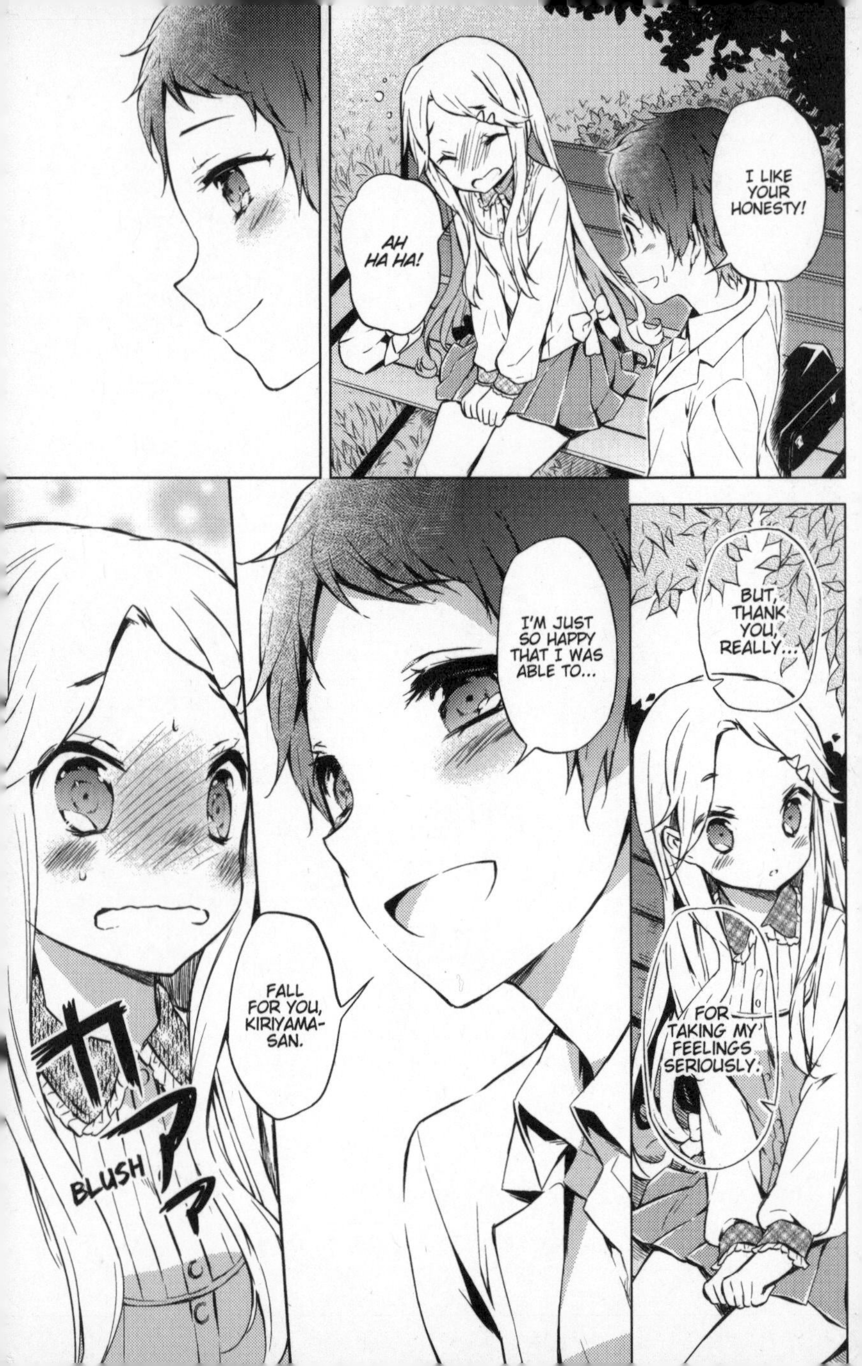
I LIKE YOUR HONESTY!
AH HA HA!
BUT, THANK YOU, REALLY...
FOR TAKING MY FEELINGS SERIOUSLY.
I'M JUST SO HAPPY THAT I WAS ABLE TO...
FALL FOR YOU, KIRIYAMA-SAN.
BLUSH

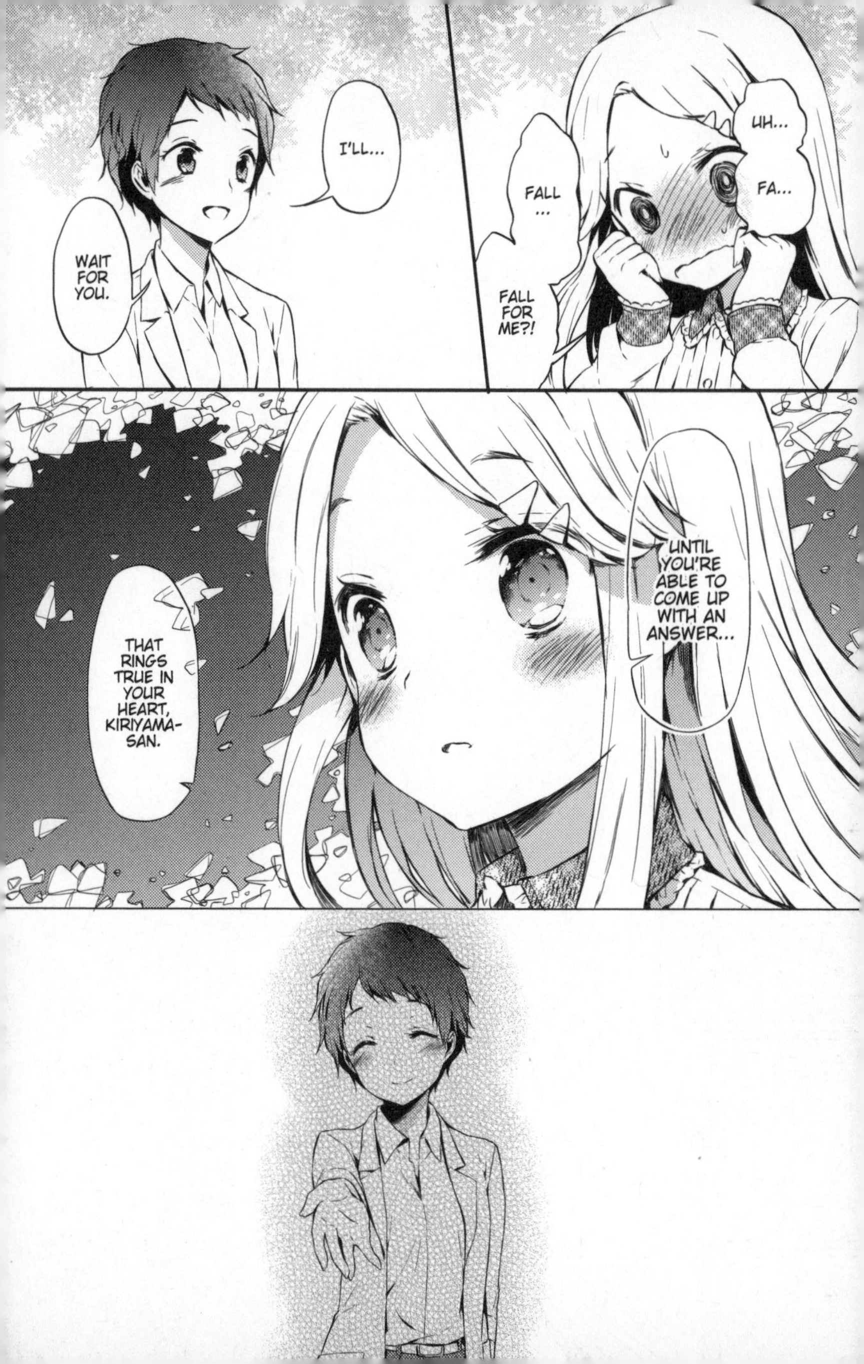
UH...
FA...
FALL ...
FALL FOR ME?!
I'LL...
WAIT FOR YOU.
UNTIL YOU'RE ABLE TO COME UP WITH AN ANSWER...
THAT RINGS TRUE IN YOUR HEART, KIRIYAMA-SAN.

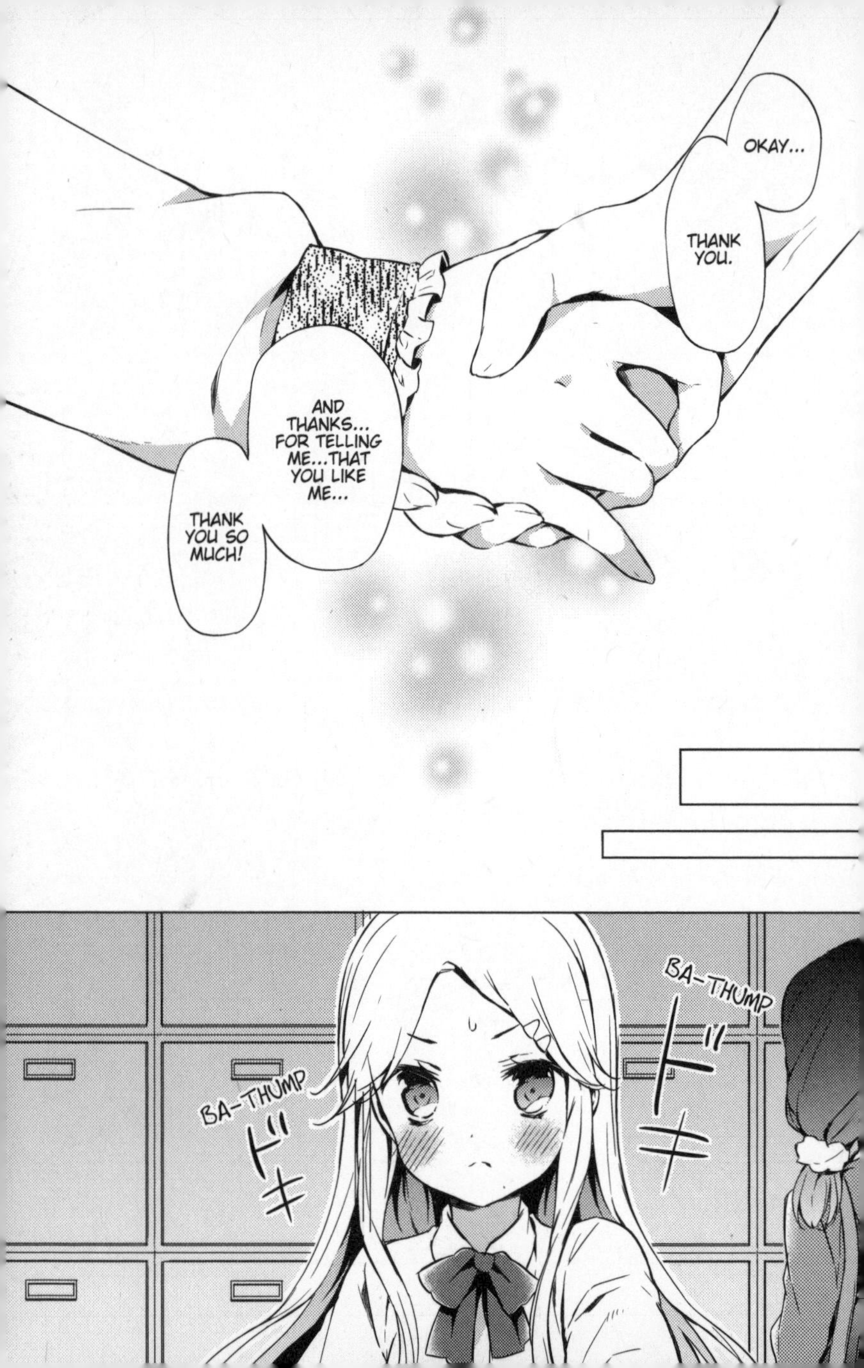
OKAY...
THANK YOU.
AND THANKS... FOR TELLING ME...THAT YOU LIKE ME...
THANK YOU SO MUCH!
BA-THUMP
ドキ
BA-THUMP
ドキ

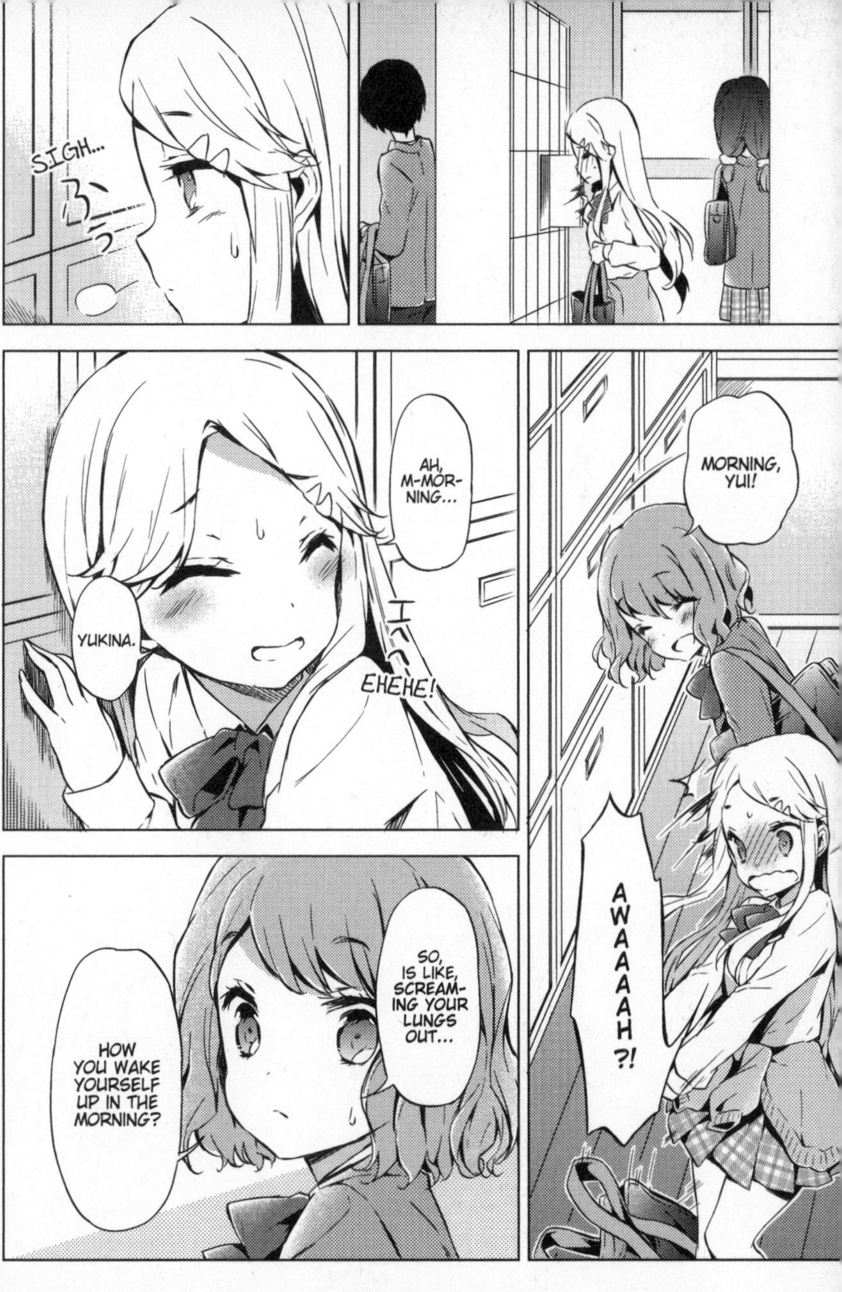
SIGH...
ふぅ
MORNING, YUI!
AWAAAAAH?!
AH, M-MOR-NING...
YUKINA.
エヘヘ
EHEHE!
SO, IS LIKE, SCREAM-ING YOUR LUNGS OUT...
HOW YOU WAKE YOURSELF UP IN THE MORNING?

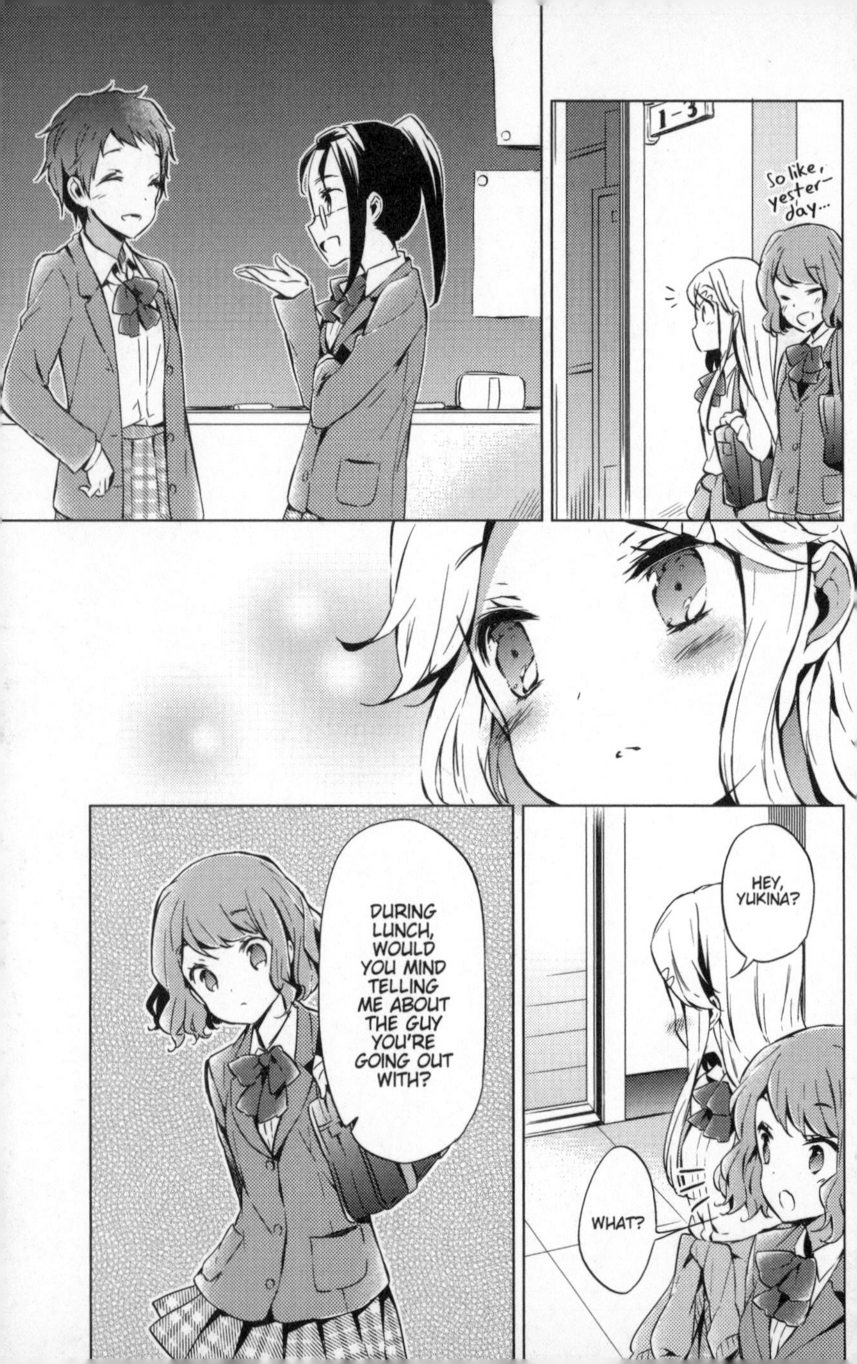
So like, yester-day...
HEY, YUKINA?
WHAT?
DURING LUNCH, WOULD YOU MIND TELLING ME ABOUT THE GUY YOU'RE GOING OUT WITH?

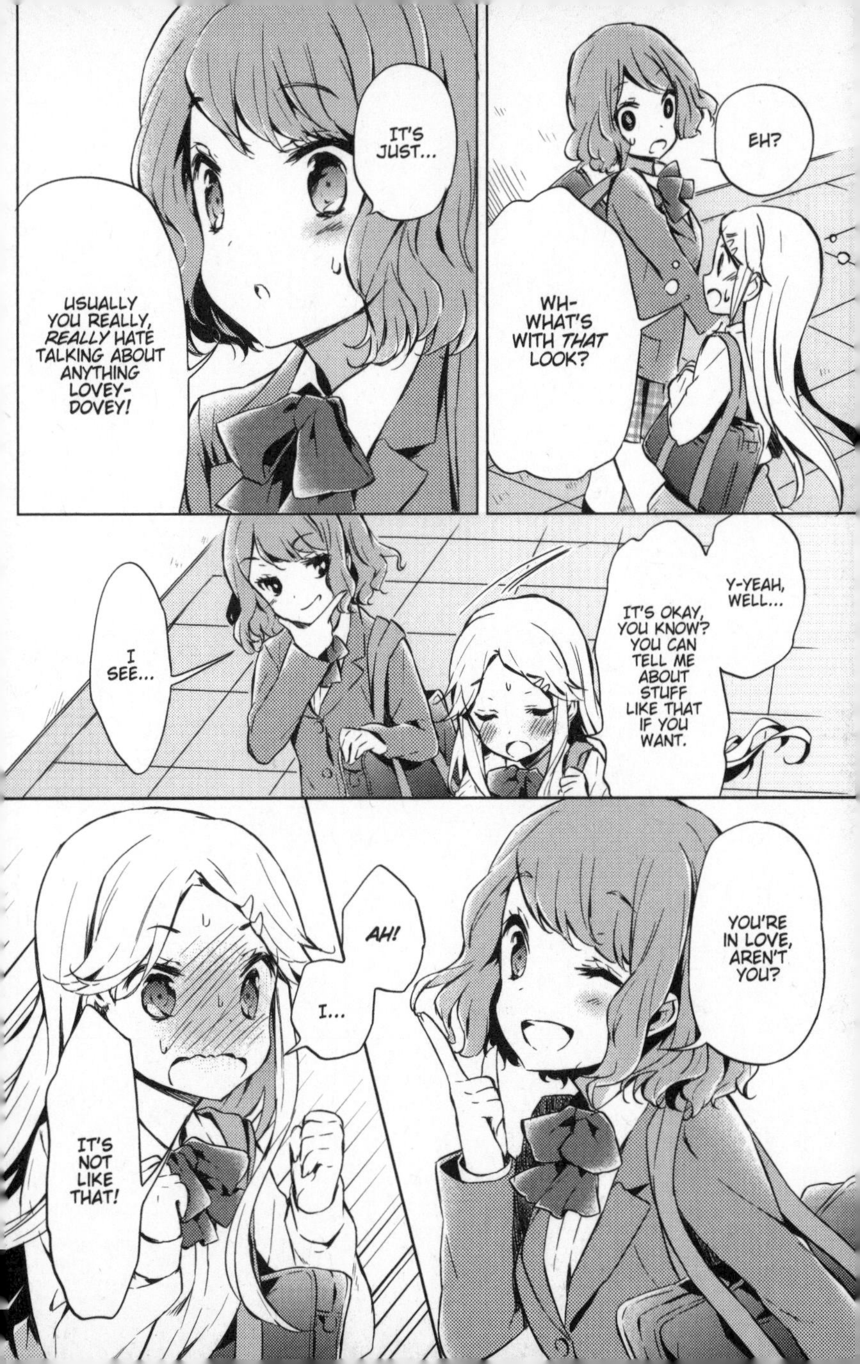
EH?
WH-WHAT'S WITH *THAT* LOOK?
IT'S JUST...
USUALLY YOU REALLY, *REALLY* HATE TALKING ABOUT ANYTHING LOVEY-DOVEY!
Y-YEAH, WELL...
IT'S OKAY, YOU KNOW? YOU CAN TELL ME ABOUT STUFF LIKE THAT IF YOU WANT.
I SEE...
YOU'RE IN LOVE, AREN'T YOU?
AH!
I...
IT'S NOT LIKE THAT!

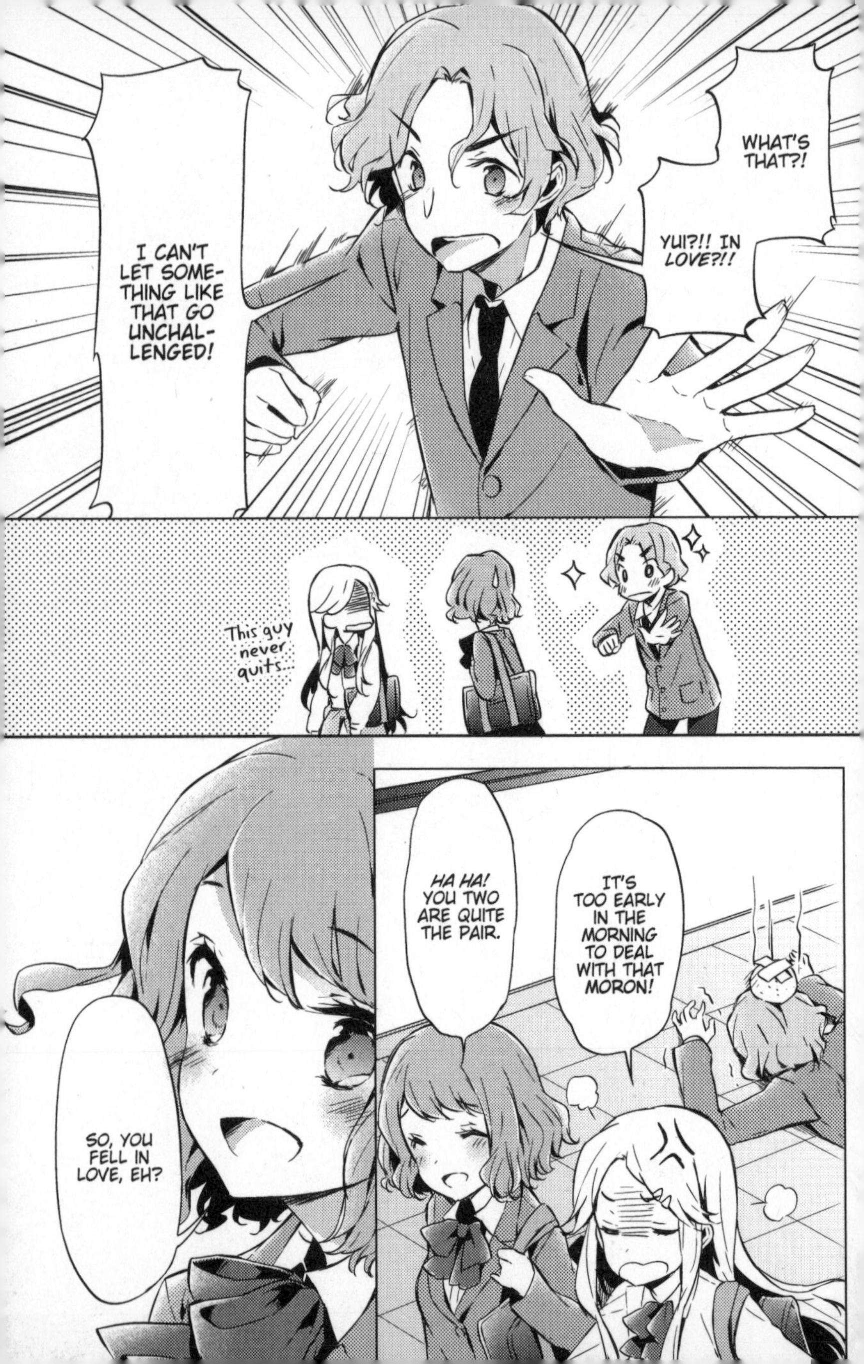
WHAT'S THAT?!
YUI?!! IN LOVE?!!
I CAN'T LET SOMETHING LIKE THAT GO UNCHALLENGED!
This guy never quits...
IT'S TOO EARLY IN THE MORNING TO DEAL WITH THAT MORON!
HA HA! YOU TWO ARE QUITE THE PAIR.
SO, YOU FELL IN LOVE, EH?

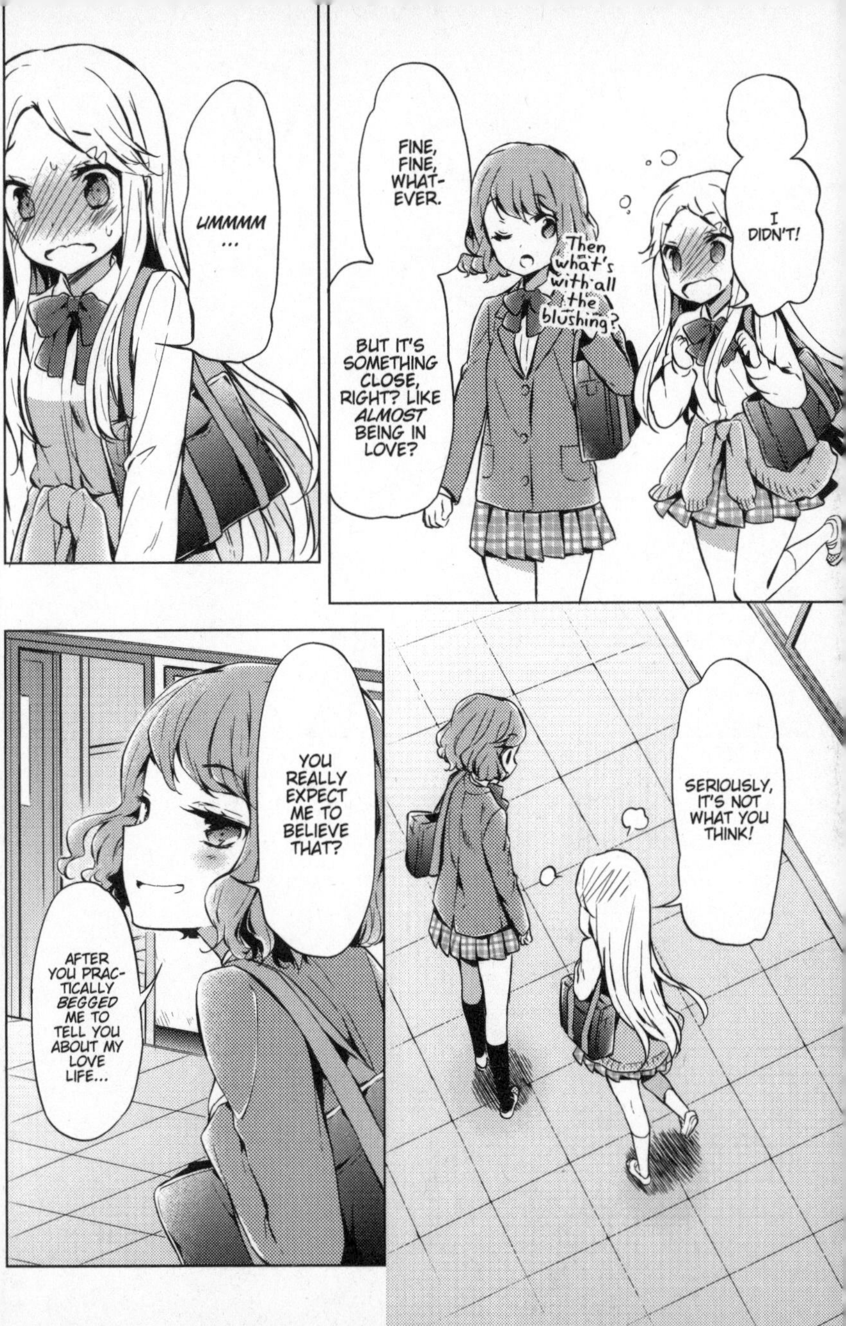
I DIDN'T!
Then what's with all the blushing?
FINE, FINE, WHATEVER.
BUT IT'S SOMETHING CLOSE, RIGHT? LIKE *ALMOST* BEING IN LOVE?
UMMMM...
SERIOUSLY, IT'S NOT WHAT YOU THINK!
YOU REALLY EXPECT ME TO BELIEVE THAT?
AFTER YOU PRACTICALLY *BEGGED* ME TO TELL YOU ABOUT MY LOVE LIFE...

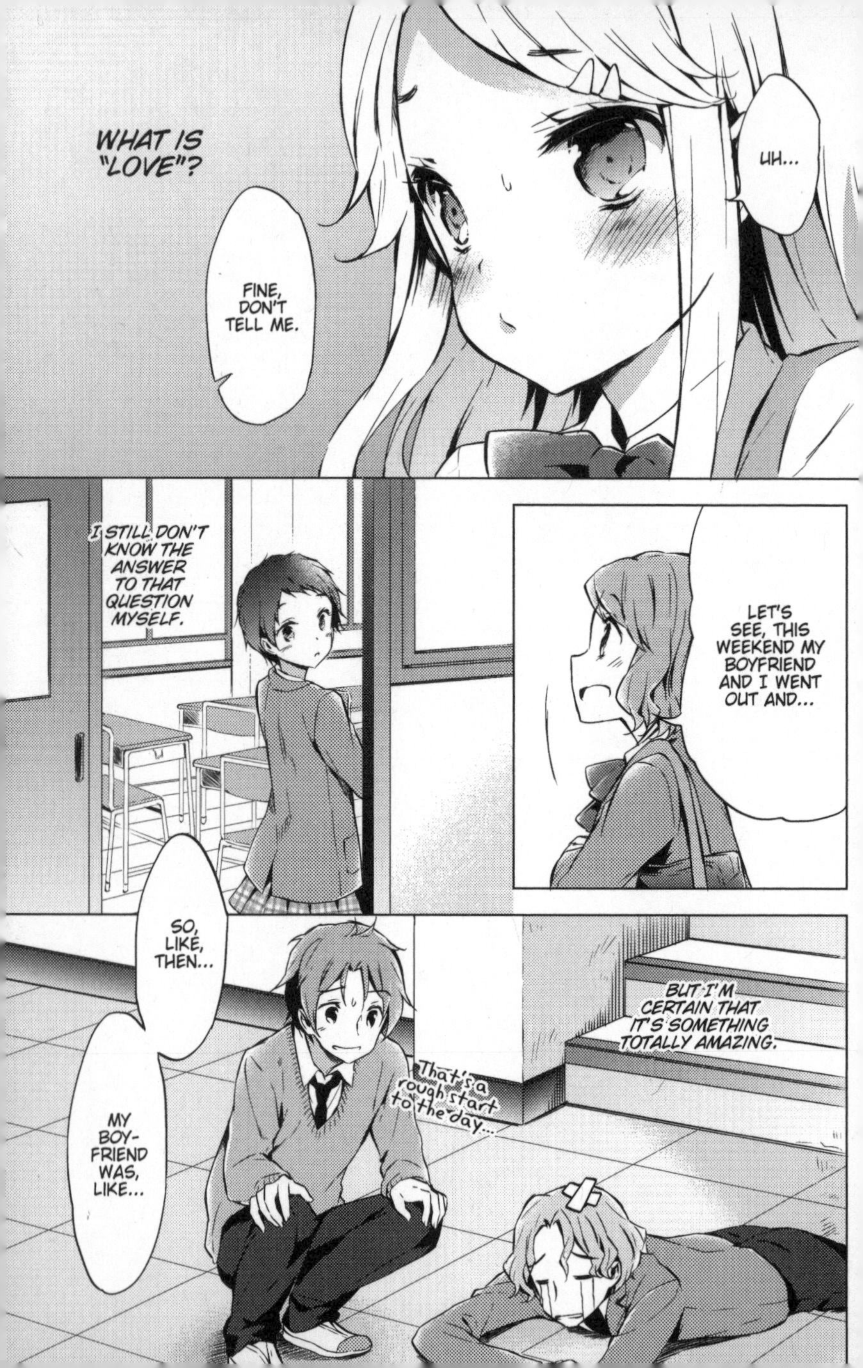
UH...
WHAT IS "LOVE"?
FINE, DON'T TELL ME.
LET'S SEE, THIS WEEKEND MY BOYFRIEND AND I WENT OUT AND...
I STILL DON'T KNOW THE ANSWER TO THAT QUESTION MYSELF.
BUT I'M CERTAIN THAT IT'S SOMETHING TOTALLY AMAZING.
That's a rough start to the day...
SO, LIKE, THEN...
MY BOY-FRIEND WAS, LIKE...

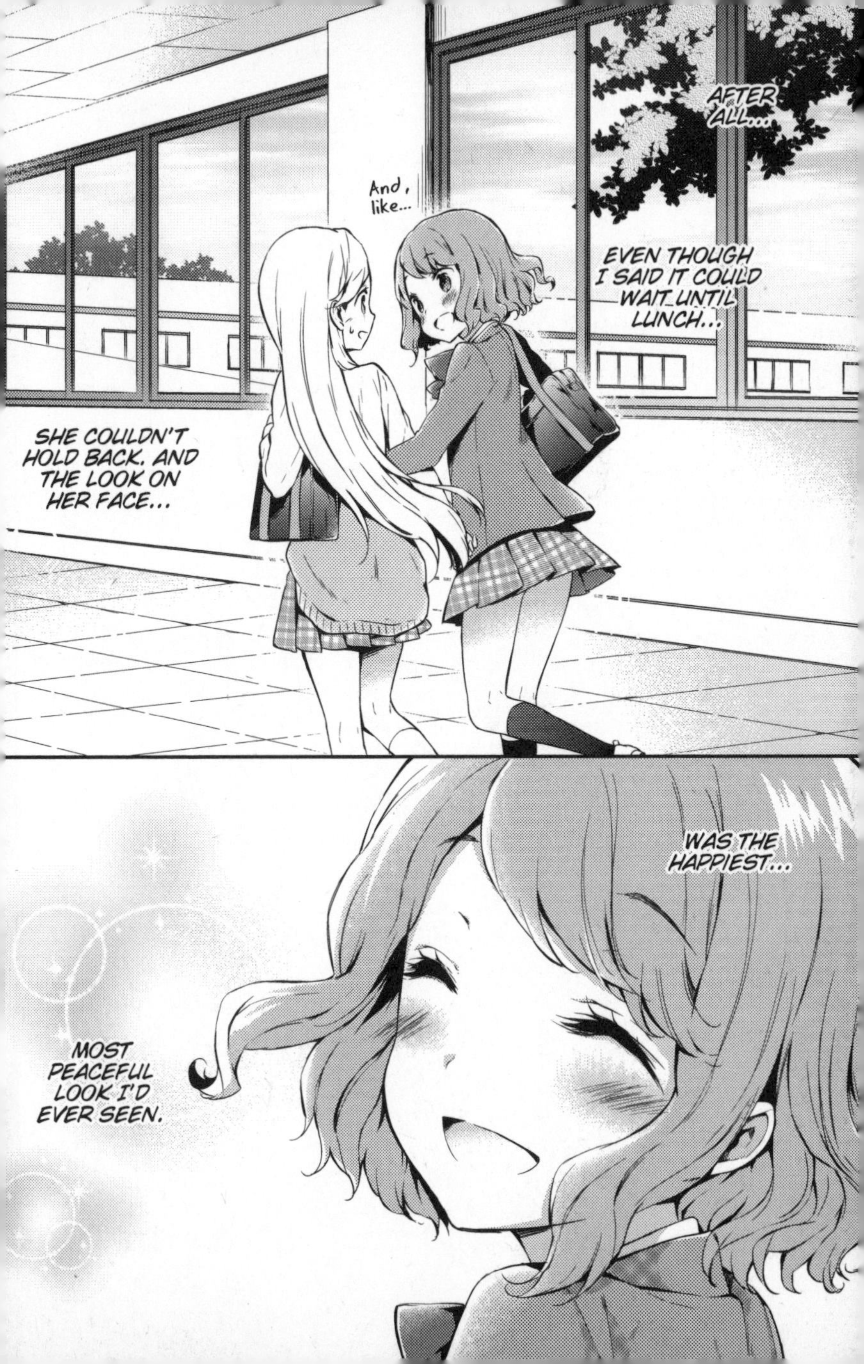
AFTER ALL...
EVEN THOUGH I SAID IT COULD WAIT UNTIL LUNCH...
And, like...
SHE COULDN'T HOLD BACK. AND THE LOOK ON HER FACE...
WAS THE HAPPIEST...
MOST PEACEFUL LOOK I'D EVER SEEN.

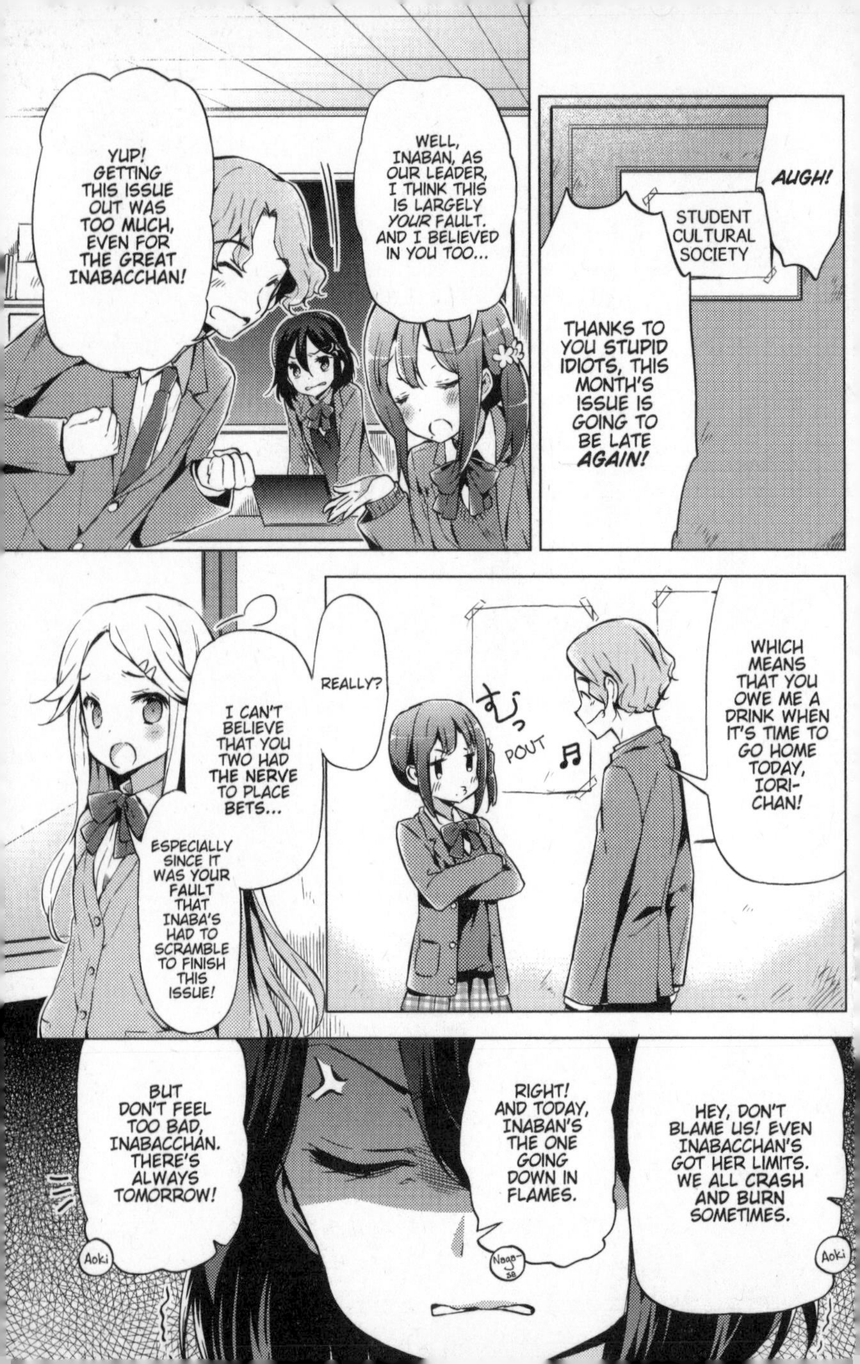
AUGH!
STUDENT CULTURAL SOCIETY
THANKS TO YOU STUPID IDIOTS, THIS MONTH'S ISSUE IS GOING TO BE LATE *AGAIN!*
WELL, INABAN, AS OUR LEADER, I THINK THIS IS LARGELY *YOUR* FAULT. AND I BELIEVED IN YOU TOO...
YUP! GETTING THIS ISSUE OUT WAS TOO MUCH, EVEN FOR THE GREAT INABACCHAN!
WHICH MEANS THAT YOU OWE ME A DRINK WHEN IT'S TIME TO GO HOME TODAY, IORI-CHAN!
むっ
POUT
REALLY?
I CAN'T BELIEVE THAT YOU TWO HAD THE NERVE TO PLACE BETS...
ESPECIALLY SINCE IT WAS YOUR FAULT THAT INABA'S HAD TO SCRAMBLE TO FINISH THIS ISSUE!
HEY, DON'T BLAME US! EVEN INABACCHAN'S GOT HER LIMITS. WE ALL CRASH AND BURN SOMETIMES.
Aoki
RIGHT! AND TODAY, INABAN'S THE ONE GOING DOWN IN FLAMES.
Naga-se
BUT DON'T FEEL TOO BAD, INABACCHAN. THERE'S ALWAYS TOMORROW!
Aoki

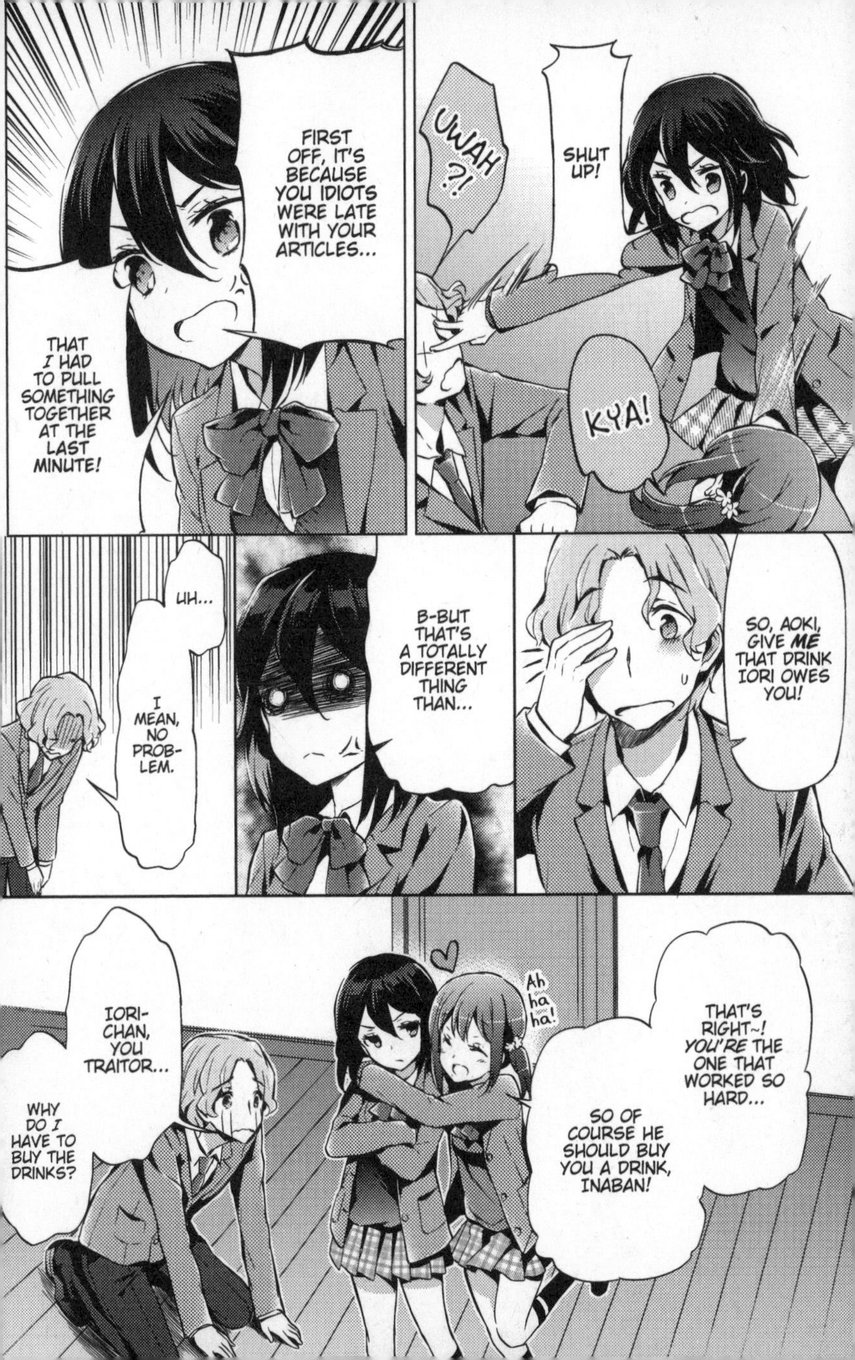
SHUT UP!
UWAH ?!
KYA!
FIRST OFF, IT'S BECAUSE YOU IDIOTS WERE LATE WITH YOUR ARTICLES...
THAT *I* HAD TO PULL SOMETHING TOGETHER AT THE LAST MINUTE!
SO, AOKI, GIVE ***ME*** THAT DRINK IORI OWES YOU!
B-BUT THAT'S A TOTALLY DIFFERENT THING THAN...
UH...
I MEAN, NO PROB-LEM.
THAT'S RIGHT~! *YOU'RE* THE ONE THAT WORKED SO HARD...
SO OF COURSE HE SHOULD BUY YOU A DRINK, INABAN!
Ah ha ha!
IORI-CHAN, YOU TRAITOR...
WHY DO *I* HAVE TO BUY THE DRINKS?

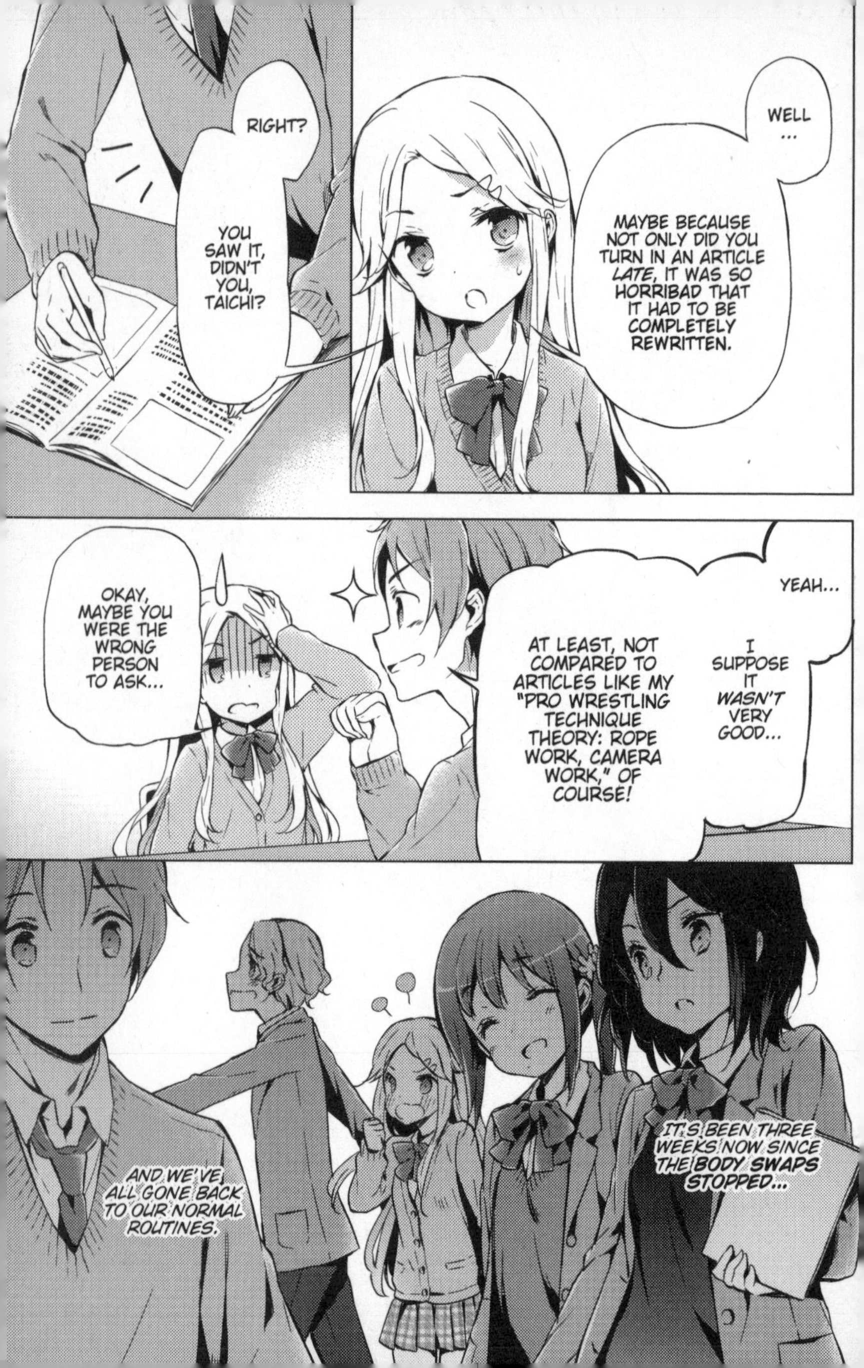
WELL ...
MAYBE BECAUSE NOT ONLY DID YOU TURN IN AN ARTICLE *LATE*, IT WAS SO HORRIBAD THAT IT HAD TO BE COMPLETELY REWRITTEN.
RIGHT?
YOU SAW IT, DIDN'T YOU, TAICHI?
YEAH...
I SUPPOSE IT *WASN'T* VERY GOOD...
AT LEAST, NOT COMPARED TO ARTICLES LIKE MY "PRO WRESTLING TECHNIQUE THEORY: ROPE WORK, CAMERA WORK," OF COURSE!
OKAY, MAYBE YOU WERE THE WRONG PERSON TO ASK...
IT'S BEEN THREE WEEKS NOW SINCE THE BODY SWAPS STOPPED...
AND WE'VE ALL GONE BACK TO OUR NORMAL ROUTINES.

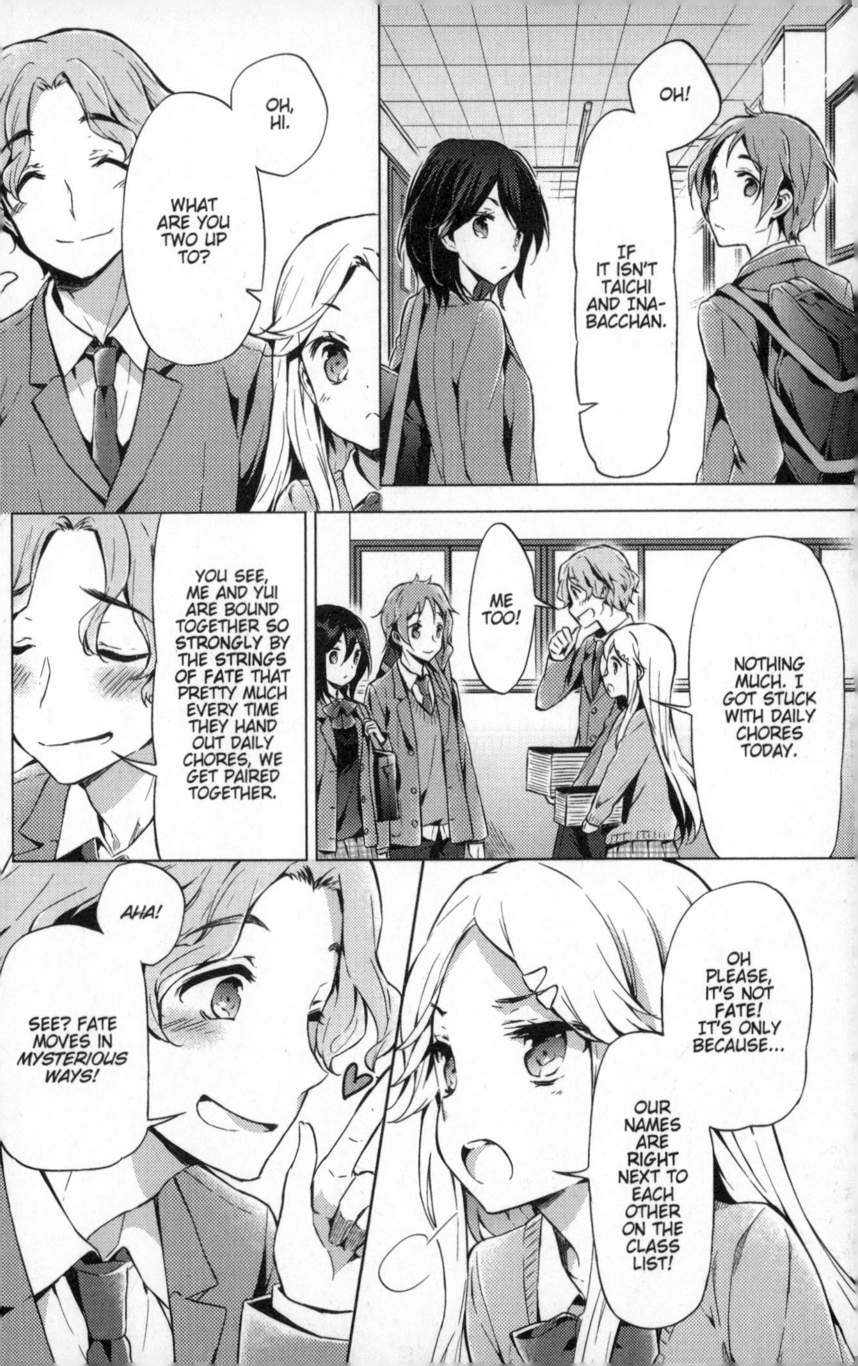
OH!
IF IT ISN'T TAICHI AND INA-BACCHAN.
OH, HI.
WHAT ARE YOU TWO UP TO?
NOTHING MUCH. I GOT STUCK WITH DAILY CHORES TODAY.
ME TOO!
YOU SEE, ME AND YUI ARE BOUND TOGETHER SO STRONGLY BY THE STRINGS OF FATE THAT PRETTY MUCH EVERY TIME THEY HAND OUT DAILY CHORES, WE GET PAIRED TOGETHER.
OH PLEASE, IT'S NOT FATE! IT'S ONLY BECAUSE...
OUR NAMES ARE RIGHT NEXT TO EACH OTHER ON THE CLASS LIST!
AHA!
SEE? FATE MOVES IN *MYSTERIOUS* WAYS!

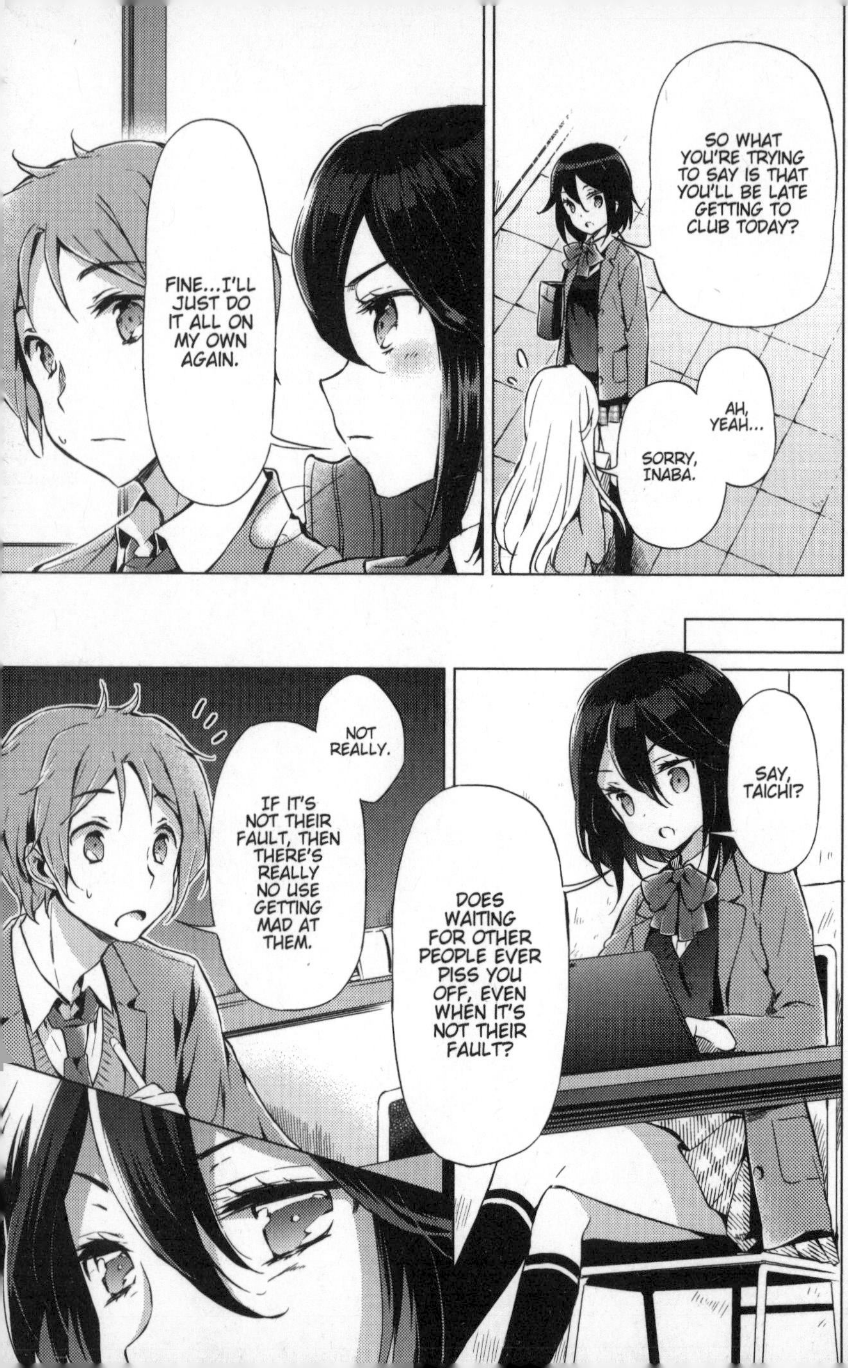
SO WHAT YOU'RE TRYING TO SAY IS THAT YOU'LL BE LATE GETTING TO CLUB TODAY?
AH, YEAH...
SORRY, INABA.
FINE...I'LL JUST DO IT ALL ON MY OWN AGAIN.
SAY, TAICHI?
DOES WAITING FOR OTHER PEOPLE EVER PISS YOU OFF, EVEN WHEN IT'S NOT THEIR FAULT?
NOT REALLY.
IF IT'S NOT THEIR FAULT, THEN THERE'S REALLY NO USE GETTING MAD AT THEM.

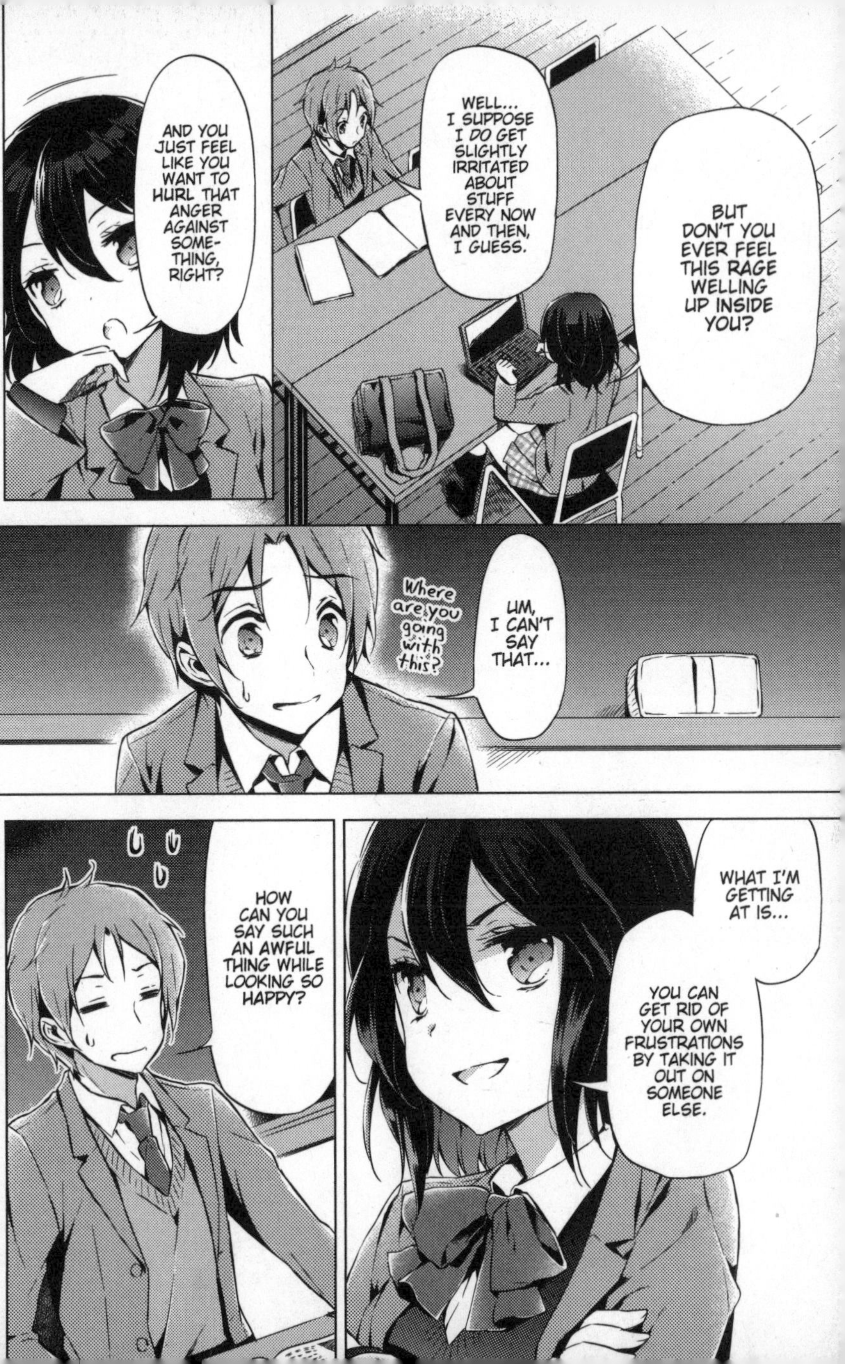
BUT DON'T YOU EVER FEEL THIS RAGE WELLING UP INSIDE YOU?
WELL... I SUPPOSE I *DO* GET SLIGHTLY IRRITATED ABOUT STUFF EVERY NOW AND THEN, I GUESS.
AND YOU JUST FEEL LIKE YOU WANT TO HURL THAT ANGER AGAINST SOME-THING, RIGHT?
UM, I CAN'T SAY THAT...
Where are you going with this?
WHAT I'M GETTING AT IS...
YOU CAN GET RID OF YOUR OWN FRUSTRATIONS BY TAKING IT OUT ON SOMEONE ELSE.
HOW CAN YOU SAY SUCH AN AWFUL THING WHILE LOOKING SO HAPPY?

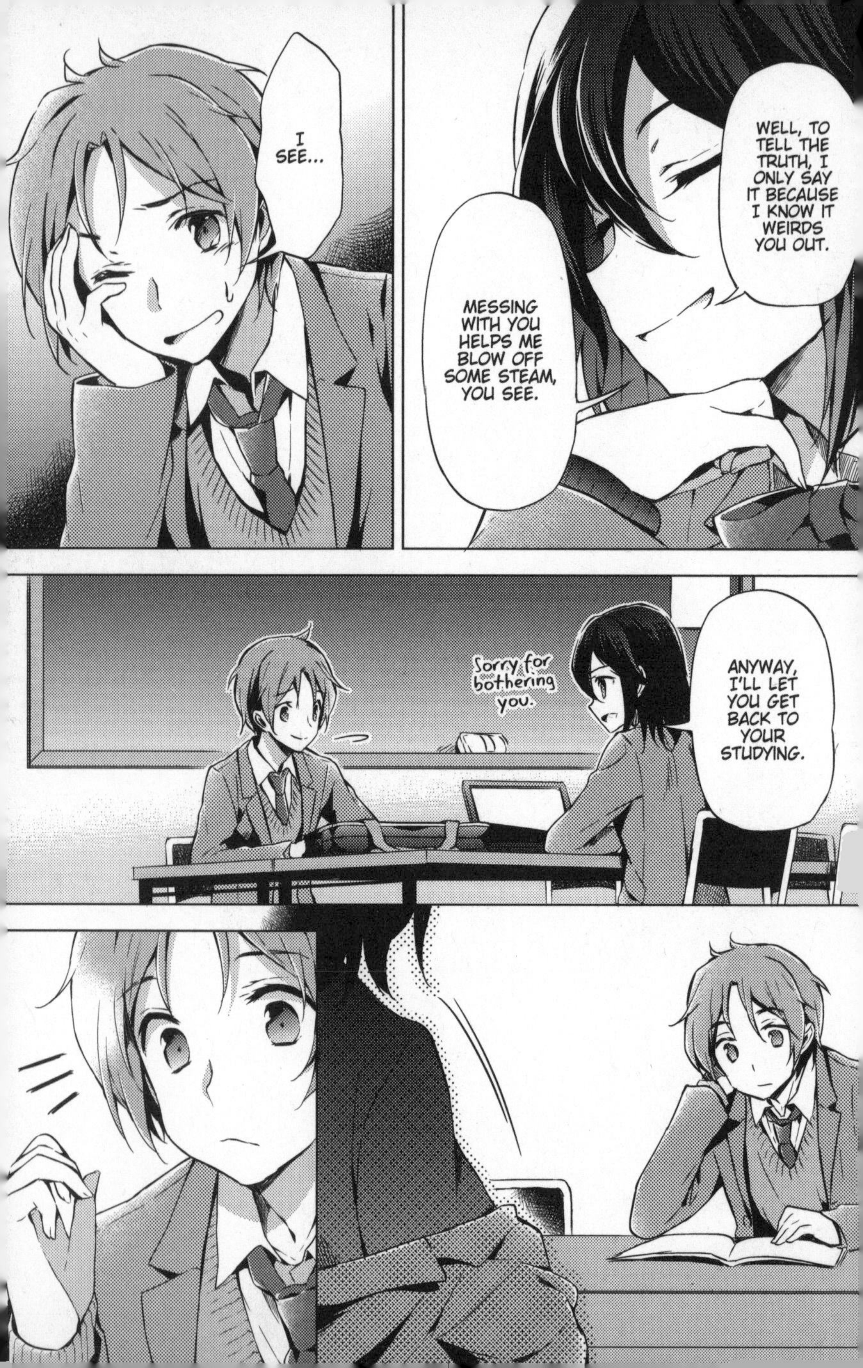
WELL, TO TELL THE TRUTH, I ONLY SAY IT BECAUSE I KNOW IT WEIRDS YOU OUT.
MESSING WITH YOU HELPS ME BLOW OFF SOME STEAM, YOU SEE.
I SEE...
ANYWAY, I'LL LET YOU GET BACK TO YOUR STUDYING.
Sorry for bothering you.

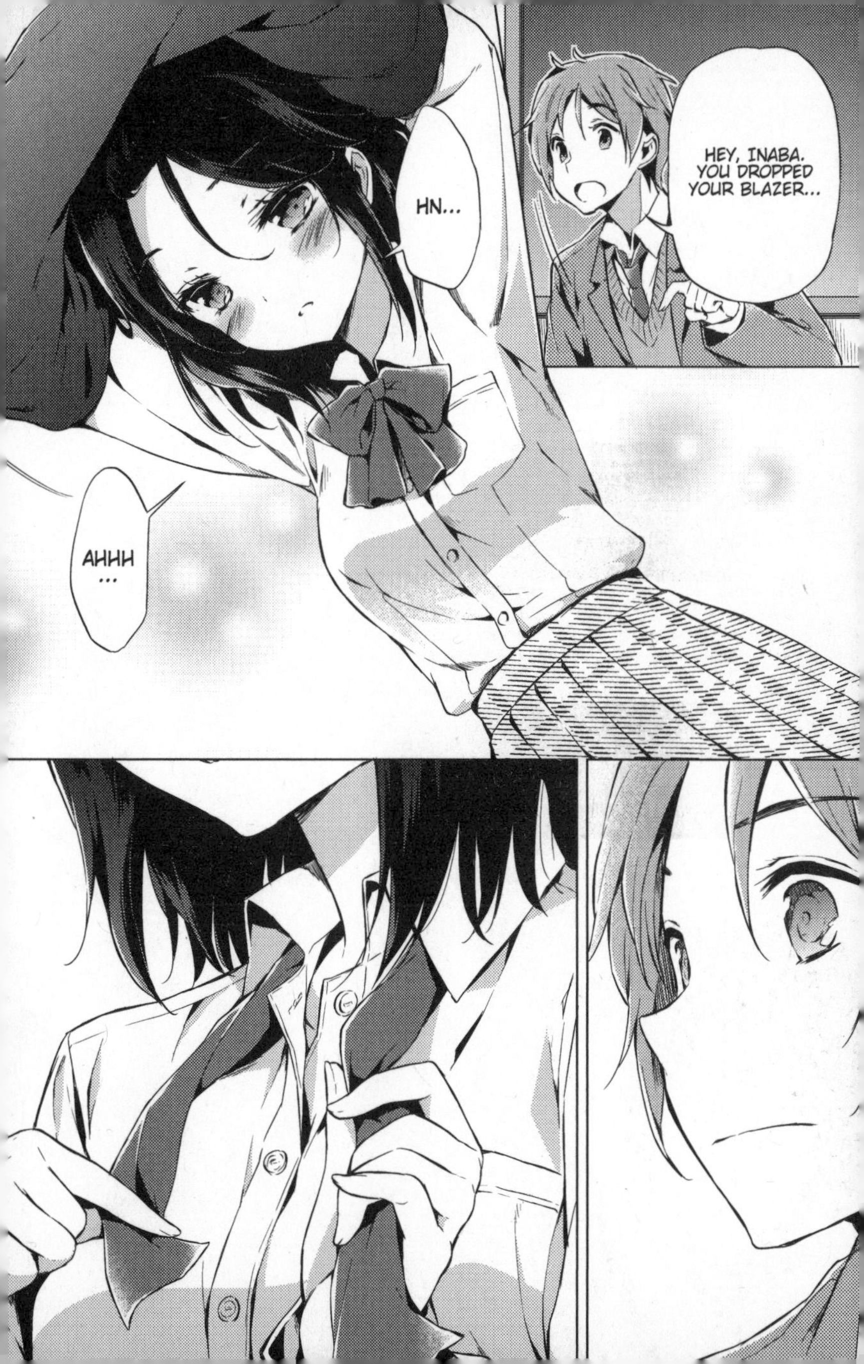
HEY, INABA. YOU DROPPED YOUR BLAZER...
HN...
AHHH ...

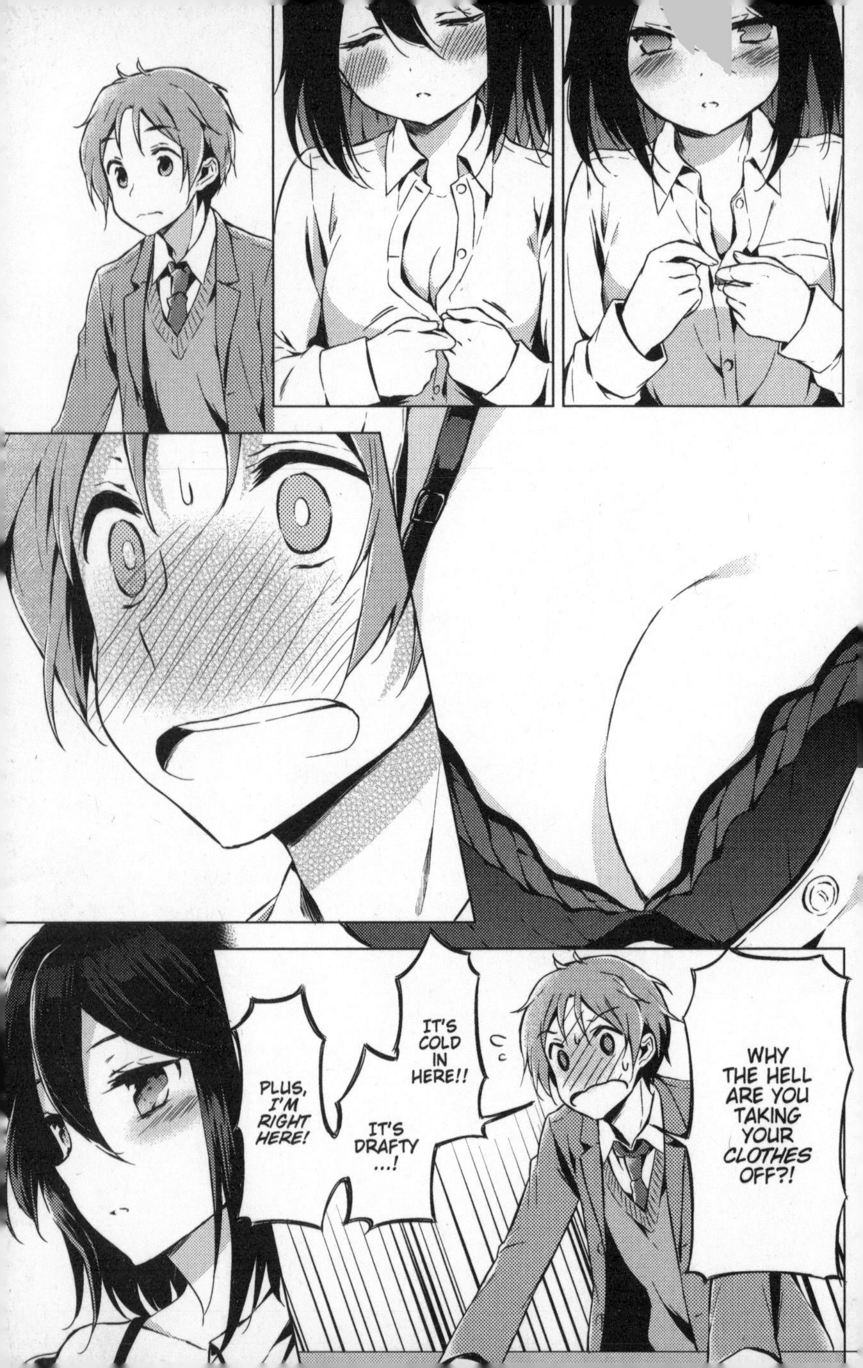
WHY THE HELL ARE YOU TAKING YOUR CLOTHES OFF?!
IT'S COLD IN HERE!!
IT'S DRAFTY ...!
PLUS, I'M RIGHT HERE!

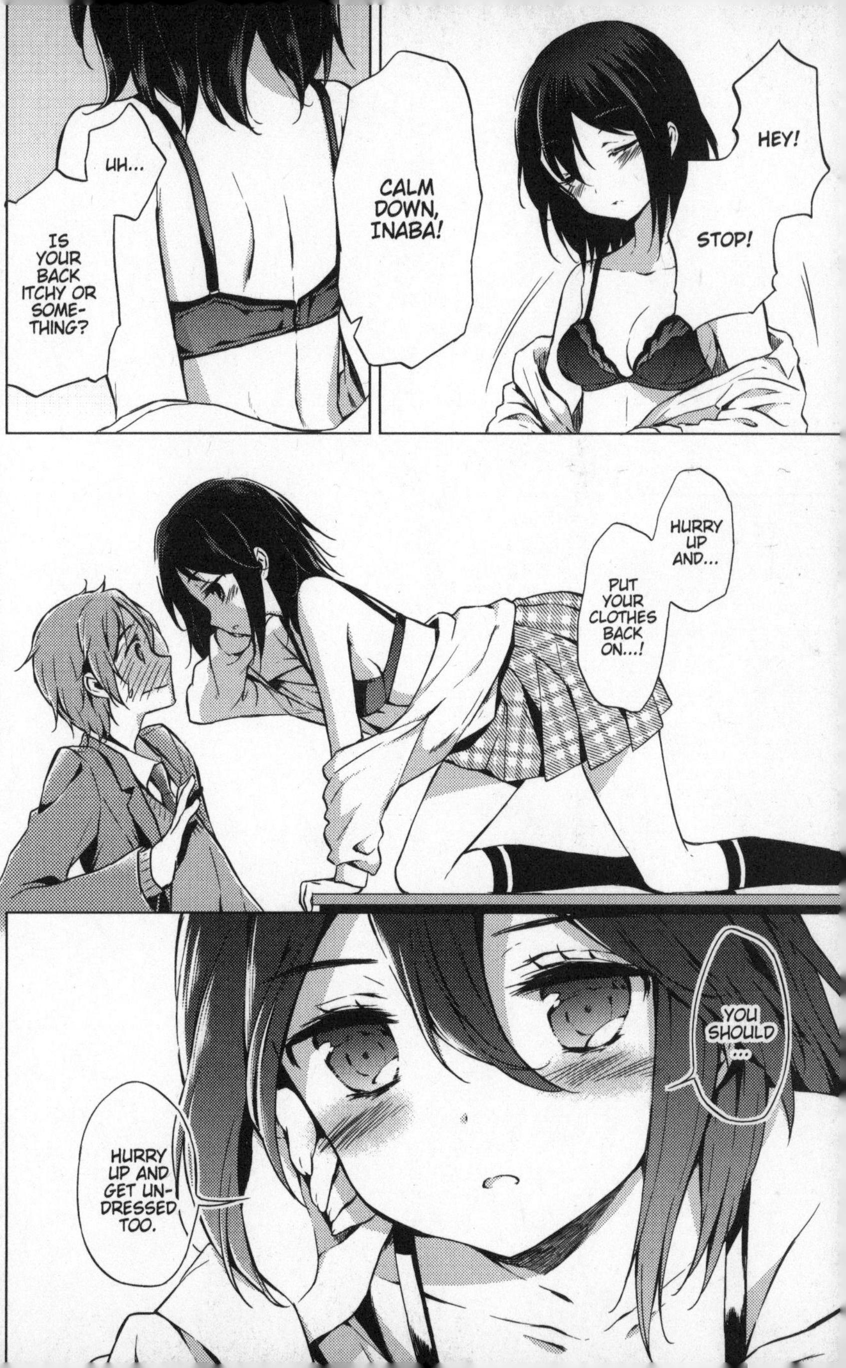
HEY!
STOP!
CALM DOWN, INABA!
UH...
IS YOUR BACK ITCHY OR SOME-THING?
HURRY UP AND...
PUT YOUR CLOTHES BACK ON...!
YOU SHOULD...
HURRY UP AND GET UN-DRESSED TOO.

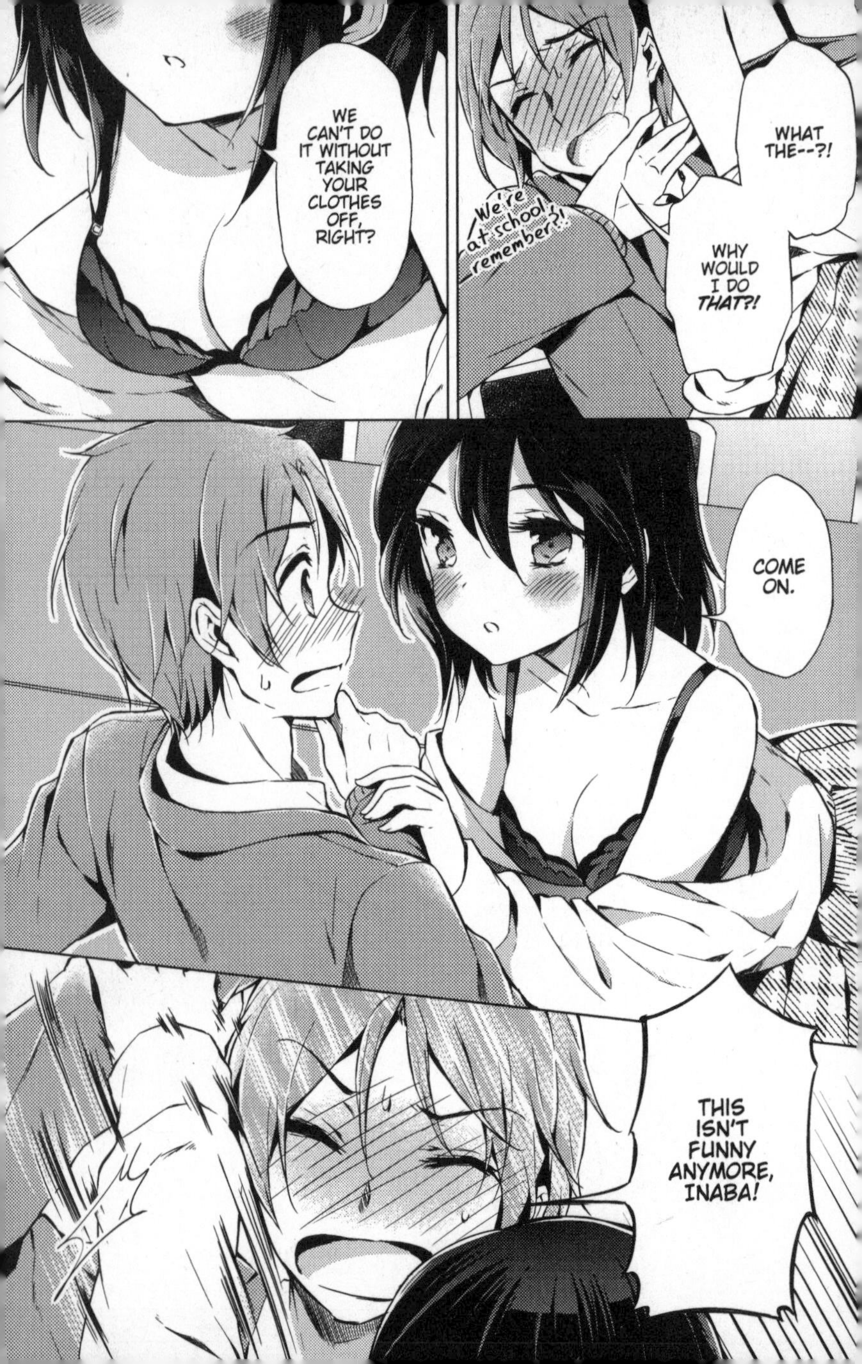
WHAT THE--?!
WHY WOULD I DO *THAT?!*
We're at school remember?!
WE CAN'T DO IT WITHOUT TAKING YOUR CLOTHES OFF, RIGHT?
COME ON.
THIS ISN'T FUNNY ANYMORE, INABA!

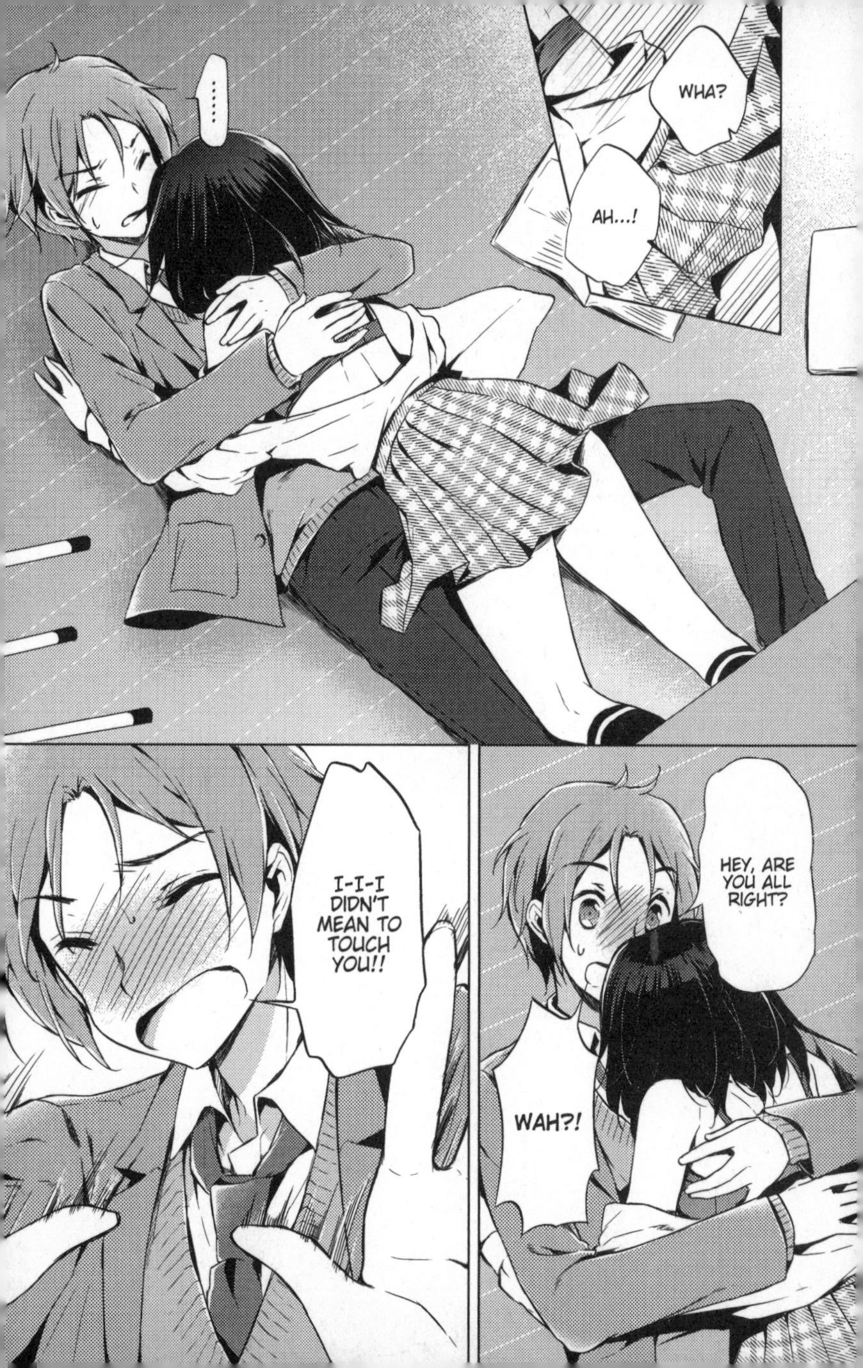
WHA?
AH...!
......
HEY, ARE YOU ALL RIGHT?
WAH?!
I-I-I DIDN'T MEAN TO TOUCH YOU!!

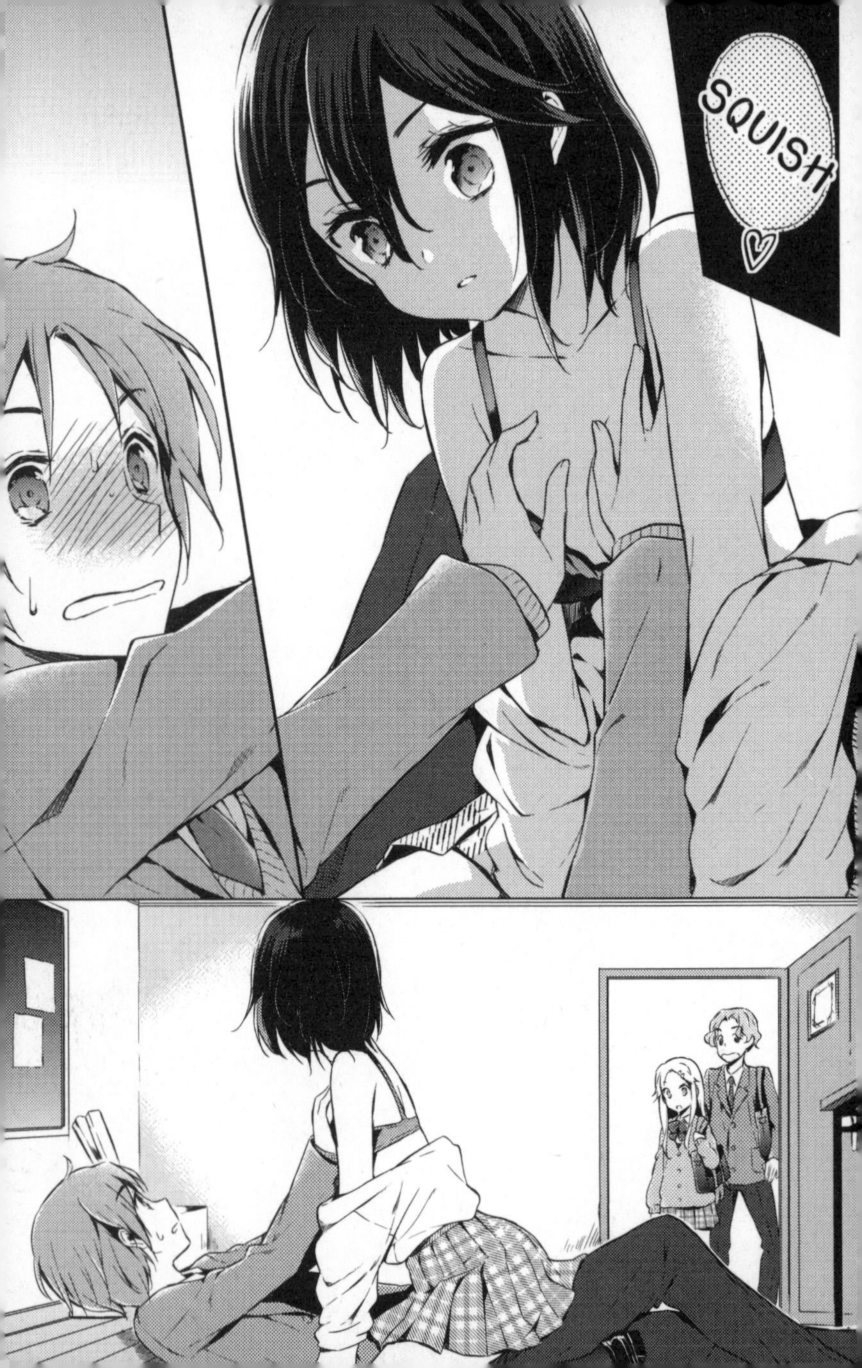
SQUISH

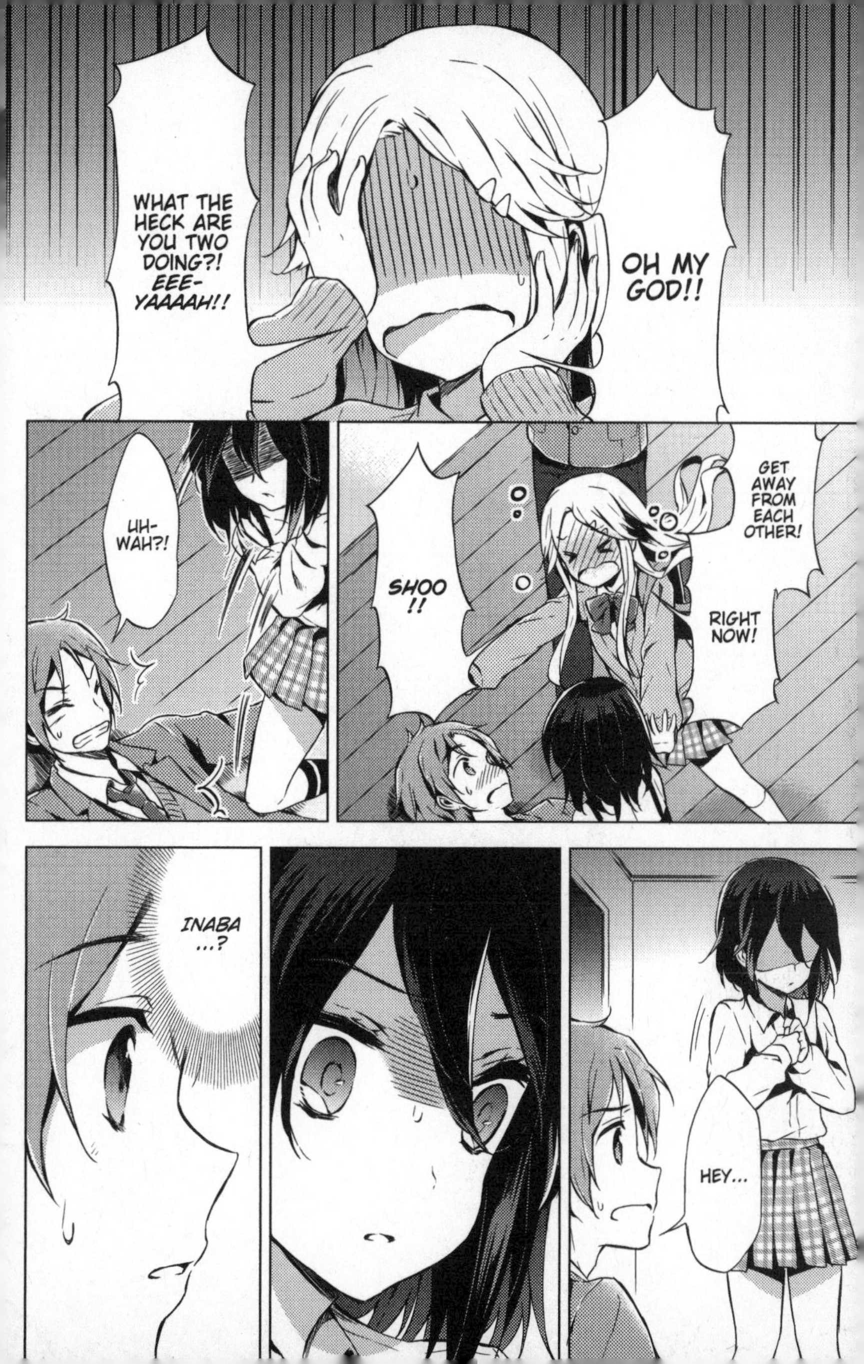
OH MY GOD!!
WHAT THE HECK ARE YOU TWO DOING?! EEE-YAAAAH!!
GET AWAY FROM EACH OTHER!
RIGHT NOW!
SHOO !!
UH-WAH?!
HEY...
INABA ...?

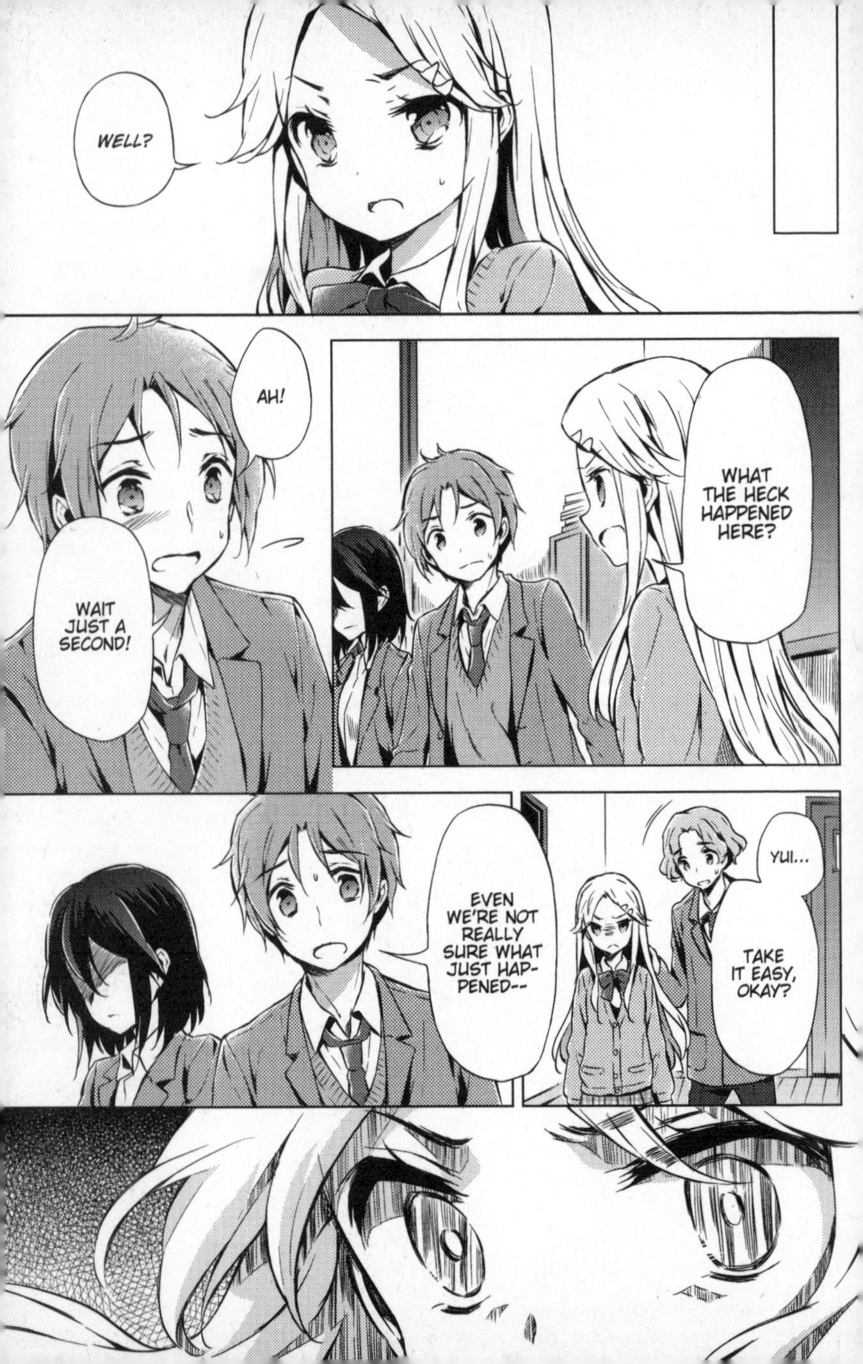
WELL?
WHAT THE HECK HAPPENED HERE?
AH!
WAIT JUST A SECOND!
YUI...
TAKE IT EASY, OKAY?
EVEN WE'RE NOT REALLY SURE WHAT JUST HAP-PENED--

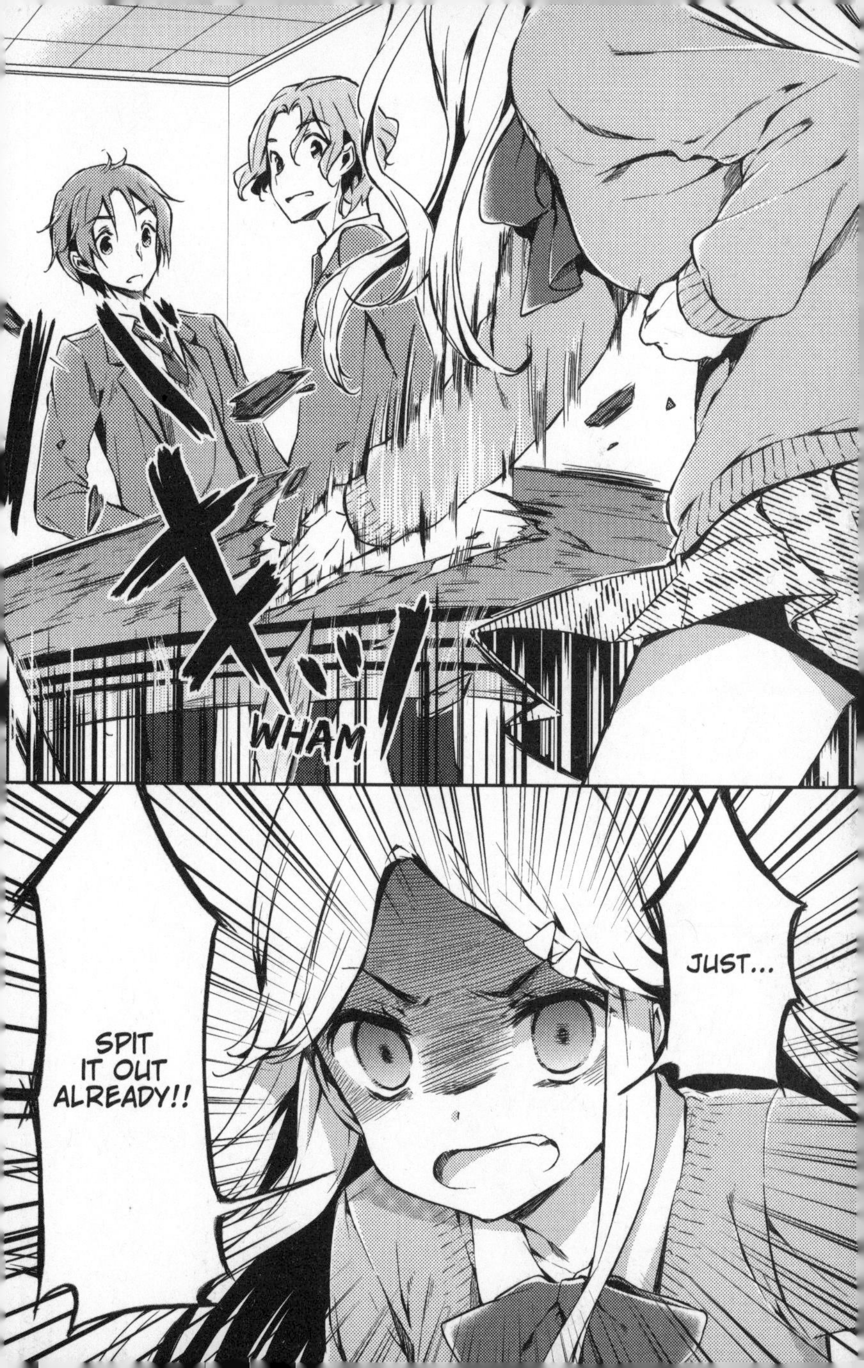
WHAM
JUST...
SPIT IT OUT ALREADY!!

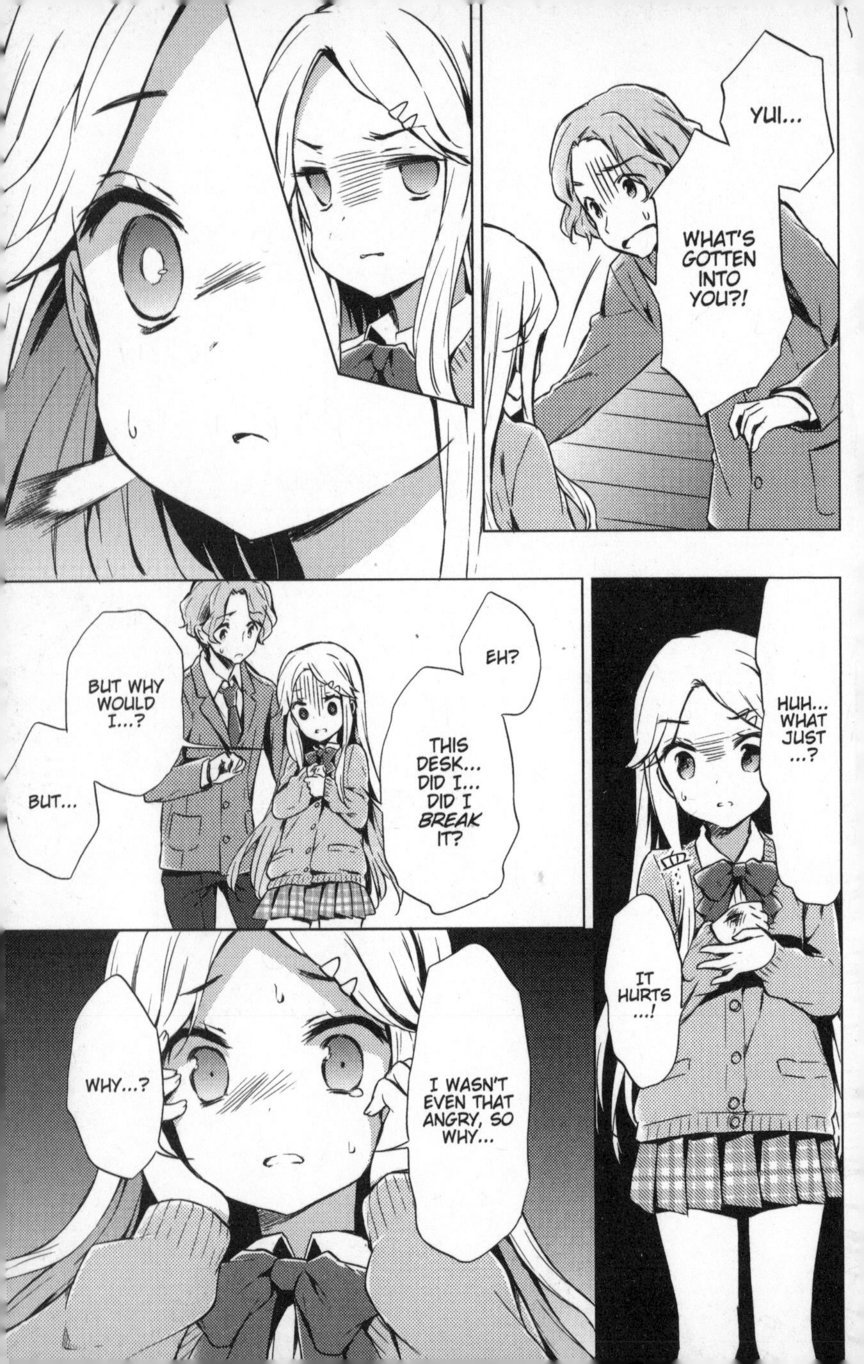
YUI...
WHAT'S GOTTEN INTO YOU?!
HUH... WHAT JUST ...?
IT HURTS ...!
EH?
THIS DESK... DID I... DID I *BREAK* IT?
BUT WHY WOULD I...?
BUT...
I WASN'T EVEN THAT ANGRY, SO WHY...
WHY...?

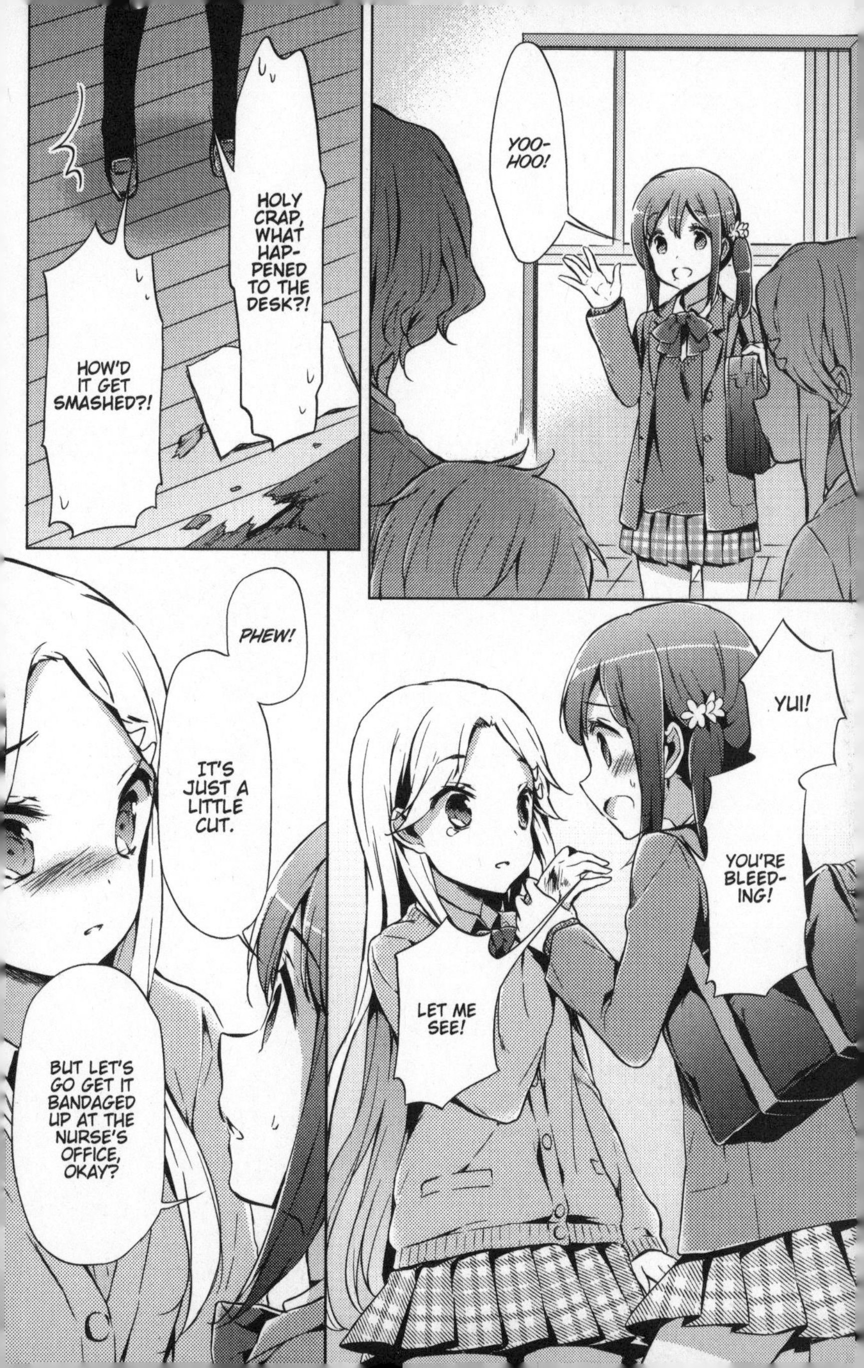
YOO-HOO!
HOLY CRAP, WHAT HAP-PENED TO THE DESK?!
HOW'D IT GET SMASHED?!
YUI!
YOU'RE BLEED-ING!
LET ME SEE!
PHEW!
IT'S JUST A LITTLE CUT.
BUT LET'S GO GET IT BANDAGED UP AT THE NURSE'S OFFICE, OKAY?

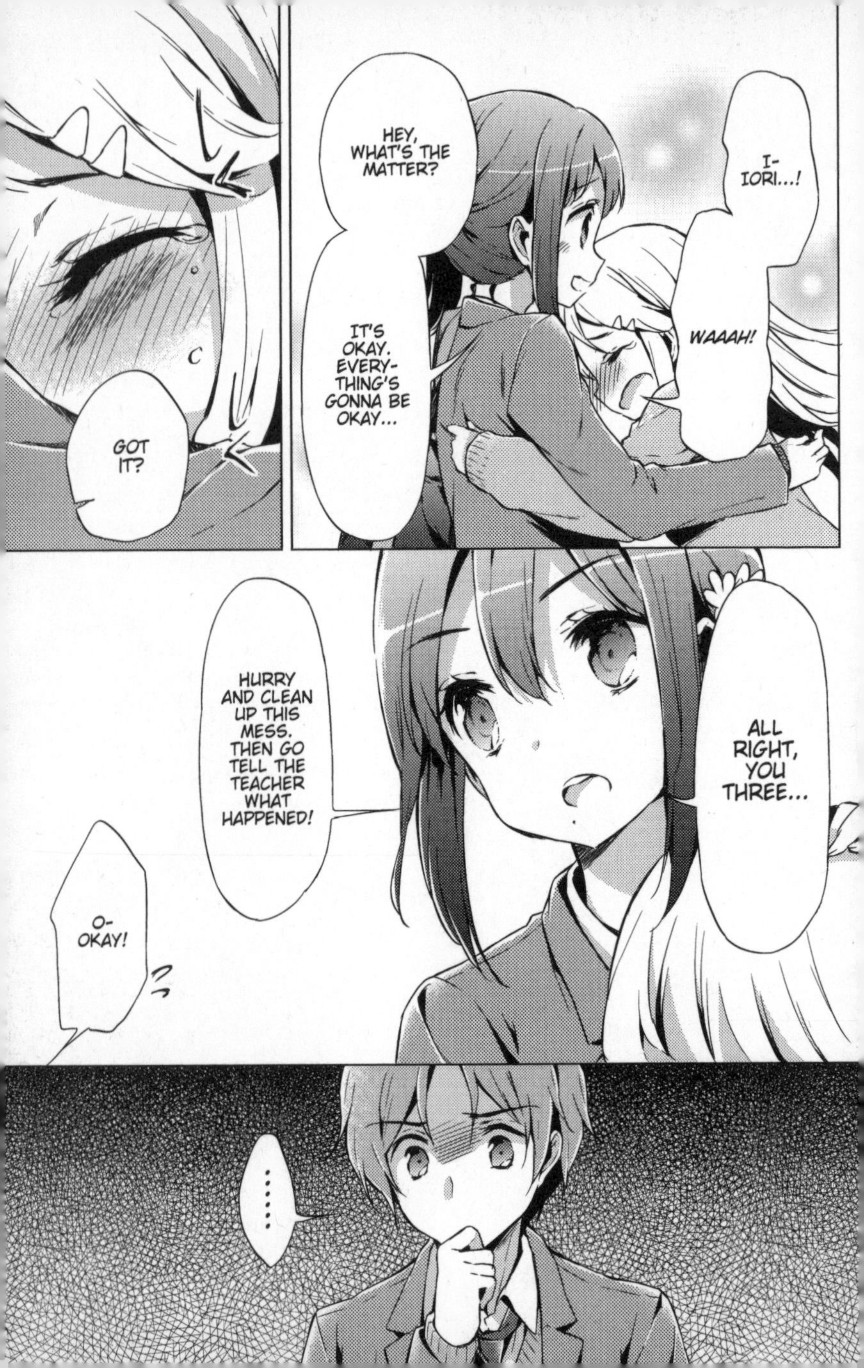
I-IORI...!
HEY, WHAT'S THE MATTER?
WAAAH!
IT'S OKAY. EVERYTHING'S GONNA BE OKAY...
GOT IT?
ALL RIGHT, YOU THREE...
HURRY AND CLEAN UP THIS MESS. THEN GO TELL THE TEACHER WHAT HAPPENED!
O-OKAY!
......

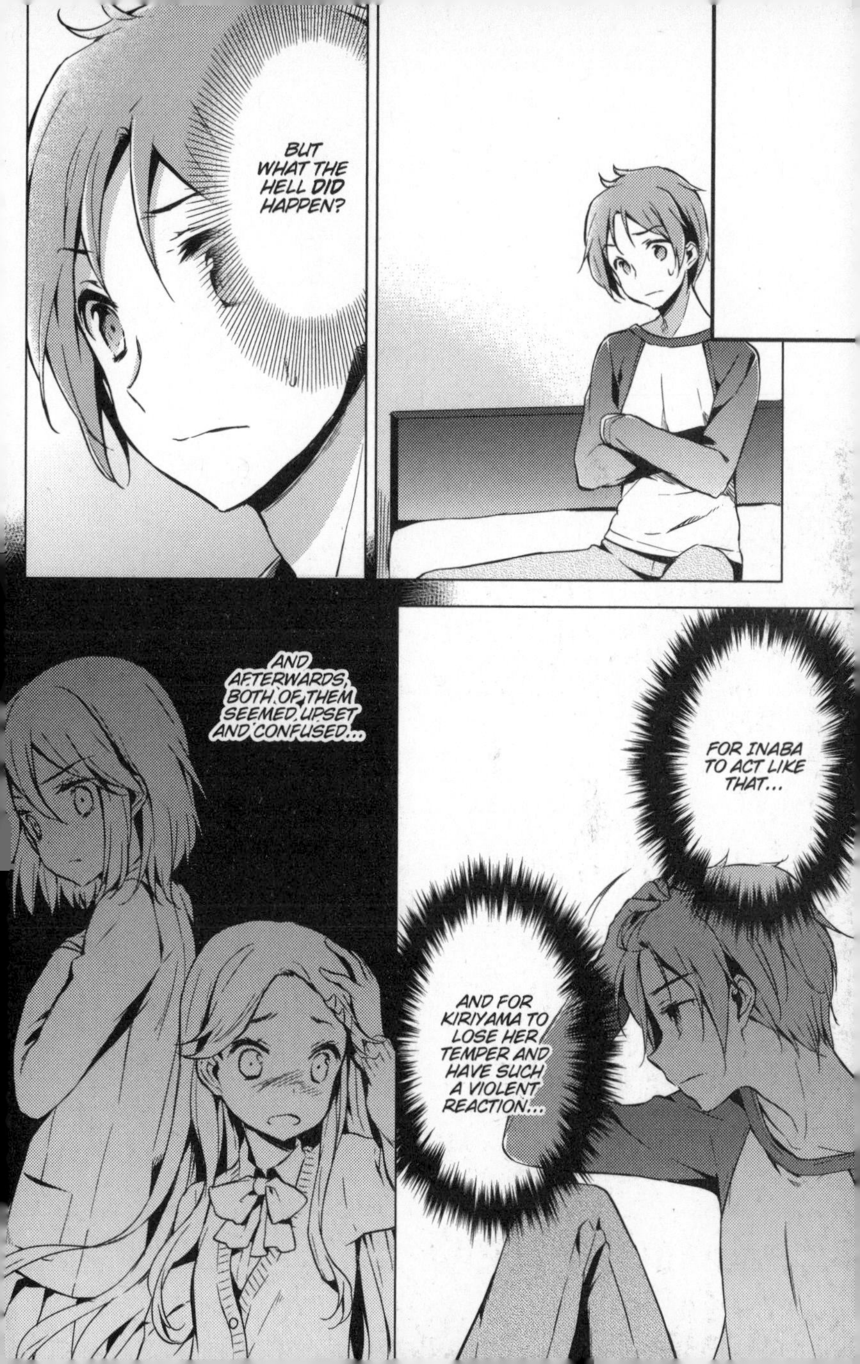
BUT WHAT THE HELL DID HAPPEN?
FOR INABA TO ACT LIKE THAT...
AND FOR KIRIYAMA TO LOSE HER TEMPER AND HAVE SUCH A VIOLENT REACTION...
AND AFTERWARDS, BOTH OF THEM SEEMED UPSET AND CONFUSED...

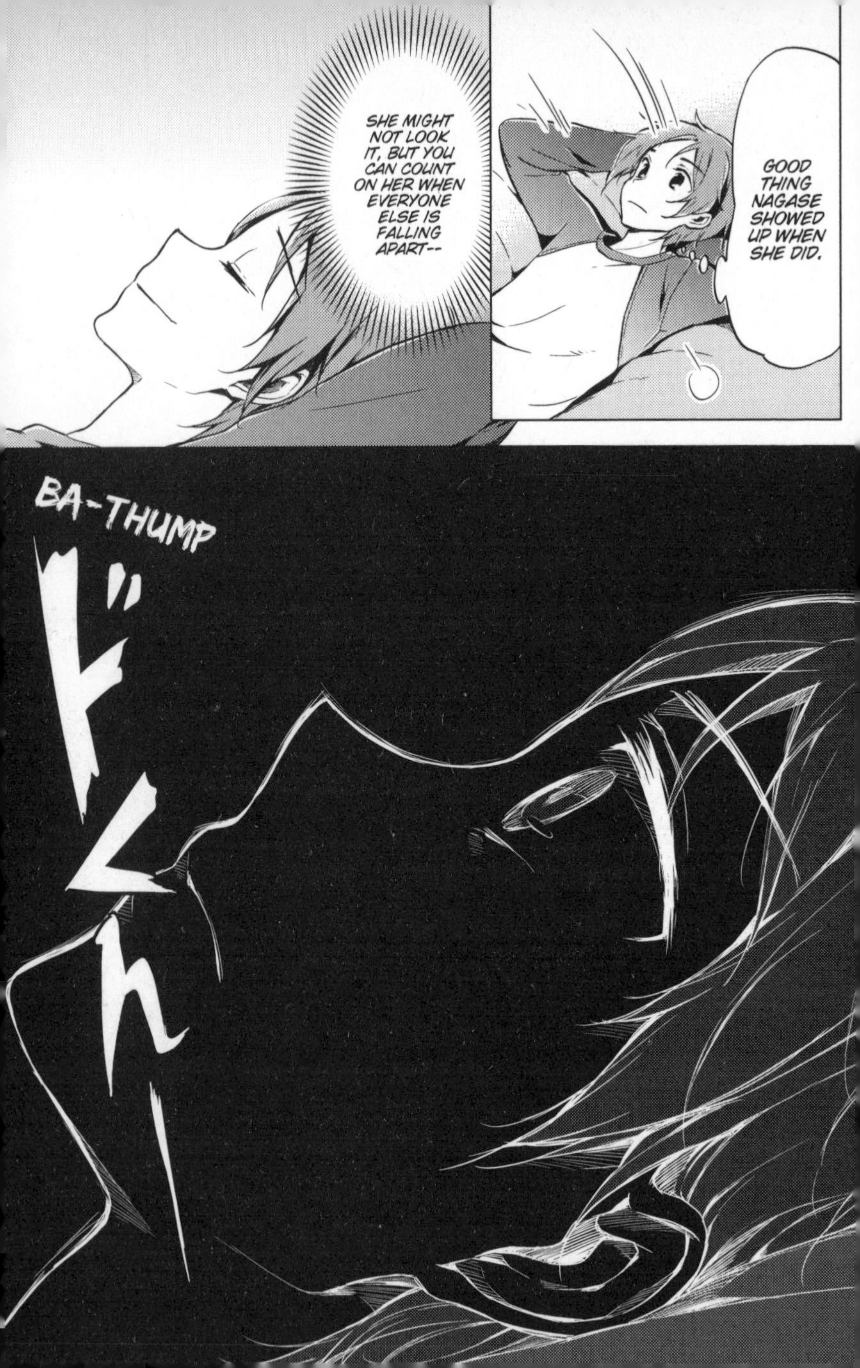
GOOD THING NAGASE SHOWED UP WHEN SHE DID.
SHE MIGHT NOT LOOK IT, BUT YOU CAN COUNT ON HER WHEN EVERYONE ELSE IS FALLING APART--
BA-THUMP
ドくん

KOKORO CONNECT

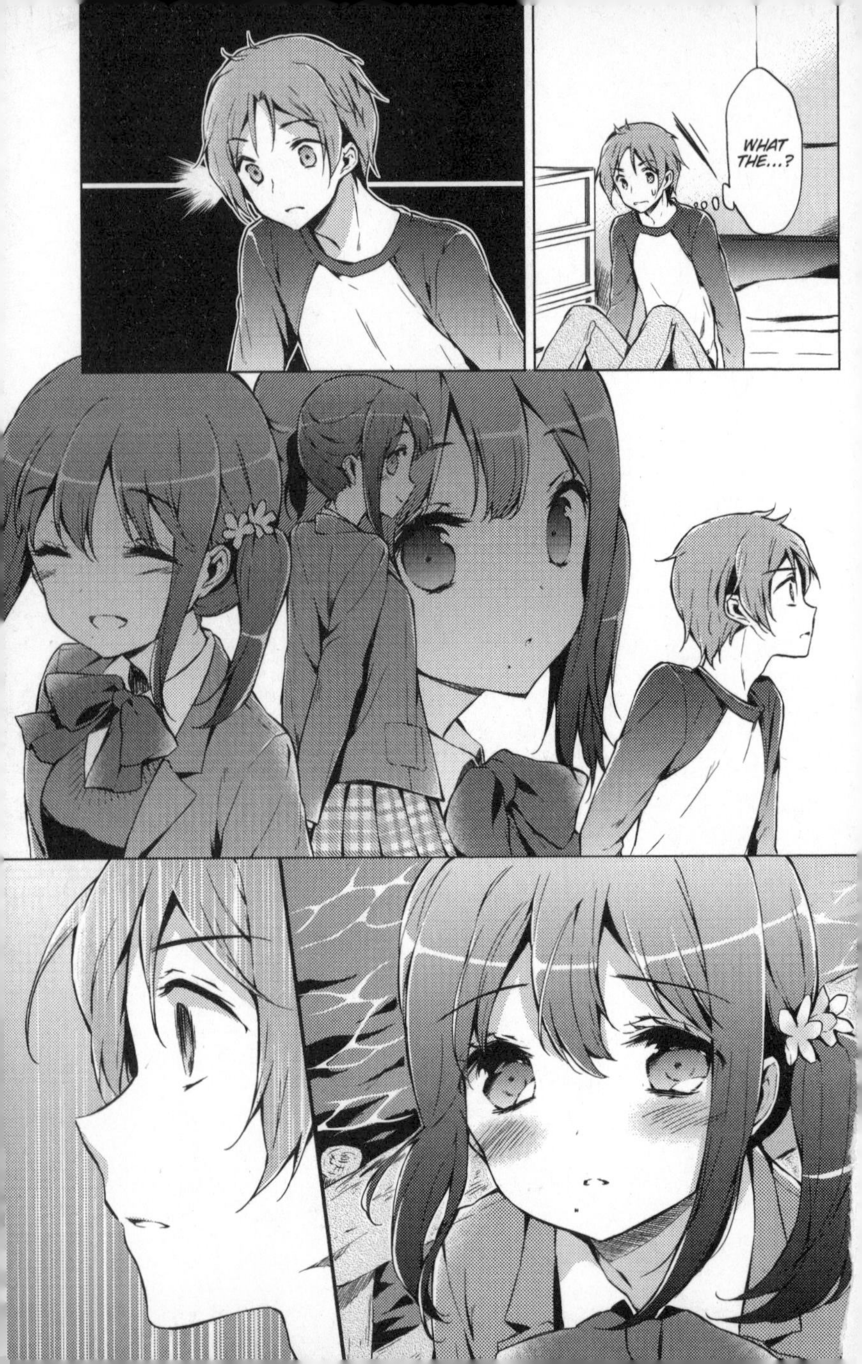
WHAT THE...?

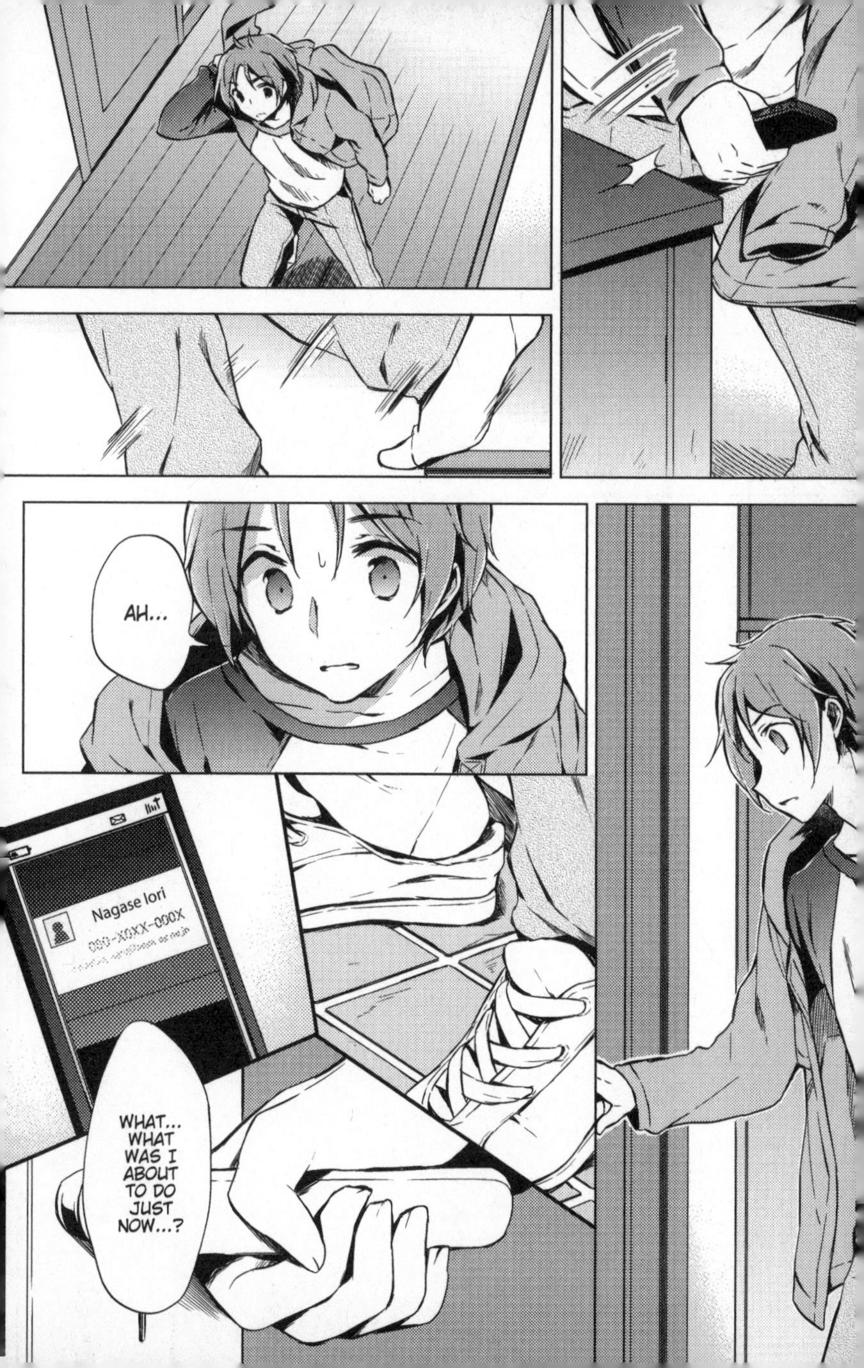
AH...
Nagase Iori
000-X0XX-000X
WHAT... WHAT WAS I ABOUT TO DO JUST NOW...?

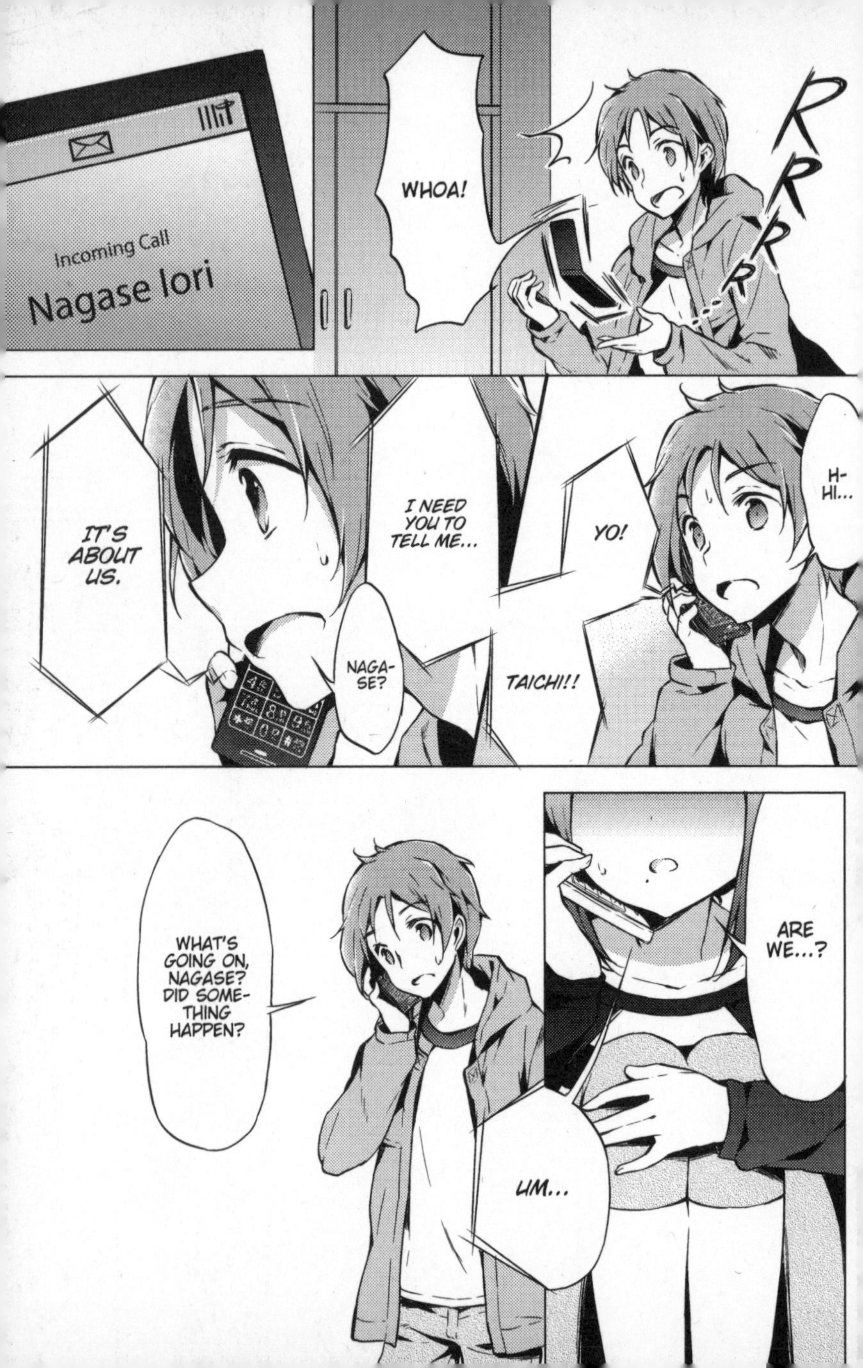
RRRR...
WHOA!
Incoming Call
Nagase Iori
H-HI...
YO!
TAICHI!!
I NEED YOU TO TELL ME...
NAGA-SE?
IT'S ABOUT US.
ARE WE...?
UM...
WHAT'S GOING ON, NAGASE? DID SOME-THING HAPPEN?

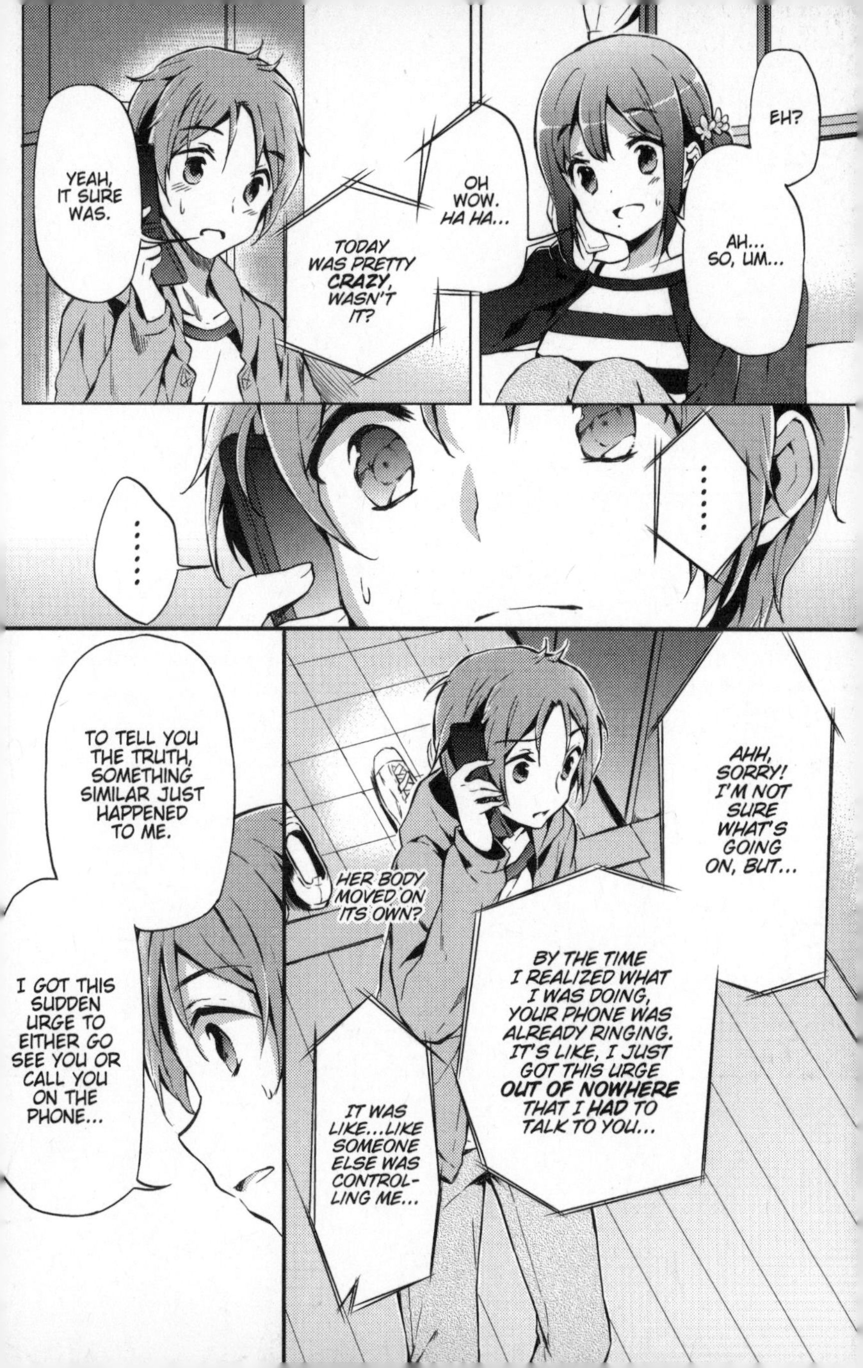
EH?
AH... SO, UM...
OH WOW. HA HA...
TODAY WAS PRETTY CRAZY, WASN'T IT?
YEAH, IT SURE WAS.
......
......
AHH, SORRY! I'M NOT SURE WHAT'S GOING ON, BUT...
BY THE TIME I REALIZED WHAT I WAS DOING, YOUR PHONE WAS ALREADY RINGING. IT'S LIKE, I JUST GOT THIS URGE OUT OF NOWHERE THAT I HAD TO TALK TO YOU...
HER BODY MOVED ON ITS OWN?
IT WAS LIKE...LIKE SOMEONE ELSE WAS CONTROL-LING ME...
TO TELL YOU THE TRUTH, SOMETHING SIMILAR JUST HAPPENED TO ME.
I GOT THIS SUDDEN URGE TO EITHER GO SEE YOU OR CALL YOU ON THE PHONE...

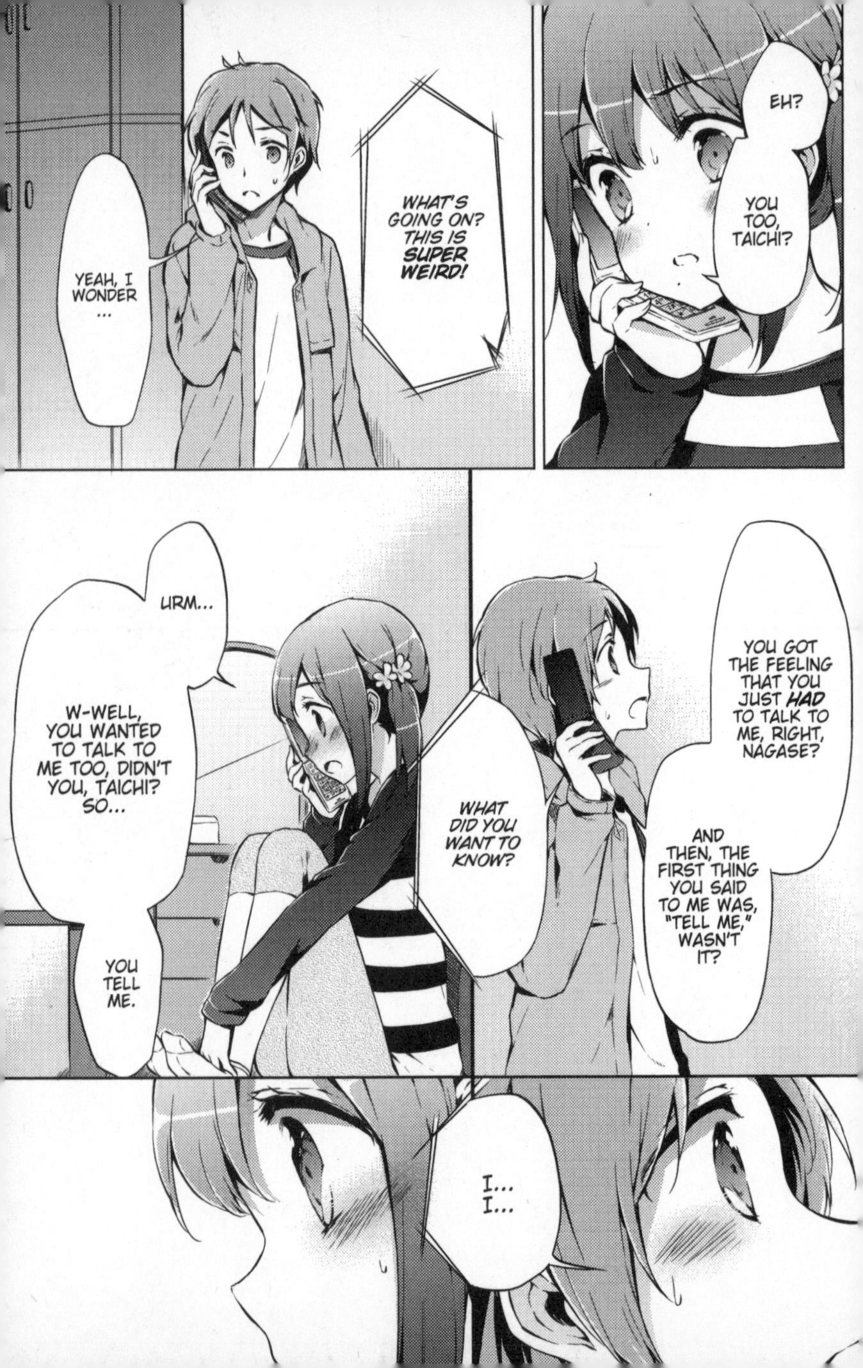
EH?
YOU TOO, TAICHI?
WHAT'S GOING ON? THIS IS **SUPER WEIRD!**
YEAH, I WONDER ...
YOU GOT THE FEELING THAT YOU JUST ***HAD*** TO TALK TO ME, RIGHT, NAGASE?
AND THEN, THE FIRST THING YOU SAID TO ME WAS, "TELL ME," WASN'T IT?
WHAT DID YOU WANT TO KNOW?
URM...
W-WELL, YOU WANTED TO TALK TO ME TOO, DIDN'T YOU, TAICHI? SO...
YOU TELL ME.
I... I...

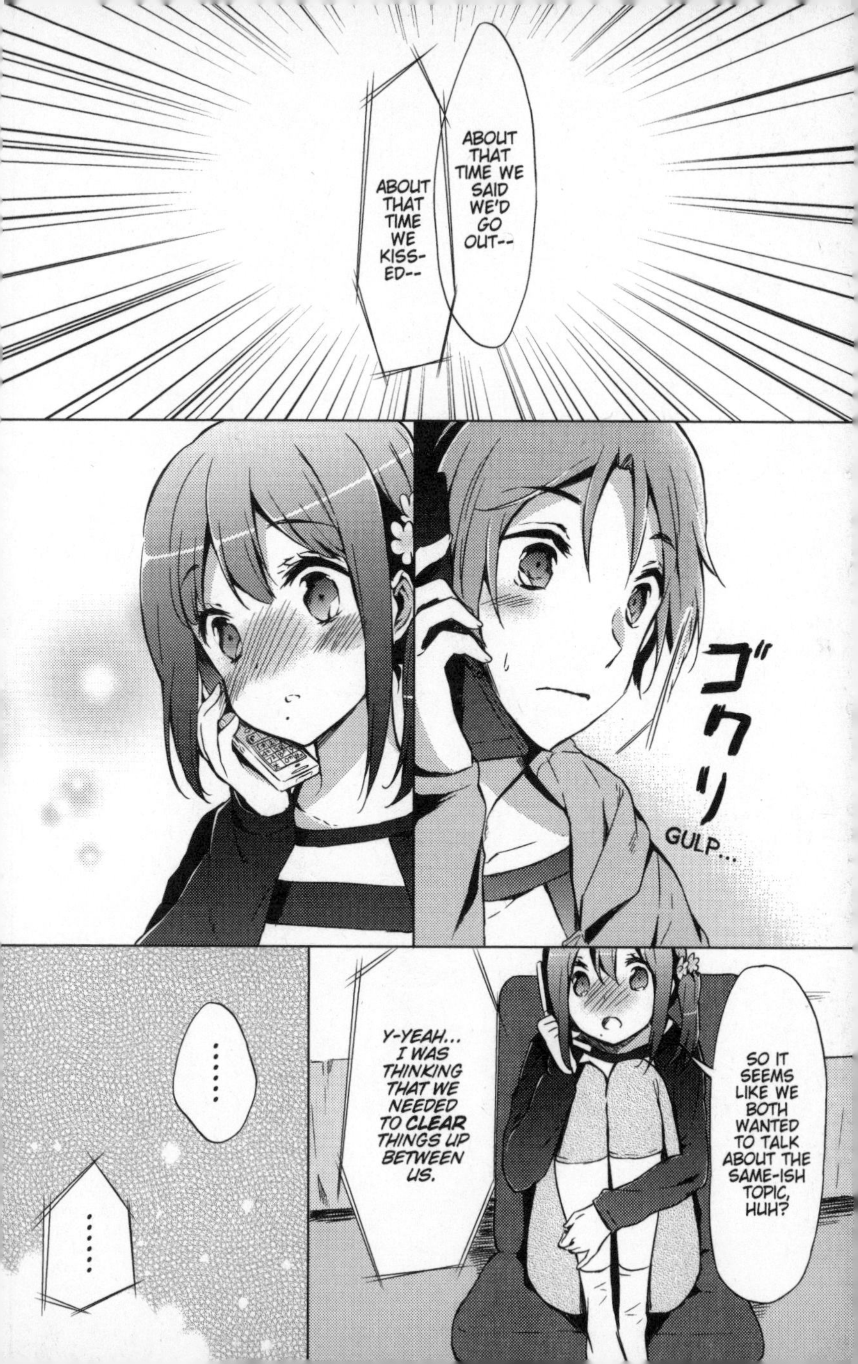
ABOUT THAT TIME WE SAID WE'D GO OUT--
ABOUT THAT TIME WE KISS-ED--
ゴクリ
GULP...
SO IT SEEMS LIKE WE BOTH WANTED TO TALK ABOUT THE SAME-ISH TOPIC, HUH?
Y-YEAH... I WAS THINKING THAT WE NEEDED TO CLEAR THINGS UP BETWEEN US.
......
......

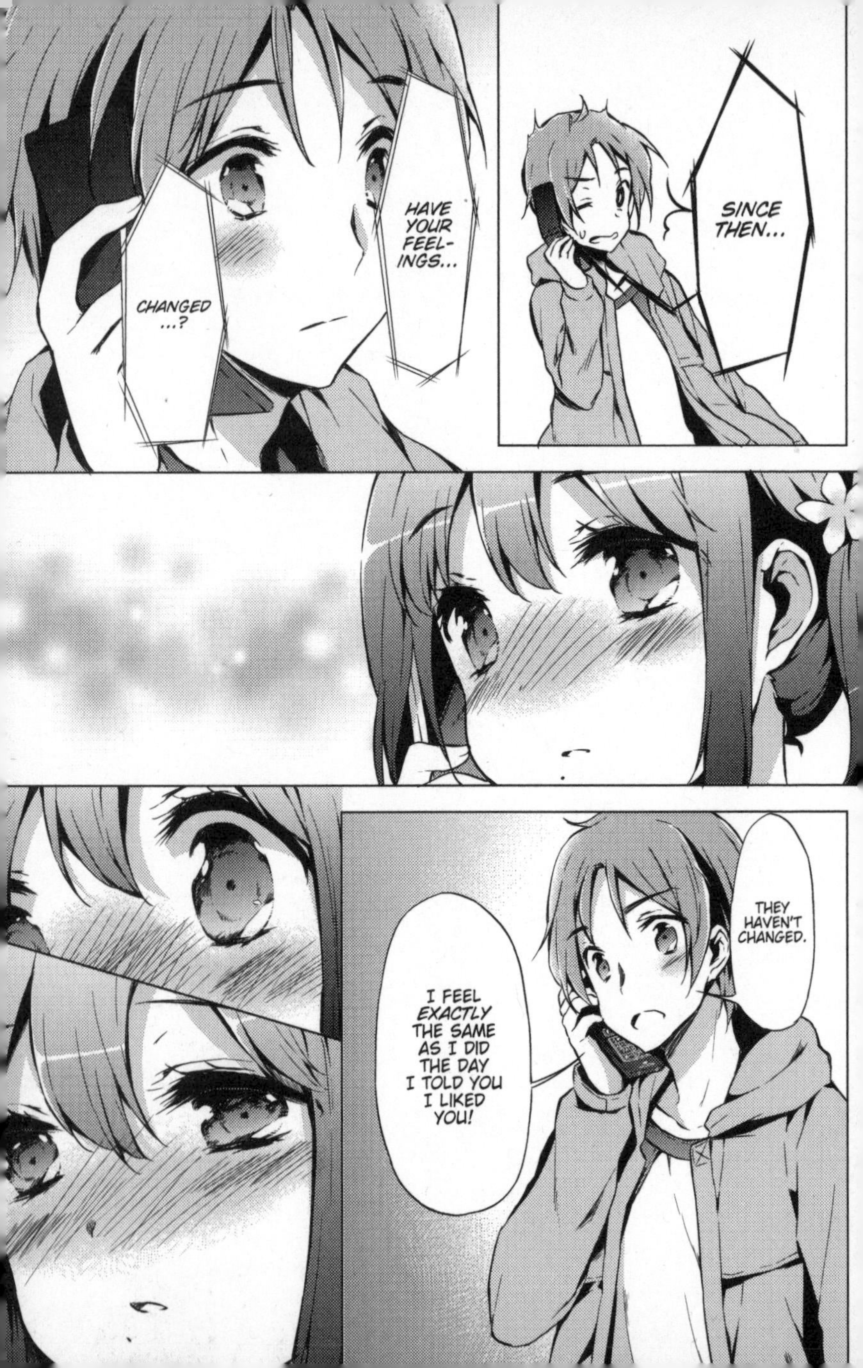
SINCE THEN...
HAVE YOUR FEEL-INGS...
CHANGED ...?
THEY HAVEN'T CHANGED.
I FEEL *EXACTLY* THE SAME AS I DID THE DAY I TOLD YOU I LIKED YOU!

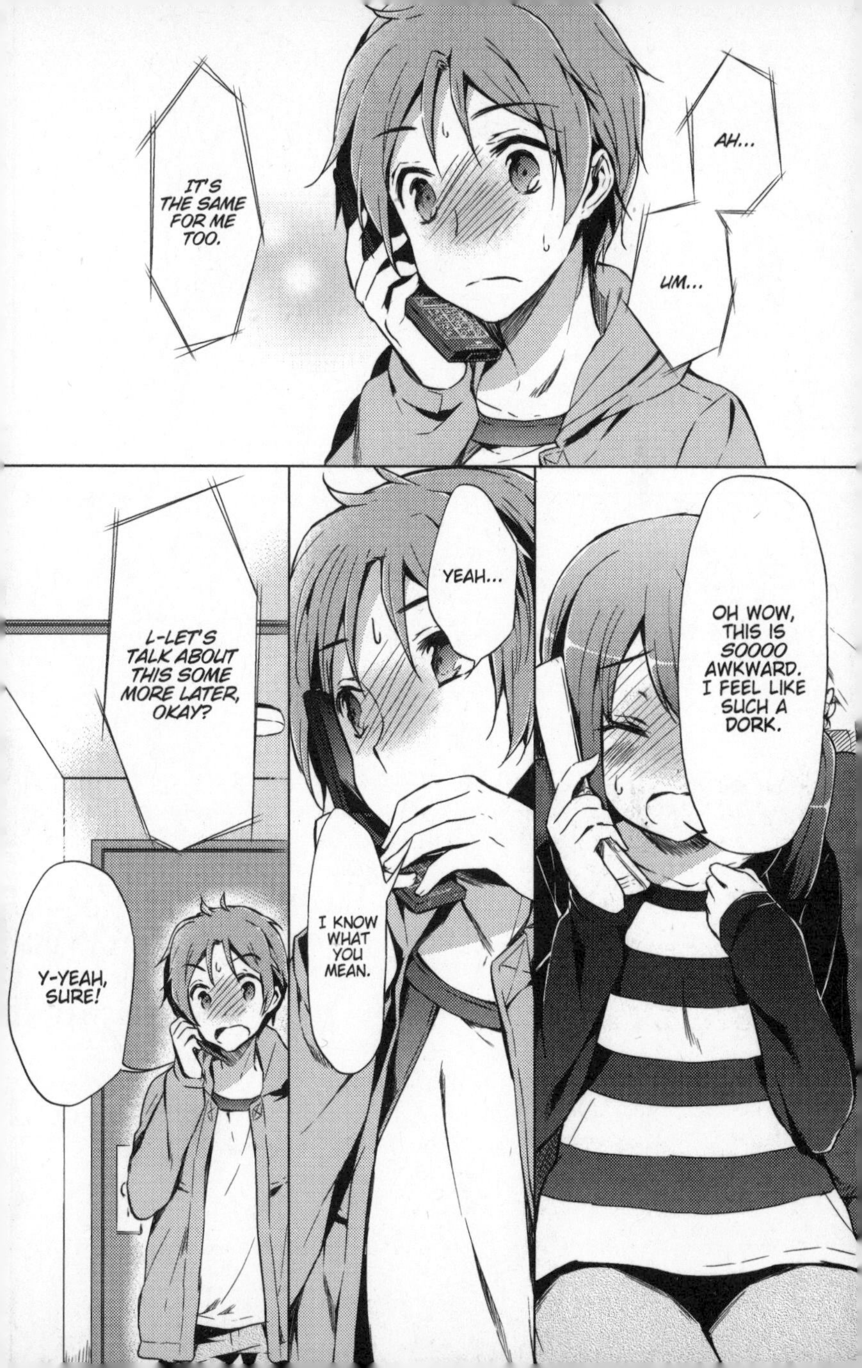
AH...
UM...
IT'S THE SAME FOR ME TOO.
OH WOW, THIS IS SOOOO AWKWARD. I FEEL LIKE SUCH A DORK.
YEAH...
I KNOW WHAT YOU MEAN.
L-LET'S TALK ABOUT THIS SOME MORE LATER, OKAY?
Y-YEAH, SURE!

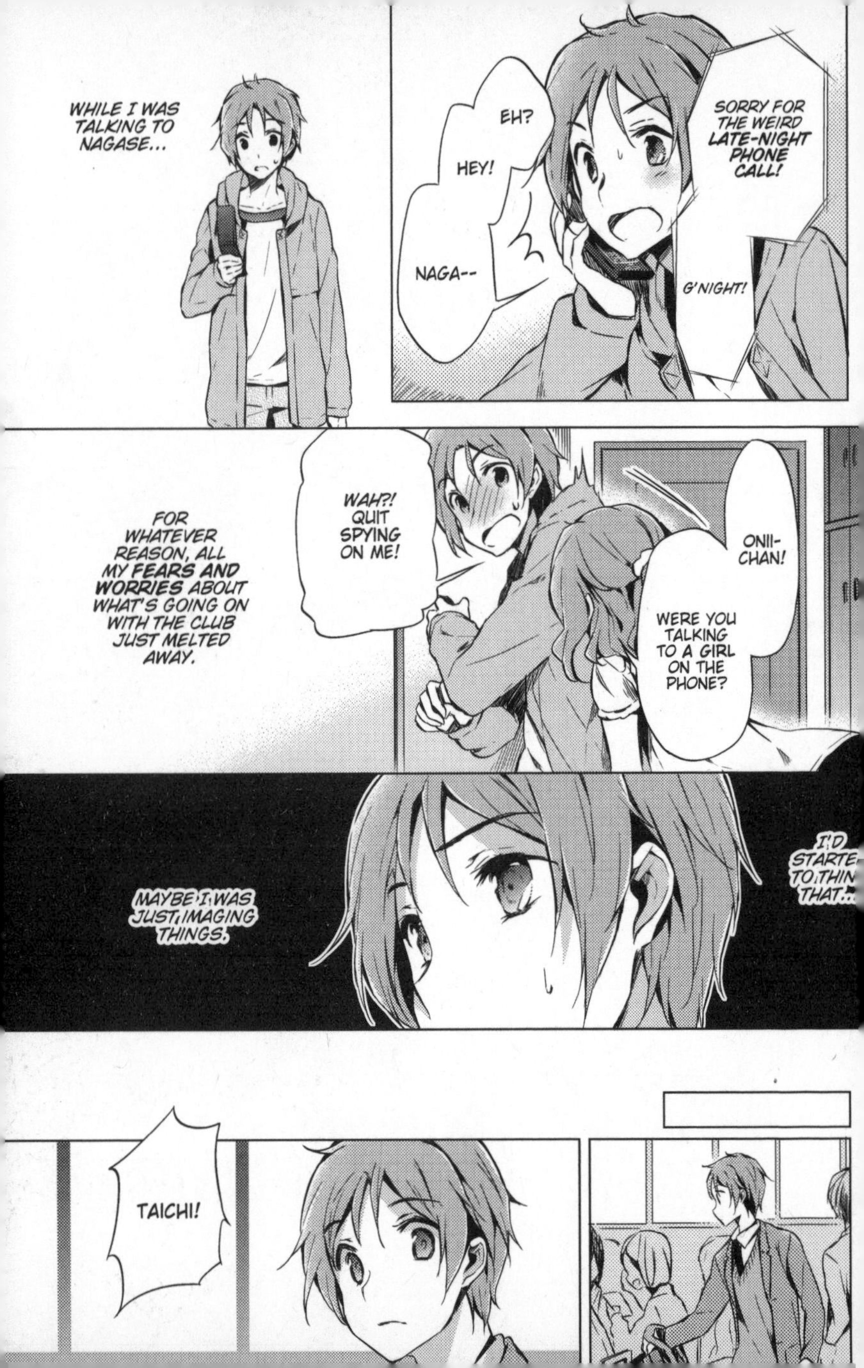
SORRY FOR THE WEIRD LATE-NIGHT PHONE CALL!
G'NIGHT!
EH?
HEY!
NAGA--
WHILE I WAS TALKING TO NAGASE...
ONII-CHAN!
WERE YOU TALKING TO A GIRL ON THE PHONE?
WAH?! QUIT SPYING ON ME!
FOR WHATEVER REASON, ALL MY FEARS AND WORRIES ABOUT WHAT'S GOING ON WITH THE CLUB JUST MELTED AWAY.
I'D STARTE TO THIN THAT...
MAYBE I WAS JUST IMAGING THINGS.
TAICHI!

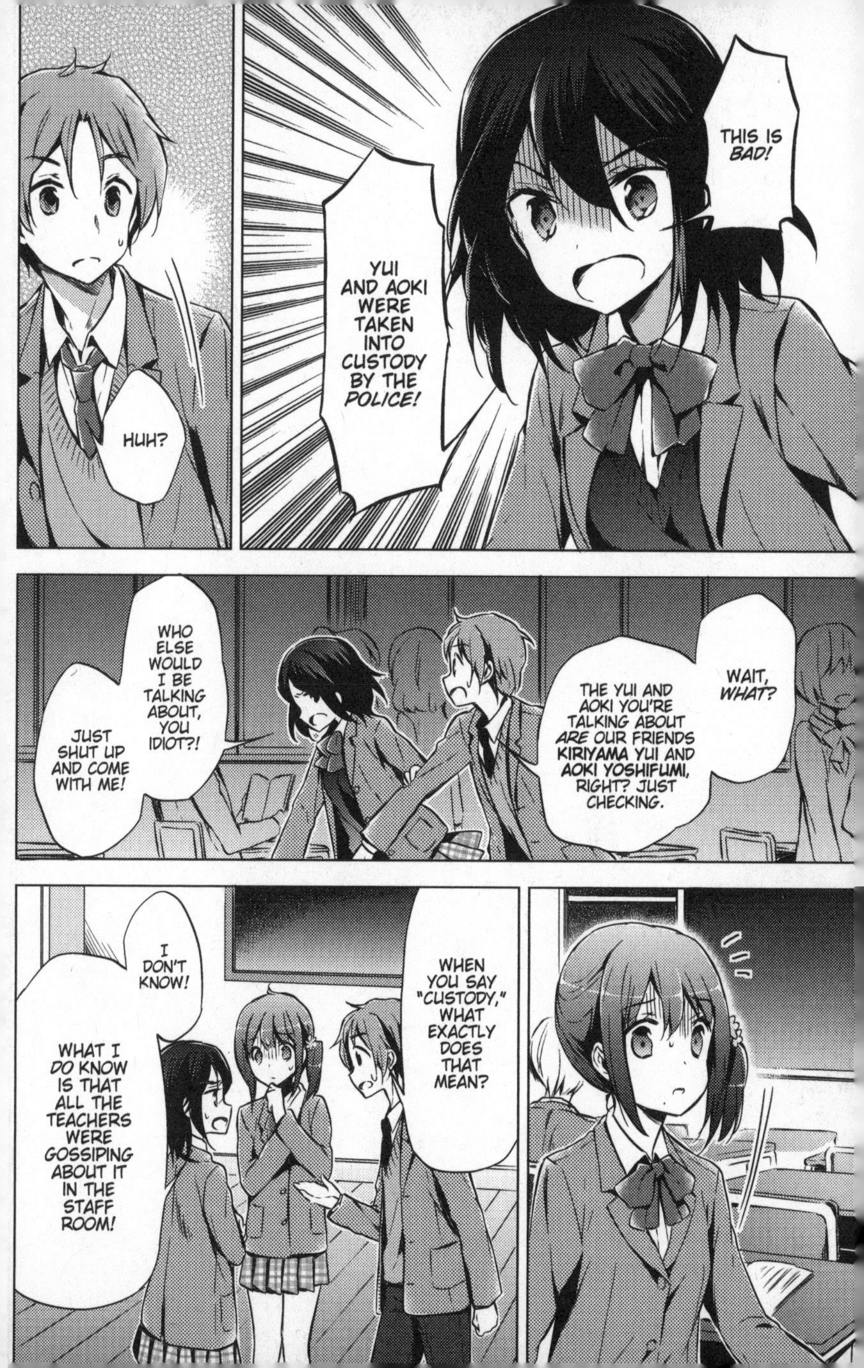
THIS IS *BAD!*
YUI AND AOKI WERE TAKEN INTO CUSTODY BY THE *POLICE!*
HUH?
WAIT, *WHAT?*
THE YUI AND AOKI YOU'RE TALKING ABOUT *ARE* OUR FRIENDS KIRIYAMA YUI AND AOKI YOSHIFUMI, RIGHT? JUST CHECKING.
WHO ELSE WOULD I BE TALKING ABOUT, YOU IDIOT?!
JUST SHUT UP AND COME WITH ME!
WHEN YOU SAY "CUSTODY," WHAT EXACTLY DOES THAT MEAN?
I DON'T KNOW!
WHAT I *DO* KNOW IS THAT ALL THE TEACHERS WERE GOSSIPING ABOUT IT IN THE STAFF ROOM!

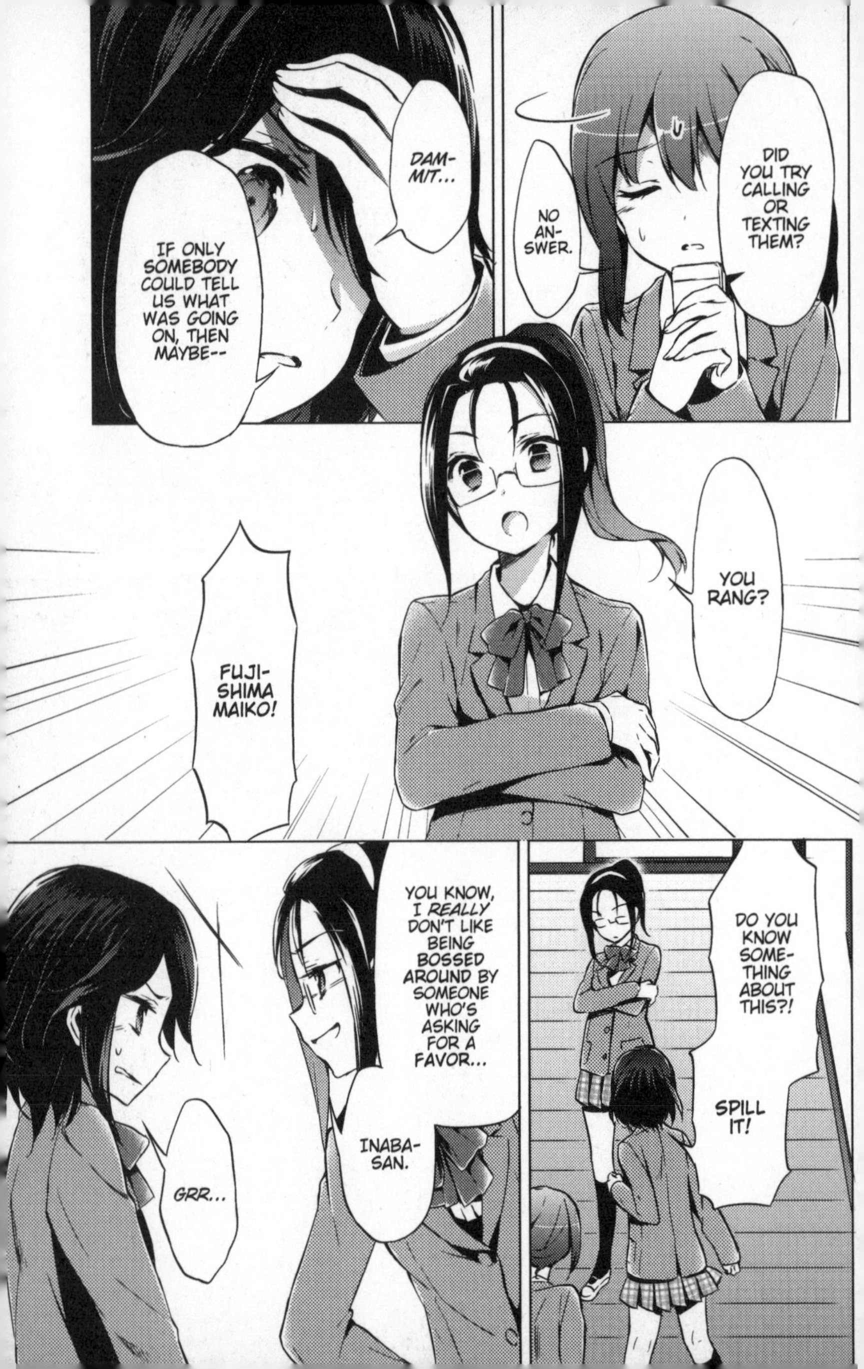
DID YOU TRY CALLING OR TEXTING THEM?
NO ANSWER.
DAMMIT...
IF ONLY SOMEBODY COULD TELL US WHAT WAS GOING ON, THEN MAYBE--
YOU RANG?
FUJISHIMA MAIKO!
DO YOU KNOW SOMETHING ABOUT THIS?!
SPILL IT!
YOU KNOW, I *REALLY* DON'T LIKE BEING BOSSED AROUND BY SOMEONE WHO'S ASKING FOR A FAVOR...
INABA-SAN.
GRR...

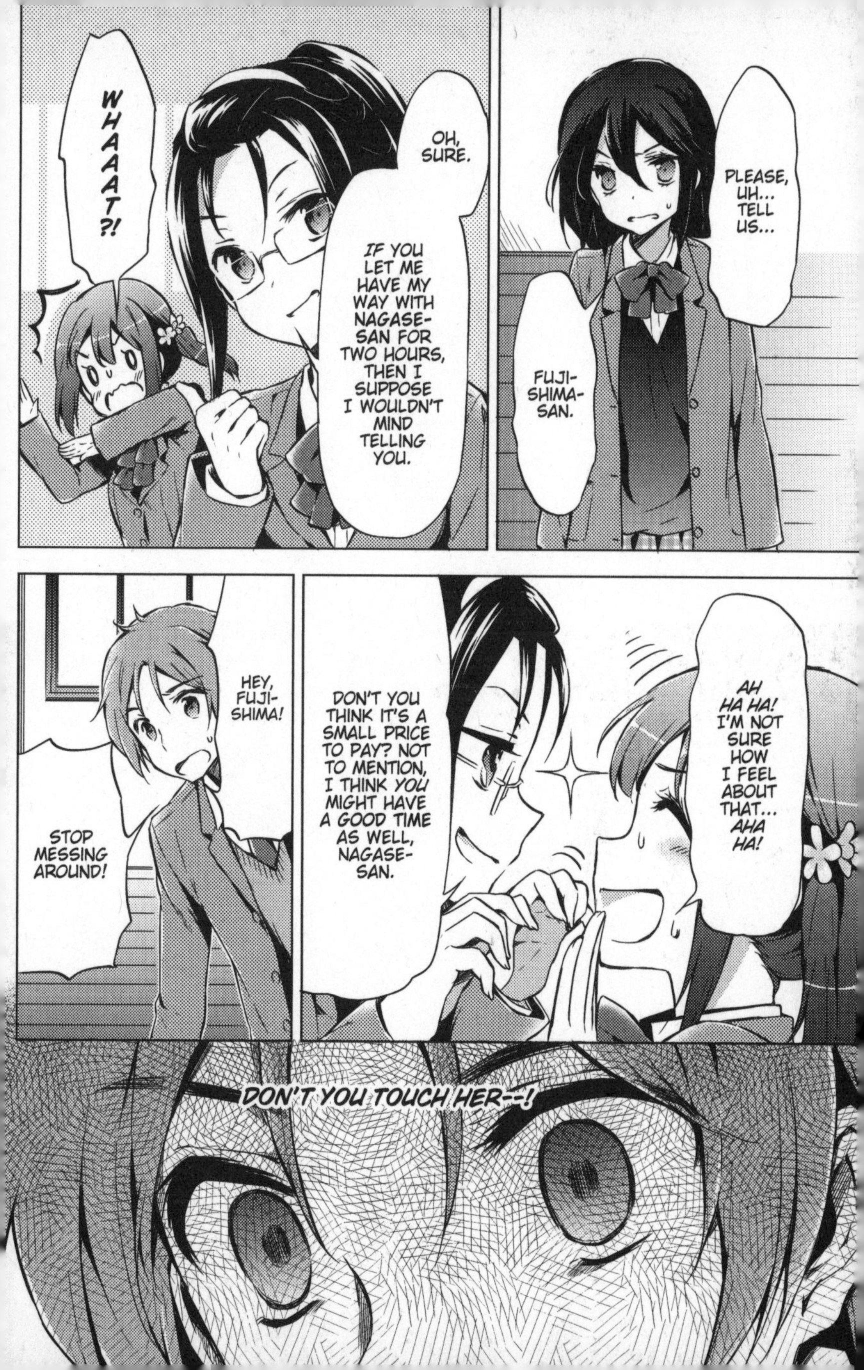
PLEASE, UH... TELL US...
FUJI-SHIMA-SAN.
OH, SURE.
IF YOU LET ME HAVE MY WAY WITH NAGASE-SAN FOR TWO HOURS, THEN I SUPPOSE I WOULDN'T MIND TELLING YOU.
WHAAAT?!
DON'T YOU THINK IT'S A SMALL PRICE TO PAY? NOT TO MENTION, I THINK *YOU* MIGHT HAVE A GOOD TIME AS WELL, NAGASE-SAN.
AH HA HA! I'M NOT SURE HOW I FEEL ABOUT THAT... *AHA HA!*
HEY, FUJI-SHIMA!
STOP MESSING AROUND!
DON'T YOU TOUCH HER--!

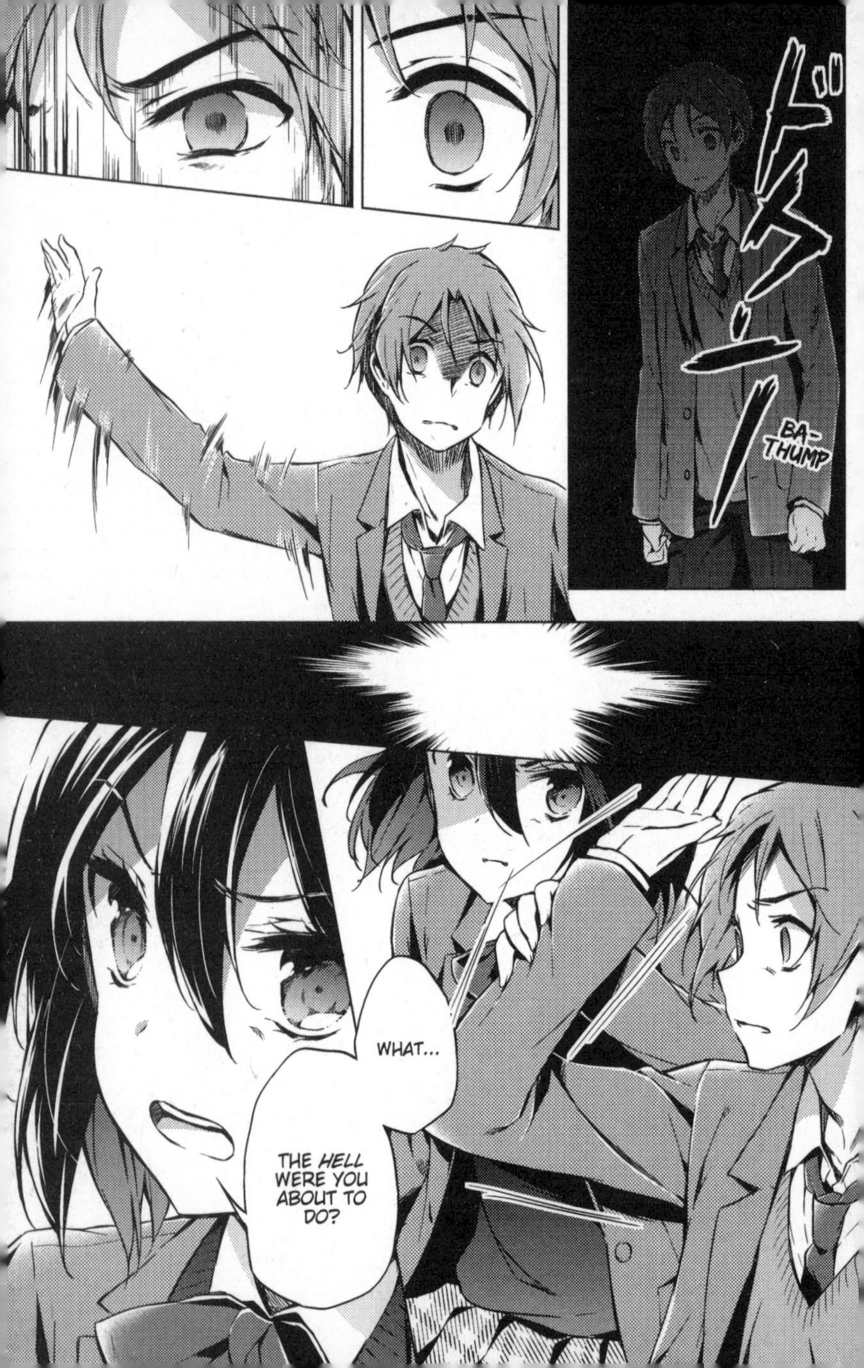
ドク
BA-THUMP
WHAT...
THE *HELL* WERE YOU ABOUT TO DO?

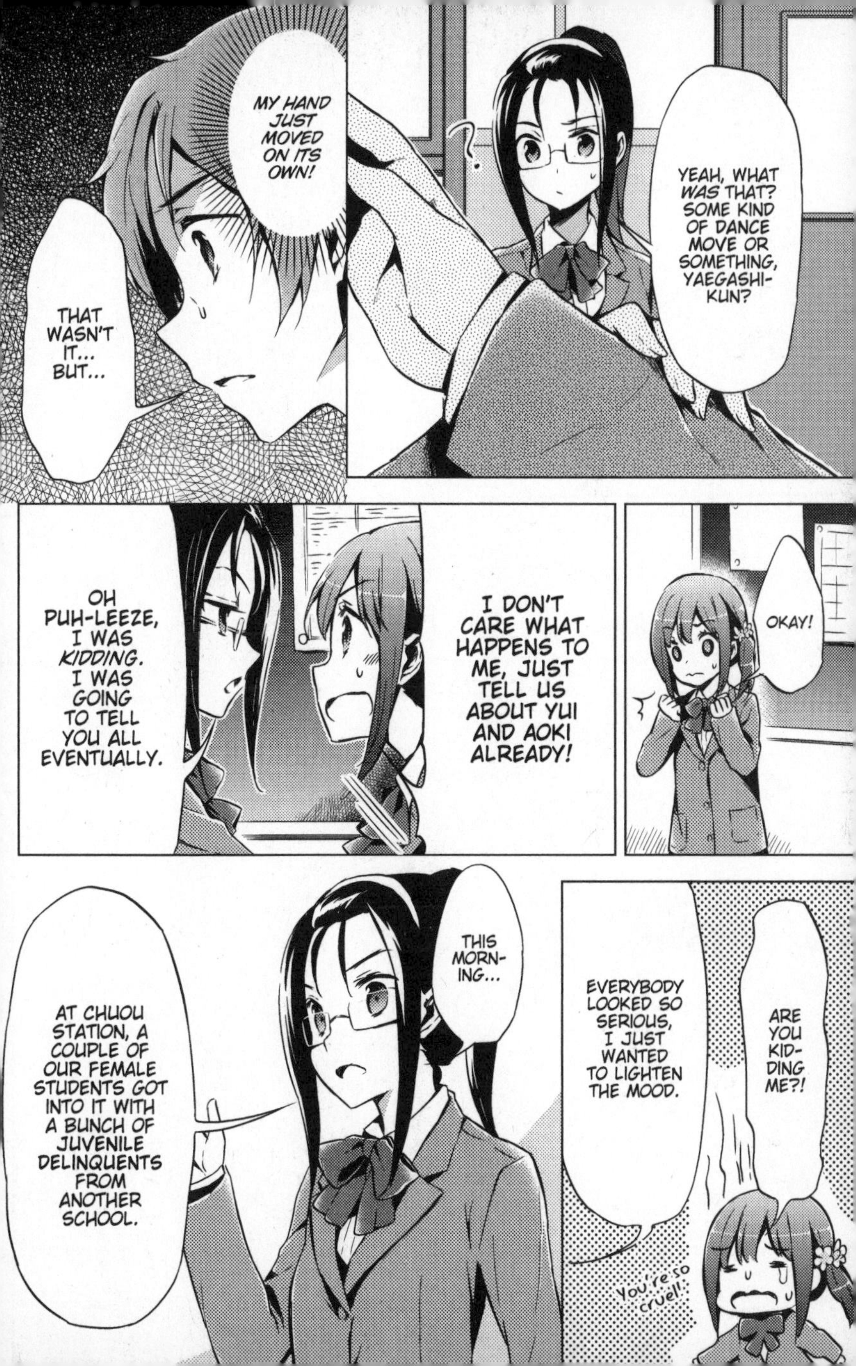
YEAH, WHAT WAS THAT? SOME KIND OF DANCE MOVE OR SOMETHING, YAEGASHI-KUN?
MY HAND JUST MOVED ON ITS OWN!
THAT WASN'T IT... BUT...
OKAY!
I DON'T CARE WHAT HAPPENS TO ME, JUST TELL US ABOUT YUI AND AOKI ALREADY!
OH PUH-LEEZE, I WAS KIDDING. I WAS GOING TO TELL YOU ALL EVENTUALLY.
ARE YOU KID-DING ME?!
EVERYBODY LOOKED SO SERIOUS, I JUST WANTED TO LIGHTEN THE MOOD.
You're so cruel!
THIS MORN-ING...
AT CHUOU STATION, A COUPLE OF OUR FEMALE STUDENTS GOT INTO IT WITH A BUNCH OF JUVENILE DELINQUENTS FROM ANOTHER SCHOOL.

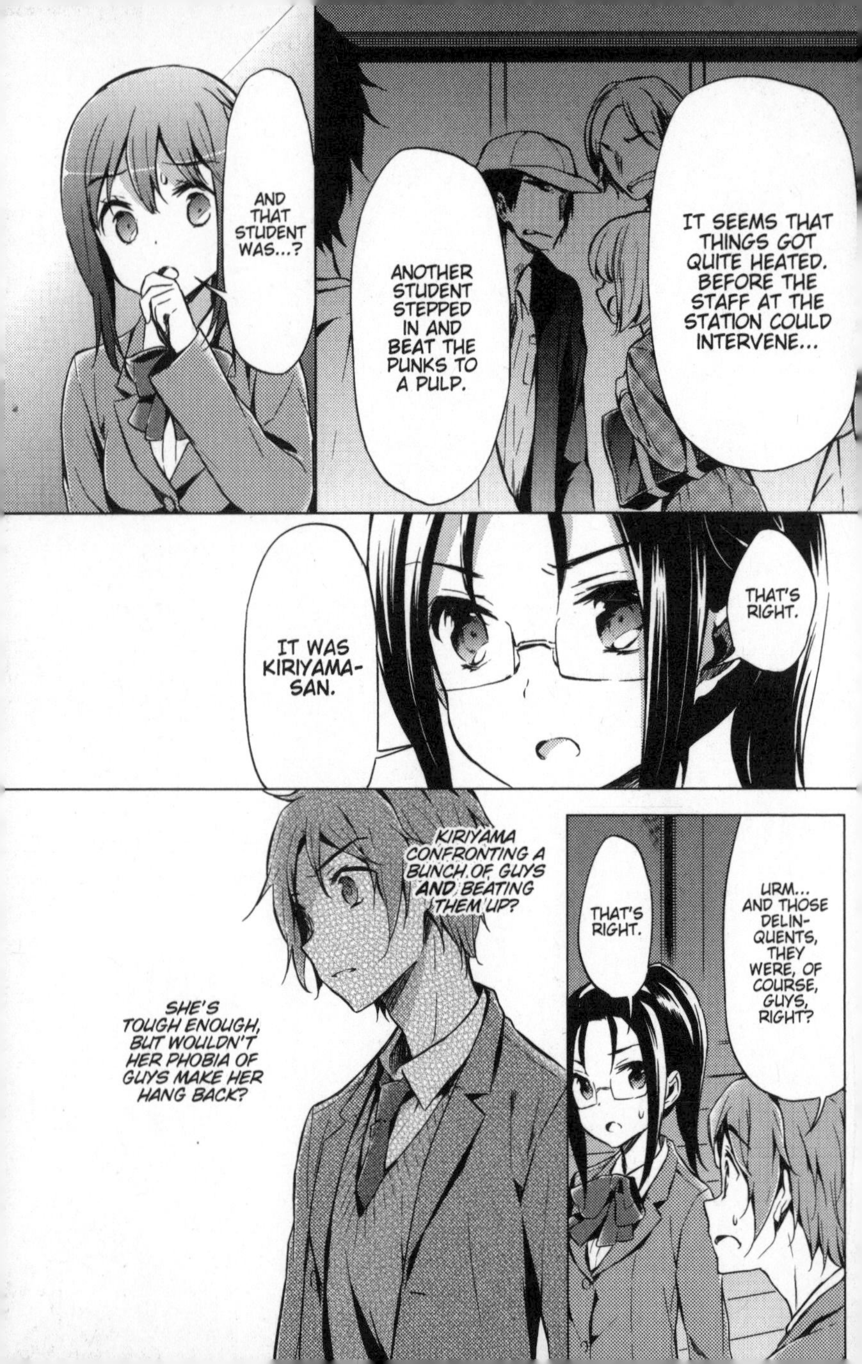
IT SEEMS THAT THINGS GOT QUITE HEATED. BEFORE THE STAFF AT THE STATION COULD INTERVENE...
ANOTHER STUDENT STEPPED IN AND BEAT THE PUNKS TO A PULP.
AND THAT STUDENT WAS...?
THAT'S RIGHT.
IT WAS KIRIYAMA-SAN.
URM... AND THOSE DELIN-QUENTS, THEY WERE, OF COURSE, GUYS, RIGHT?
THAT'S RIGHT.
KIRIYAMA CONFRONTING A BUNCH OF GUYS AND BEATING THEM UP?
SHE'S TOUGH ENOUGH, BUT WOULDN'T HER PHOBIA OF GUYS MAKE HER HANG BACK?

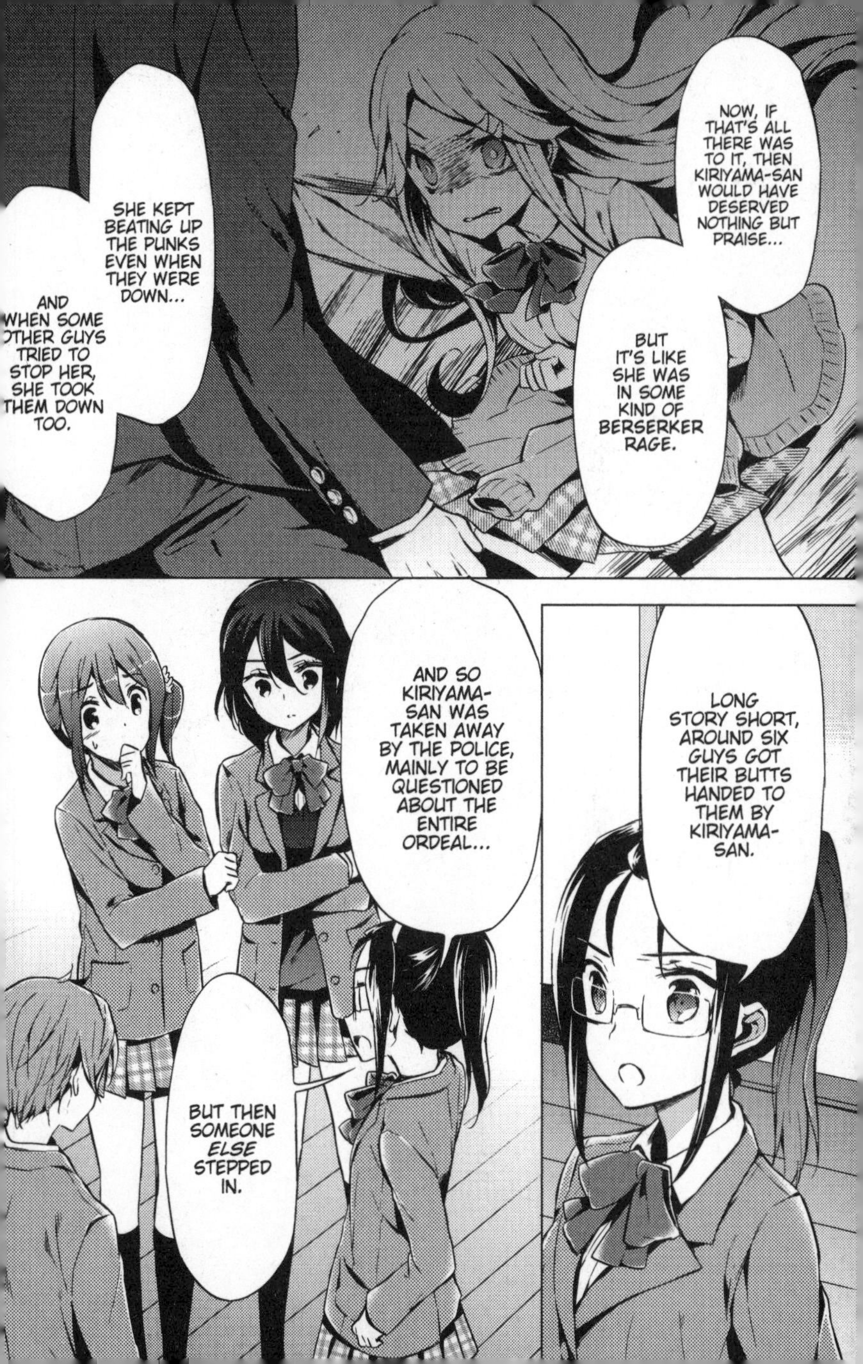
NOW, IF THAT'S ALL THERE WAS TO IT, THEN KIRIYAMA-SAN WOULD HAVE DESERVED NOTHING BUT PRAISE...
BUT IT'S LIKE SHE WAS IN SOME KIND OF BERSERKER RAGE.
SHE KEPT BEATING UP THE PUNKS EVEN WHEN THEY WERE DOWN...
AND WHEN SOME OTHER GUYS TRIED TO STOP HER, SHE TOOK THEM DOWN TOO.
LONG STORY SHORT, AROUND SIX GUYS GOT THEIR BUTTS HANDED TO THEM BY KIRIYAMA-SAN.
AND SO KIRIYAMA-SAN WAS TAKEN AWAY BY THE POLICE, MAINLY TO BE QUESTIONED ABOUT THE ENTIRE ORDEAL...
BUT THEN SOMEONE *ELSE* STEPPED IN.

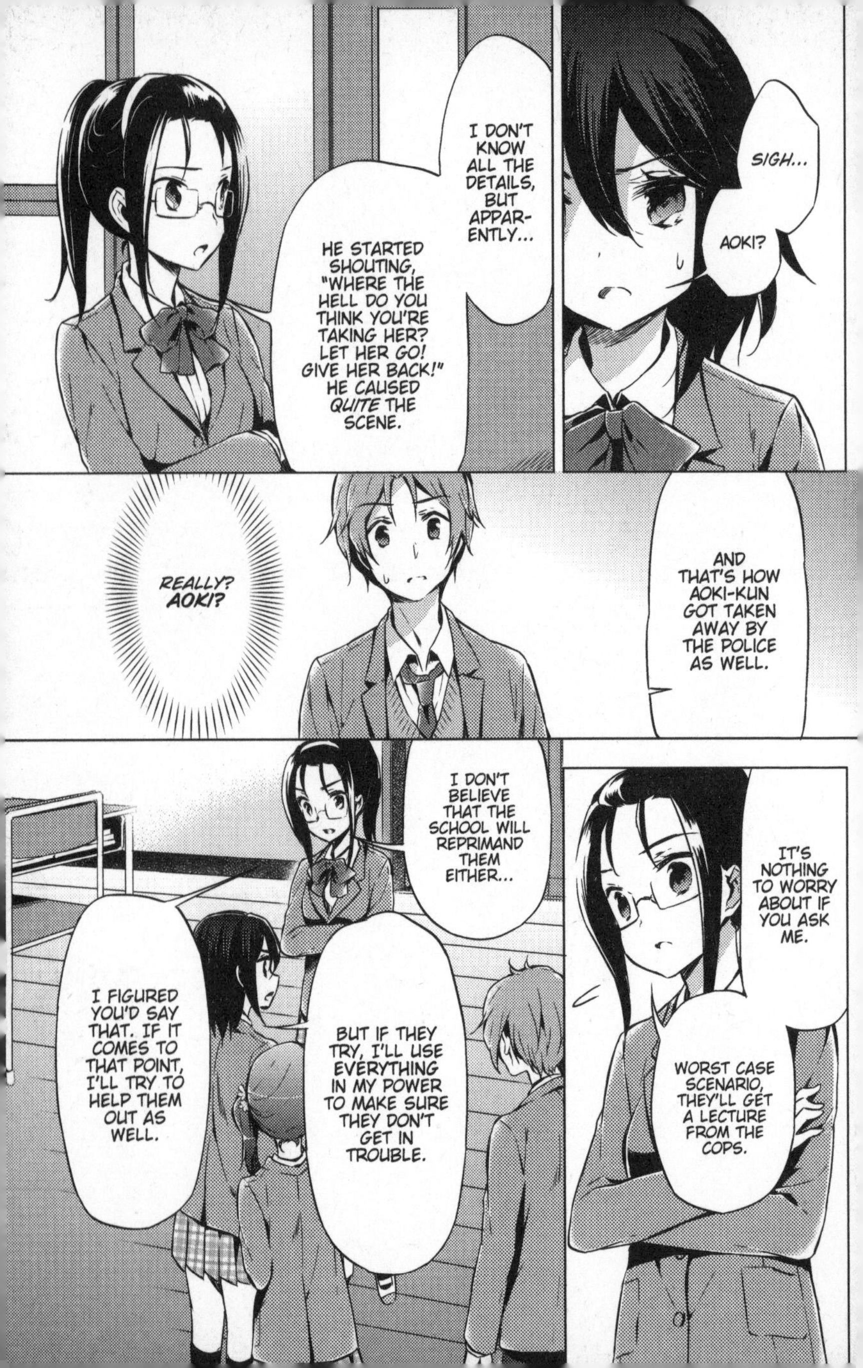
SIGH...
AOKI?
I DON'T KNOW ALL THE DETAILS, BUT APPARENTLY...
HE STARTED SHOUTING, "WHERE THE HELL DO YOU THINK YOU'RE TAKING HER? LET HER GO! GIVE HER BACK!" HE CAUSED *QUITE* THE SCENE.
AND THAT'S HOW AOKI-KUN GOT TAKEN AWAY BY THE POLICE AS WELL.
REALLY? AOKI?
IT'S NOTHING TO WORRY ABOUT IF YOU ASK ME.
WORST CASE SCENARIO, THEY'LL GET A LECTURE FROM THE COPS.
I DON'T BELIEVE THAT THE SCHOOL WILL REPRIMAND THEM EITHER...
BUT IF THEY TRY, I'LL USE EVERYTHING IN MY POWER TO MAKE SURE THEY DON'T GET IN TROUBLE.
I FIGURED YOU'D SAY THAT. IF IT COMES TO THAT POINT, I'LL TRY TO HELP THEM OUT AS WELL.

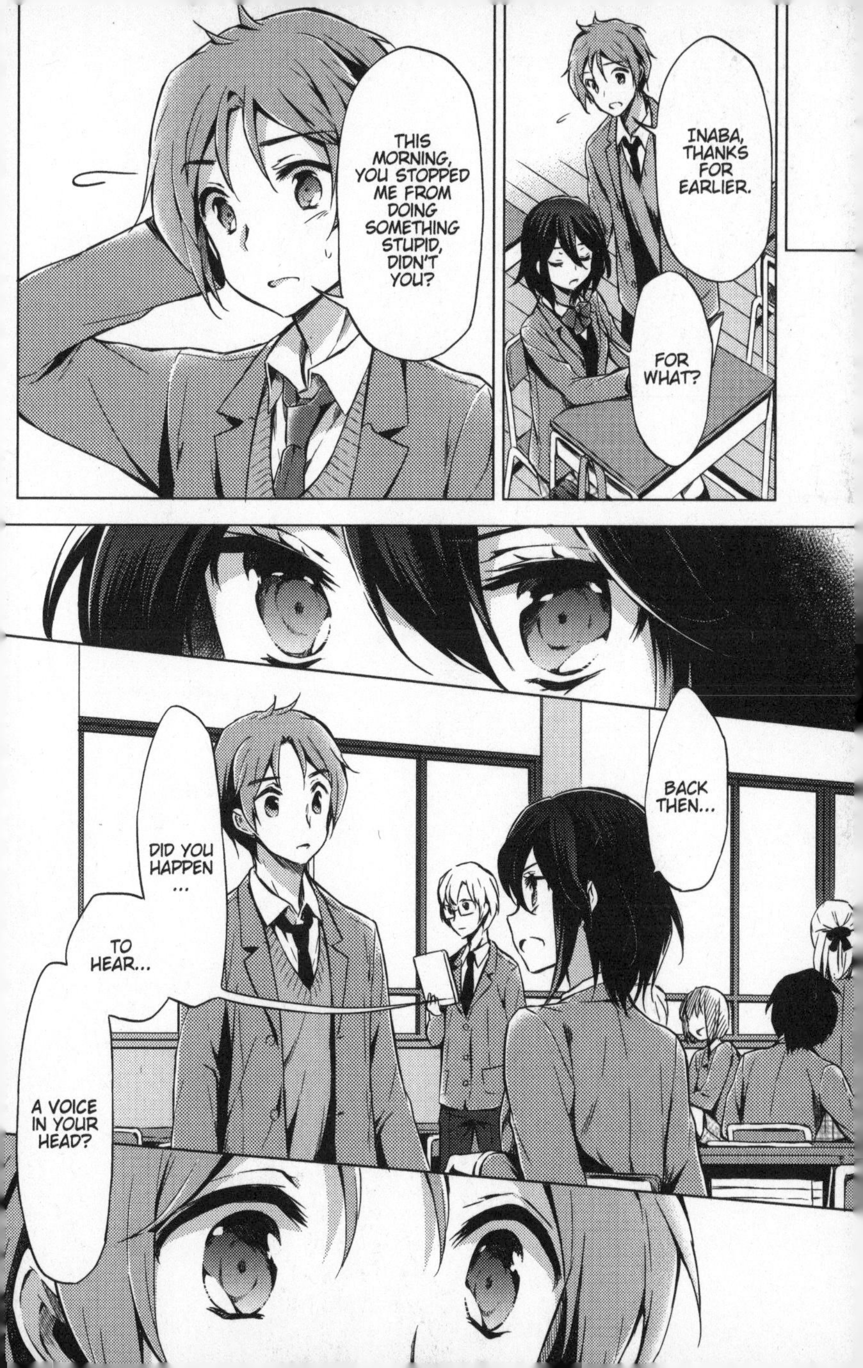
INABA, THANKS FOR EARLIER.
FOR WHAT?
THIS MORNING, YOU STOPPED ME FROM DOING SOMETHING STUPID, DIDN'T YOU?
BACK THEN...
DID YOU HAPPEN...
TO HEAR...
A VOICE IN YOUR HEAD?

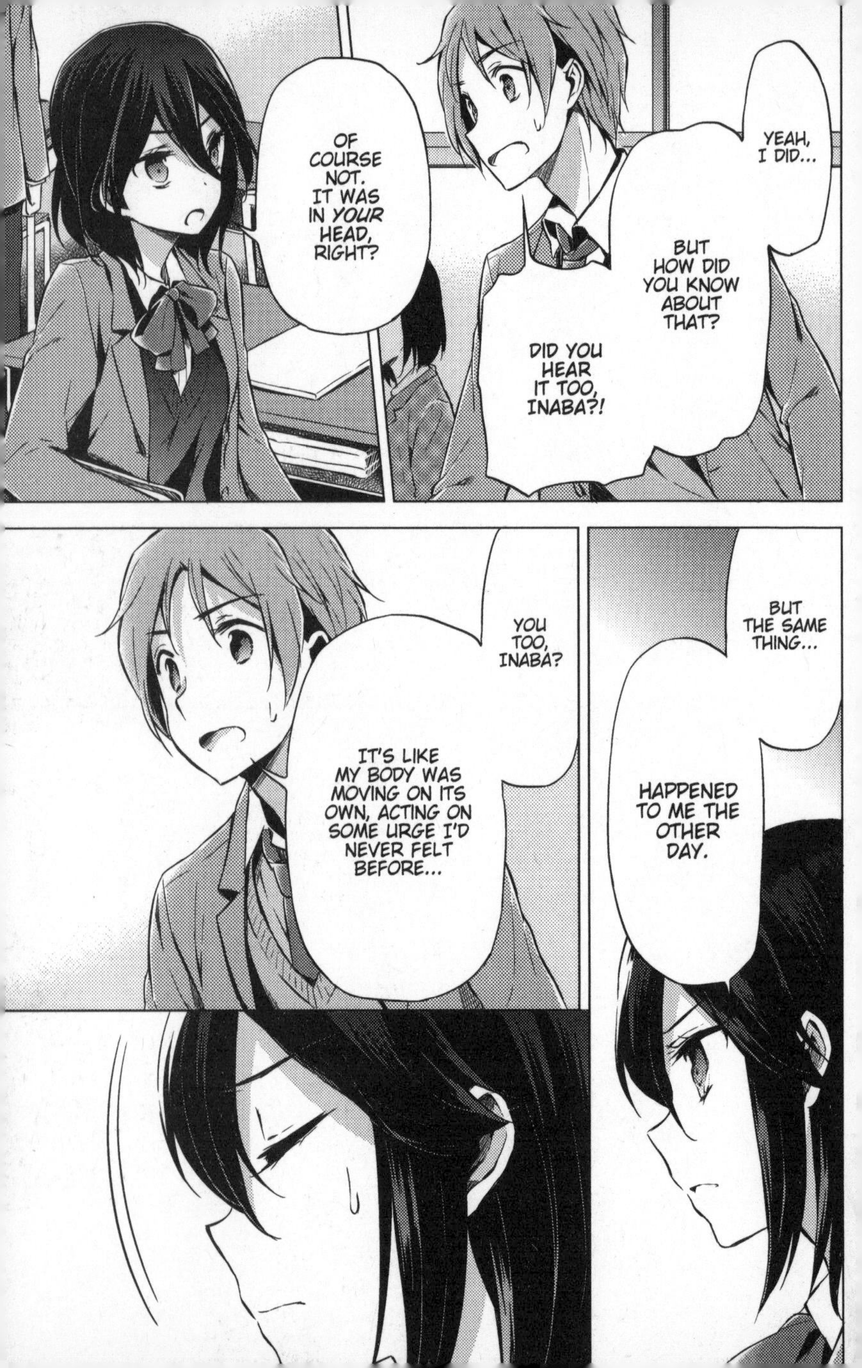
YEAH, I DID...
BUT HOW DID YOU KNOW ABOUT THAT?
DID YOU HEAR IT TOO, INABA?!
OF COURSE NOT. IT WAS IN *YOUR* HEAD, RIGHT?
BUT THE SAME THING...
HAPPENED TO ME THE OTHER DAY.
YOU TOO, INABA?
IT'S LIKE MY BODY WAS MOVING ON ITS OWN, ACTING ON SOME URGE I'D NEVER FELT BEFORE...

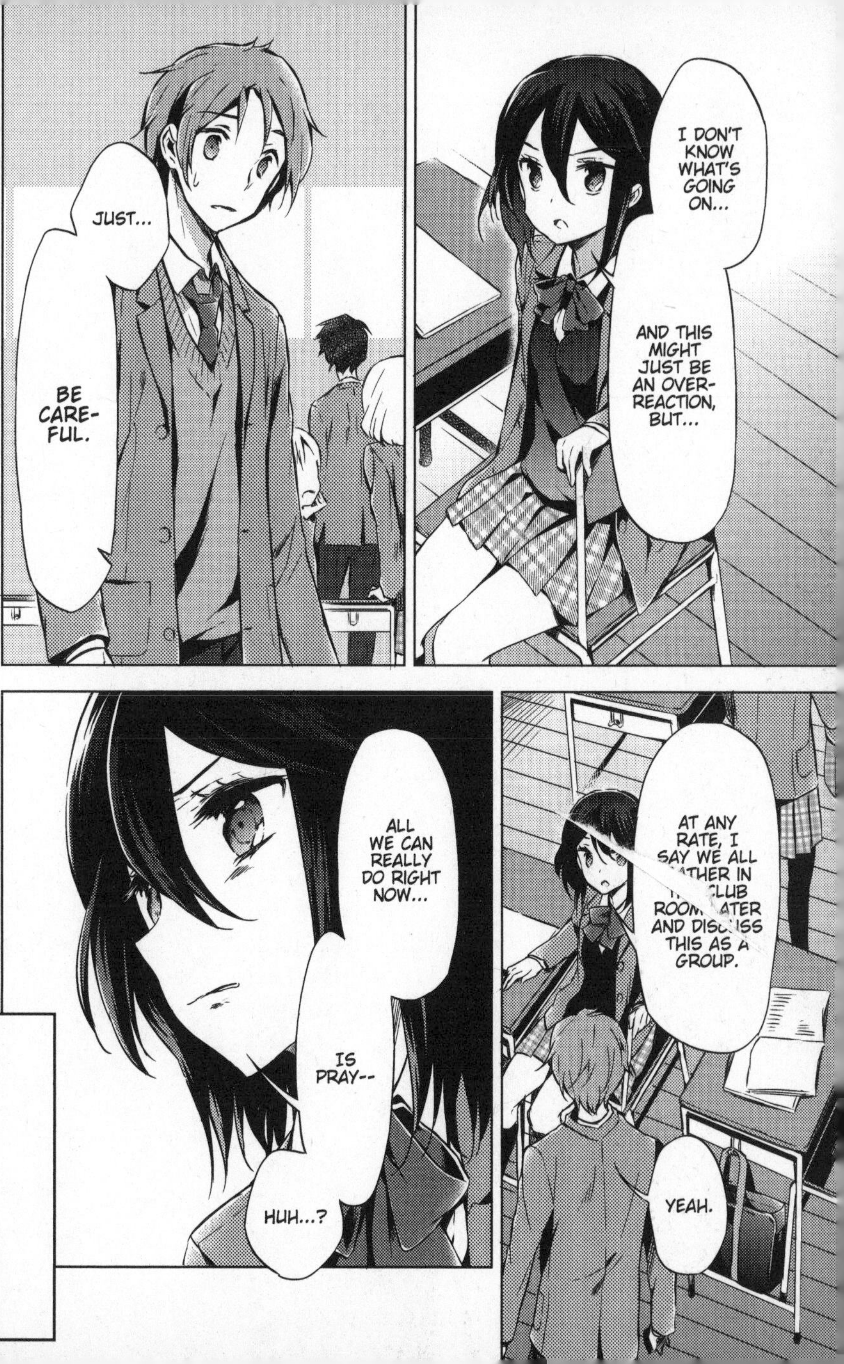
I DON'T KNOW WHAT'S GOING ON...
AND THIS MIGHT JUST BE AN OVER-REACTION, BUT...
JUST...
BE CARE-FUL.
AT ANY RATE, I SAY WE ALL GATHER IN THE CLUB ROOM LATER AND DISCUSS THIS AS A GROUP.
YEAH.
ALL WE CAN REALLY DO RIGHT NOW...
IS PRAY--
HUH...?

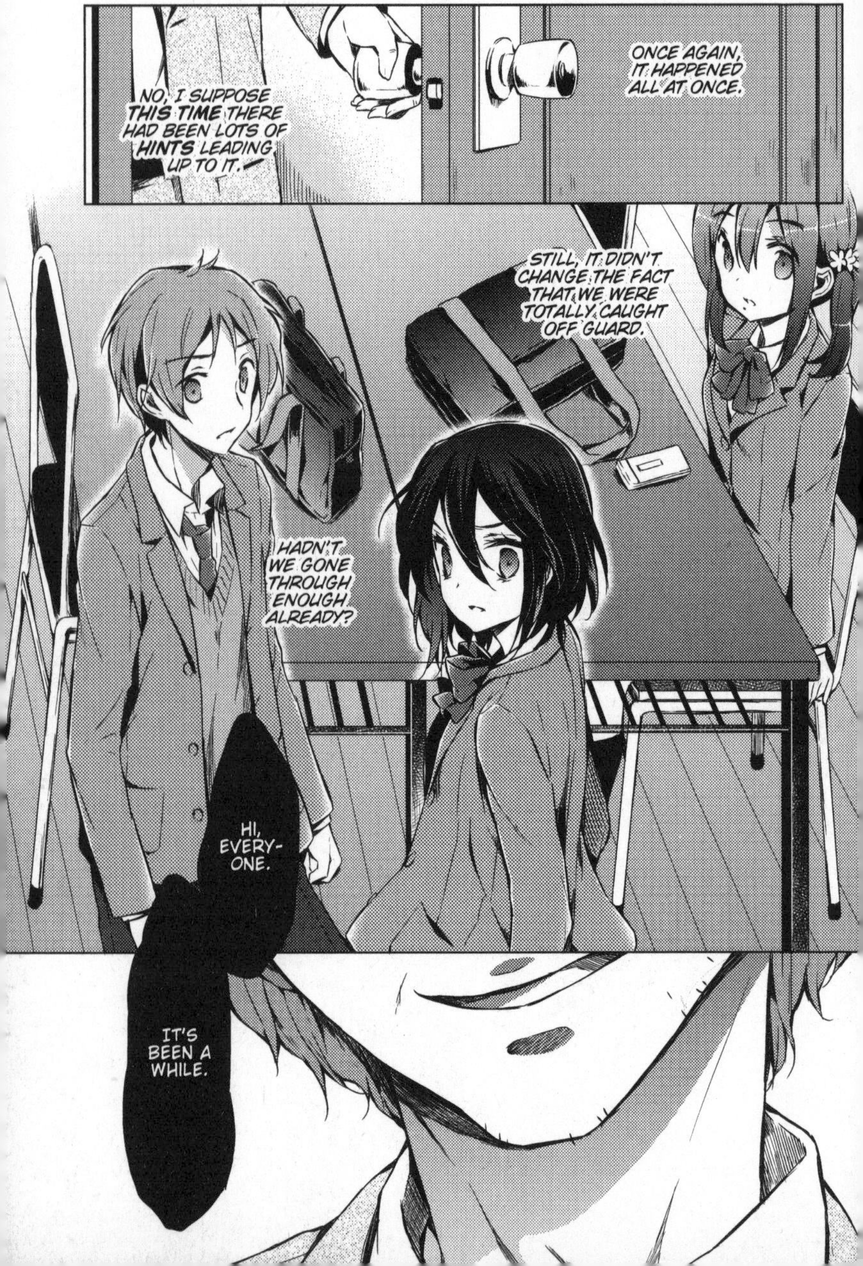
ONCE AGAIN, IT HAPPENED ALL AT ONCE.
NO, I SUPPOSE **THIS TIME** THERE HAD BEEN LOTS OF **HINTS** LEADING UP TO IT.
STILL, IT DIDN'T CHANGE THE FACT THAT WE WERE TOTALLY CAUGHT OFF GUARD.
HADN'T WE GONE THROUGH ENOUGH ALREADY?
HI, EVERY-ONE.
IT'S BEEN A WHILE.

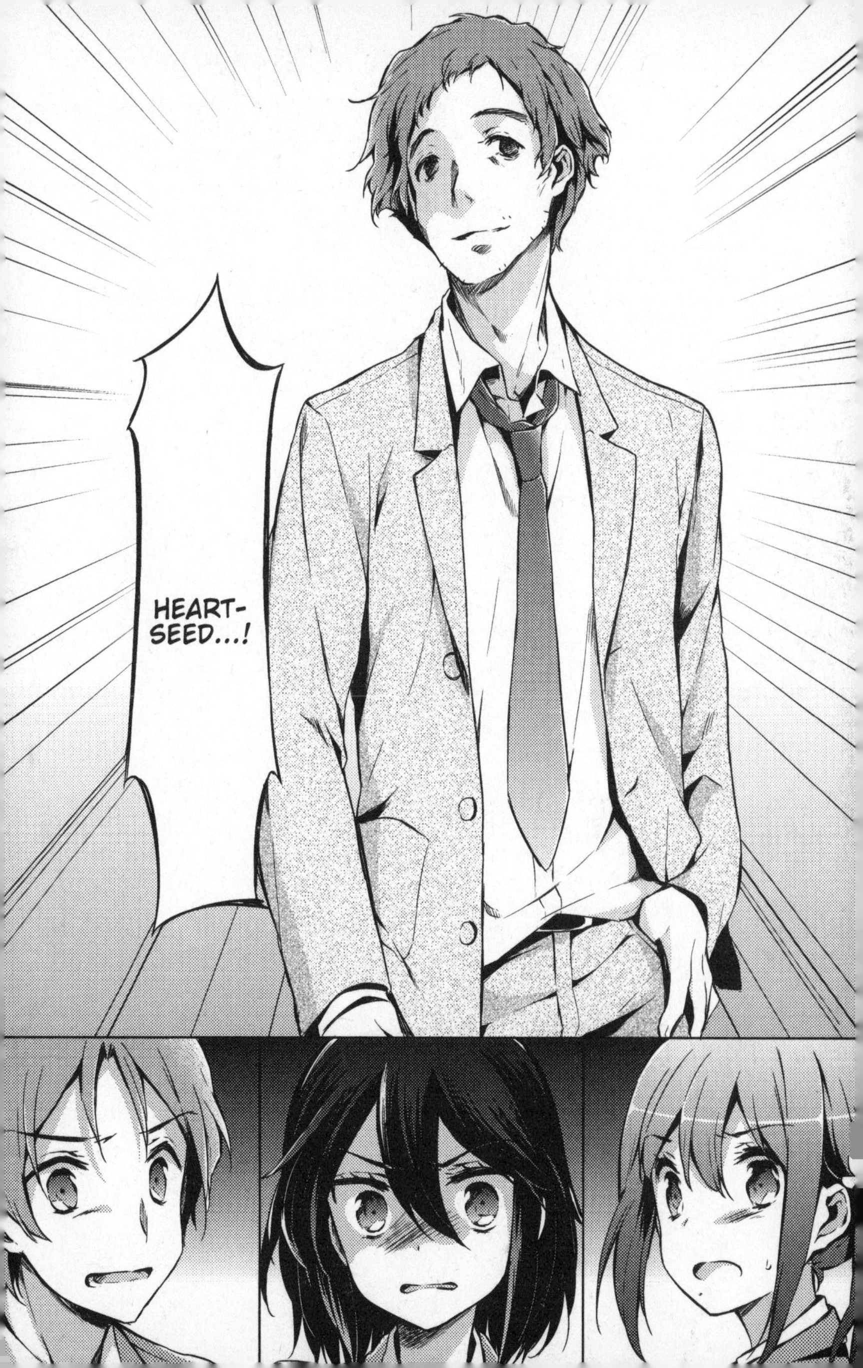
HEART-
SEED...!

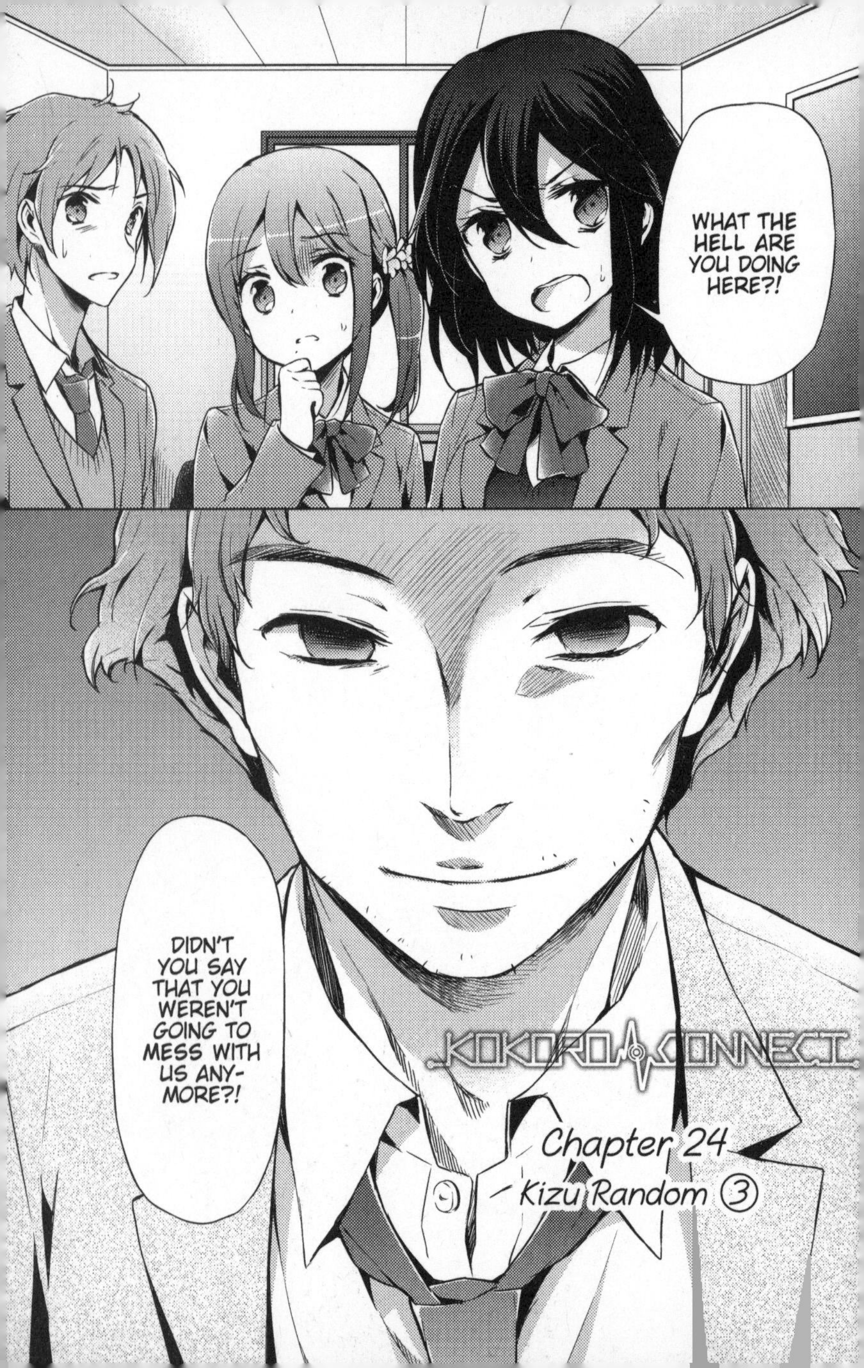
WHAT THE HELL ARE YOU DOING HERE?!
DIDN'T YOU SAY THAT YOU WEREN'T GOING TO MESS WITH US ANY-MORE?!
KOKORO CONNECT
Chapter 24
Kizu Random ③

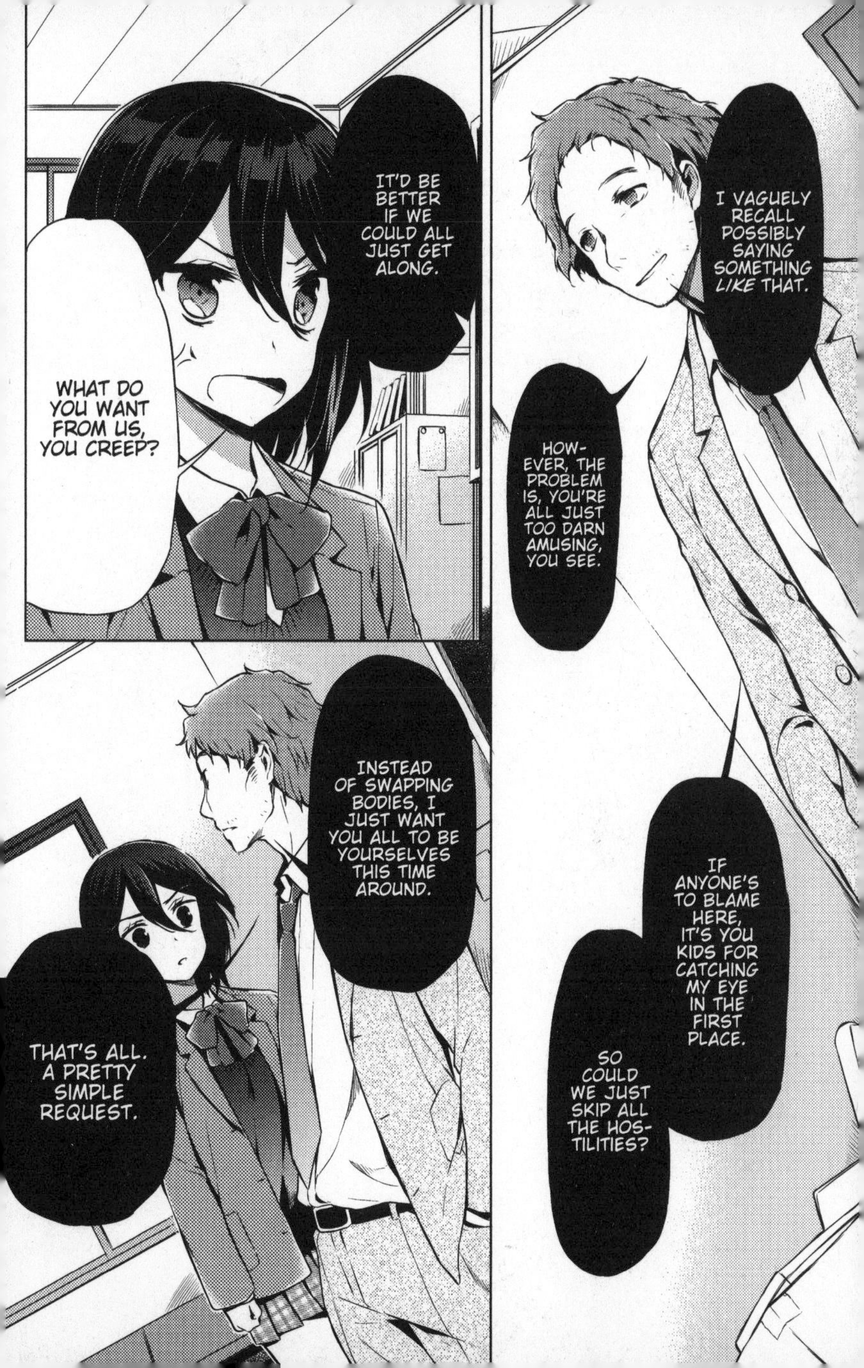
I VAGUELY RECALL POSSIBLY SAYING SOMETHING *LIKE* THAT.
HOW-EVER, THE PROBLEM IS, YOU'RE ALL JUST TOO DARN AMUSING, YOU SEE.
IF ANYONE'S TO BLAME HERE, IT'S YOU KIDS FOR CATCHING MY EYE IN THE FIRST PLACE.
SO COULD WE JUST SKIP ALL THE HOS-TILITIES?
IT'D BE BETTER IF WE COULD ALL JUST GET ALONG.
WHAT DO YOU WANT FROM US, YOU CREEP?
INSTEAD OF SWAPPING BODIES, I JUST WANT YOU ALL TO BE YOURSELVES THIS TIME AROUND.
THAT'S ALL. A PRETTY SIMPLE REQUEST.

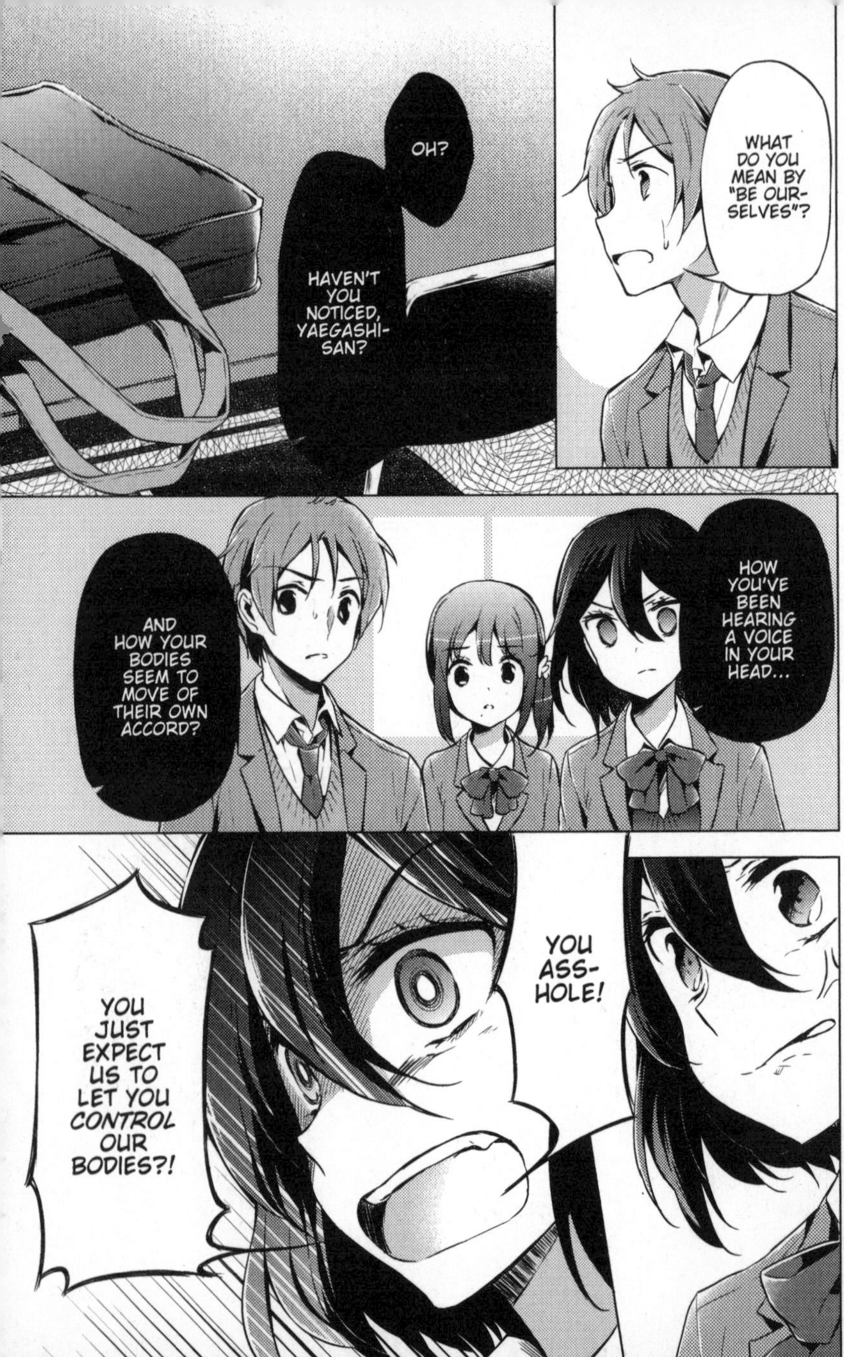
WHAT DO YOU MEAN BY "BE OUR-SELVES"?
OH?
HAVEN'T YOU NOTICED, YAEGASHI-SAN?
HOW YOU'VE BEEN HEARING A VOICE IN YOUR HEAD...
AND HOW YOUR BODIES SEEM TO MOVE OF THEIR OWN ACCORD?
YOU ASS-HOLE!
YOU JUST EXPECT US TO LET YOU *CONTROL* OUR BODIES?!

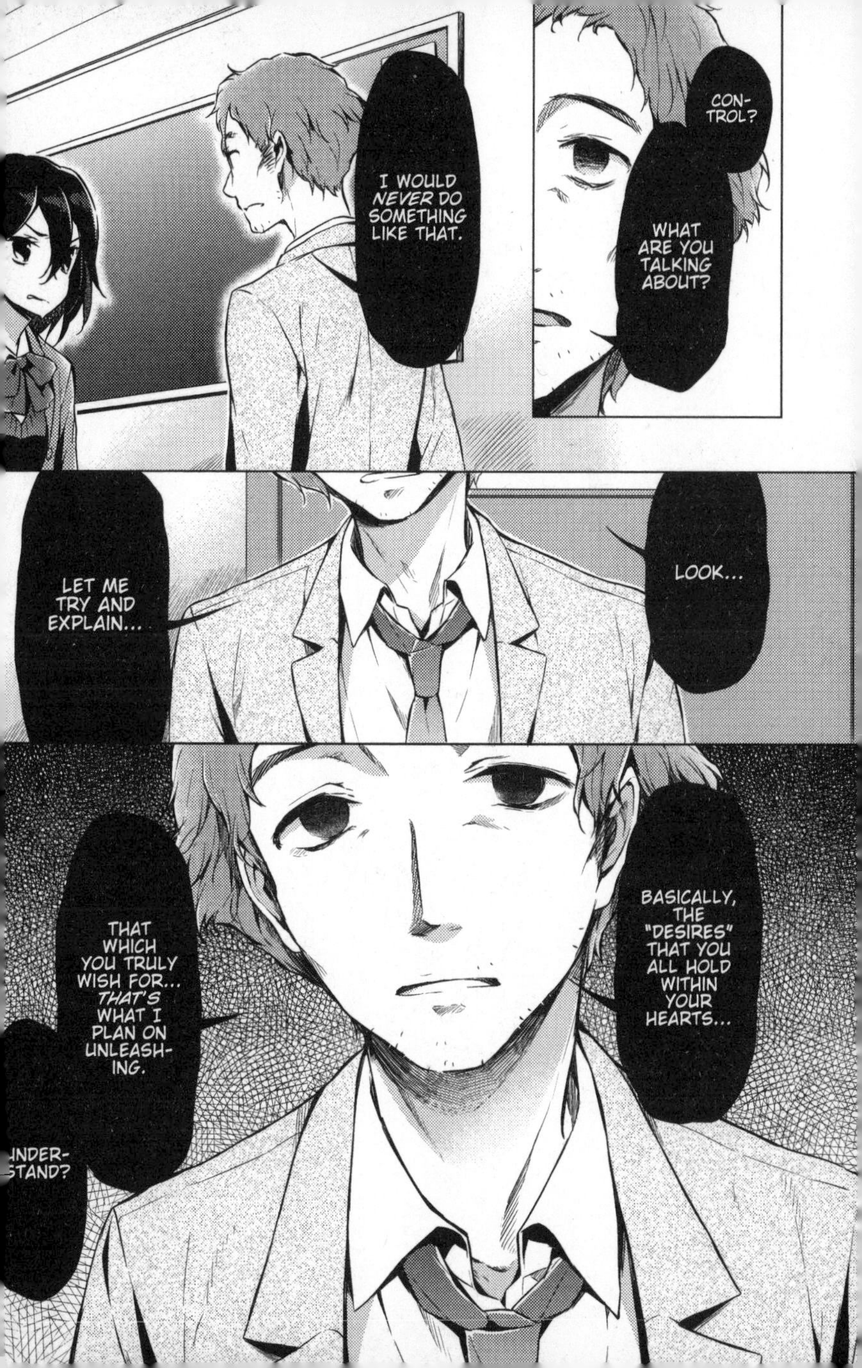
CON-TROL?
WHAT ARE YOU TALKING ABOUT?
I WOULD *NEVER* DO SOMETHING LIKE THAT.
LOOK...
LET ME TRY AND EXPLAIN...
BASICALLY, THE "DESIRES" THAT YOU ALL HOLD WITHIN YOUR HEARTS...
THAT WHICH YOU TRULY WISH FOR... *THAT'S* WHAT I PLAN ON UNLEASHING.
NDER-STAND?

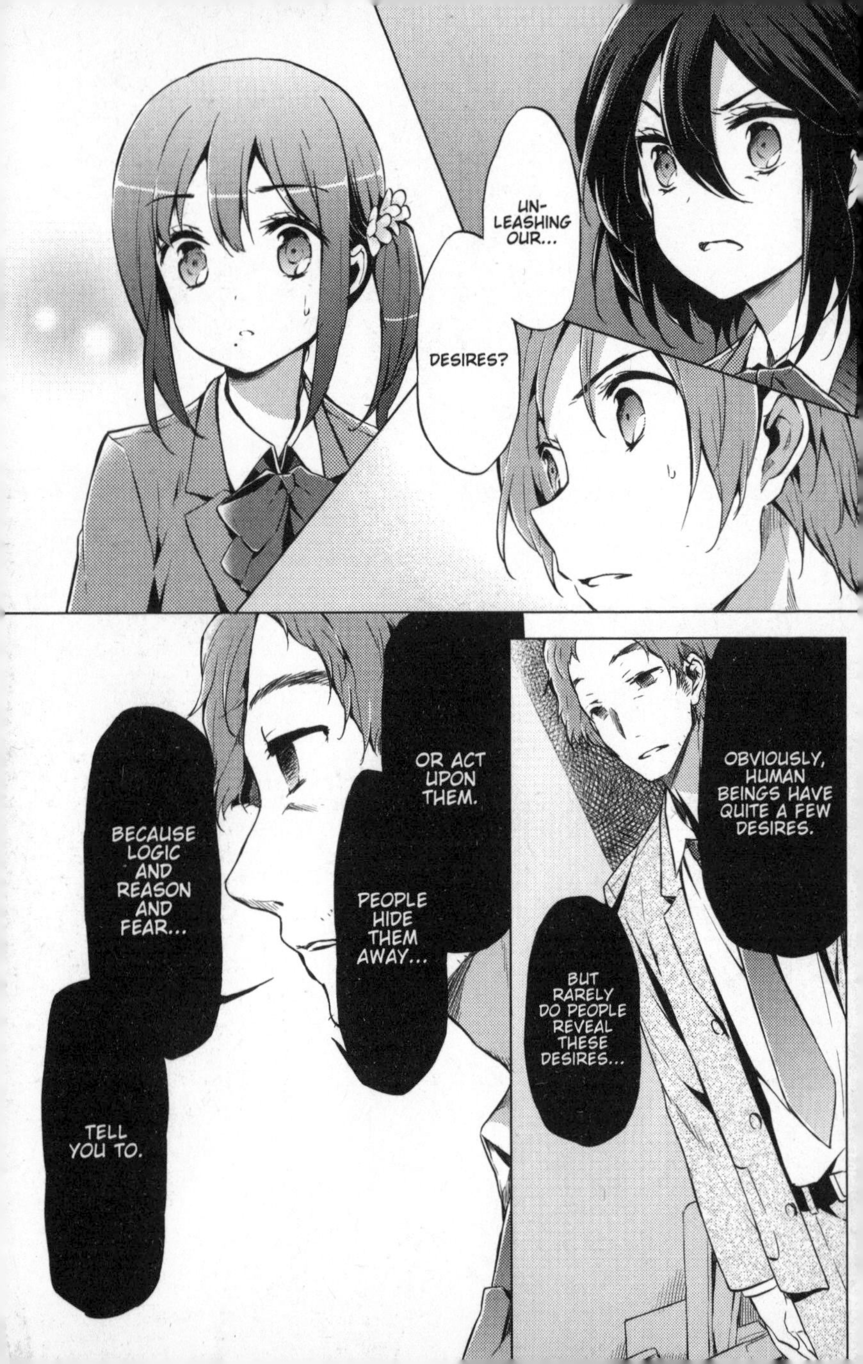
UN-LEASHING OUR... DESIRES?
OBVIOUSLY, HUMAN BEINGS HAVE QUITE A FEW DESIRES.
BUT RARELY DO PEOPLE REVEAL THESE DESIRES...
OR ACT UPON THEM.
PEOPLE HIDE THEM AWAY...
BECAUSE LOGIC AND REASON AND FEAR...
TELL YOU TO.

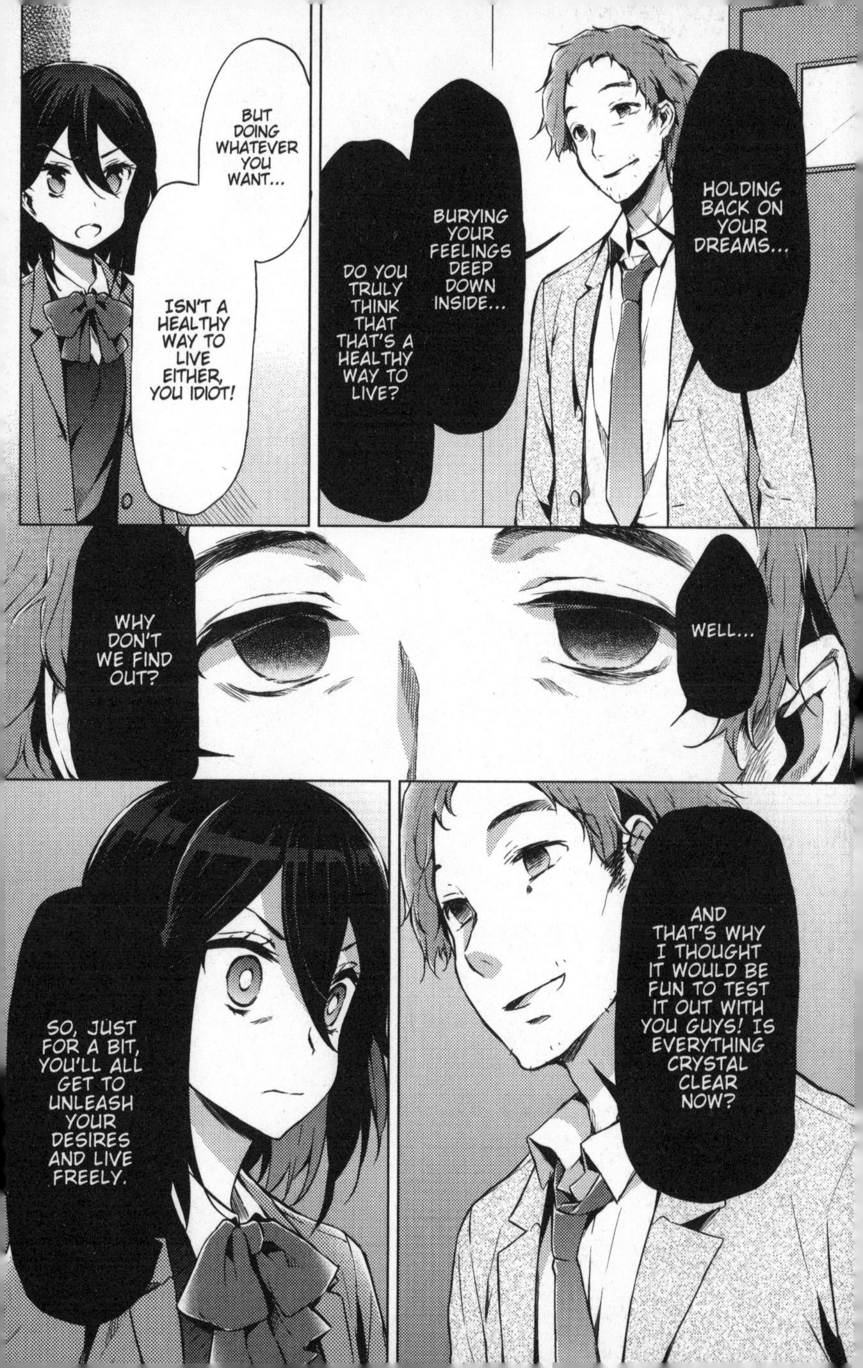
HOLDING BACK ON YOUR DREAMS...
BURYING YOUR FEELINGS DEEP DOWN INSIDE...
DO YOU TRULY THINK THAT THAT'S A HEALTHY WAY TO LIVE?
BUT DOING WHATEVER YOU WANT...
ISN'T A HEALTHY WAY TO LIVE EITHER, YOU IDIOT!
WELL...
WHY DON'T WE FIND OUT?
AND THAT'S WHY I THOUGHT IT WOULD BE FUN TO TEST IT OUT WITH YOU GUYS! IS EVERYTHING CRYSTAL CLEAR NOW?
SO, JUST FOR A BIT, YOU'LL ALL GET TO UNLEASH YOUR DESIRES AND LIVE FREELY.

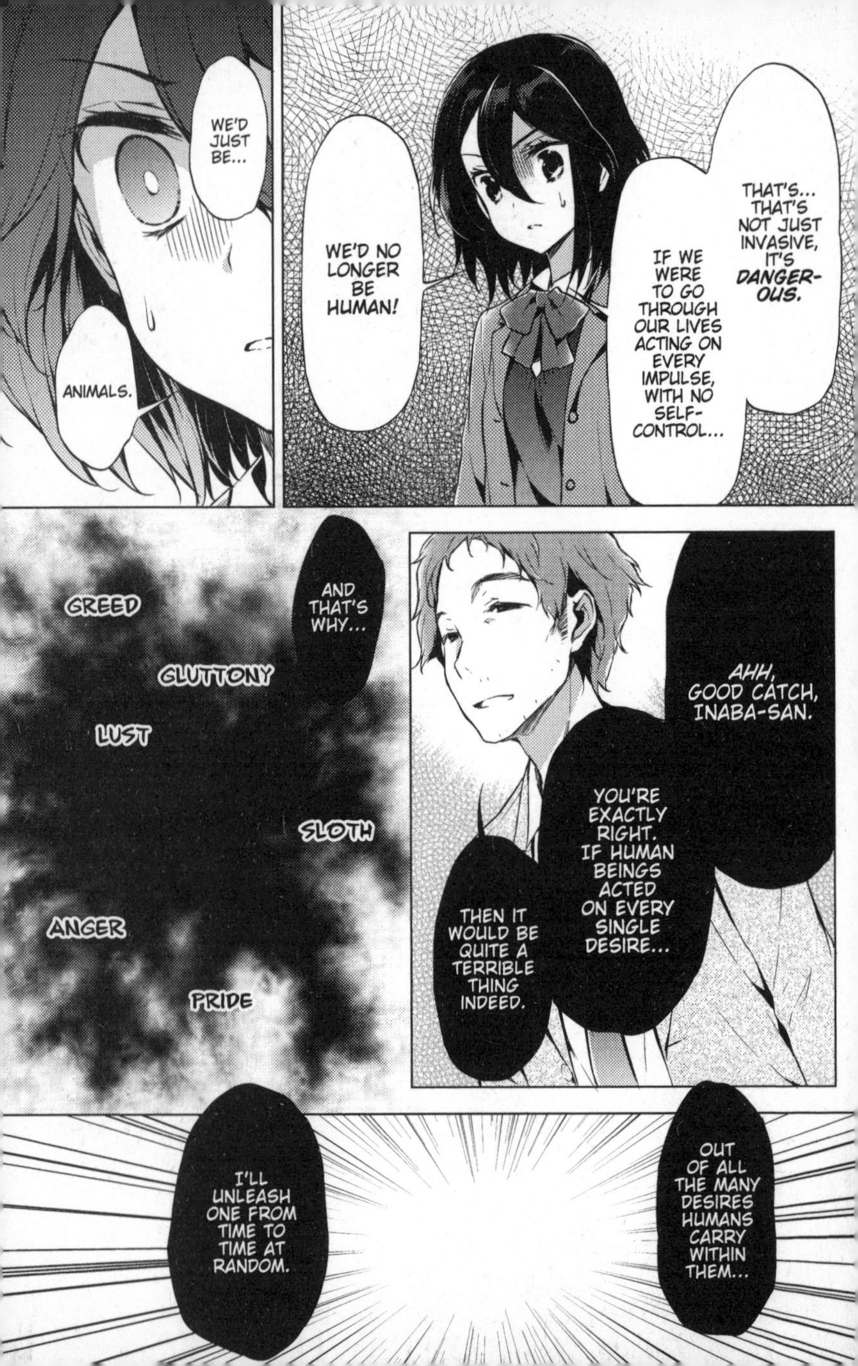
THAT'S... THAT'S NOT JUST INVASIVE, IT'S *DANGEROUS.*
IF WE WERE TO GO THROUGH OUR LIVES ACTING ON EVERY IMPULSE, WITH NO SELF-CONTROL...
WE'D NO LONGER BE HUMAN!
WE'D JUST BE...
ANIMALS.
AHH, GOOD CATCH, INABA-SAN.
YOU'RE EXACTLY RIGHT. IF HUMAN BEINGS ACTED ON EVERY SINGLE DESIRE...
THEN IT WOULD BE QUITE A TERRIBLE THING INDEED.
AND THAT'S WHY...
GREED
GLUTTONY
LUST
SLOTH
ANGER
PRIDE
OUT OF ALL THE MANY DESIRES HUMANS CARRY WITHIN THEM...
I'LL UNLEASH ONE FROM TIME TO TIME AT RANDOM.

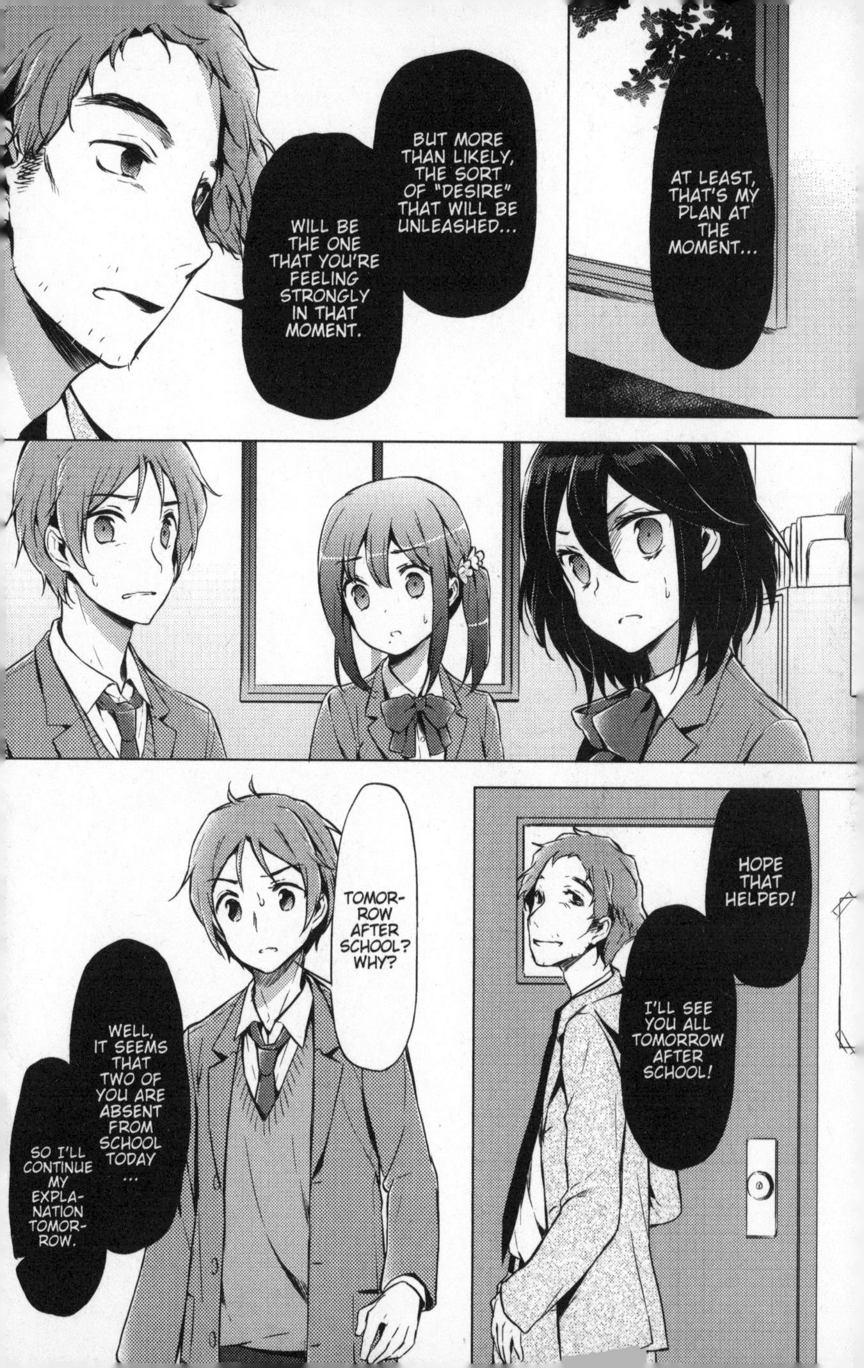
AT LEAST, THAT'S MY PLAN AT THE MOMENT...
BUT MORE THAN LIKELY, THE SORT OF "DESIRE" THAT WILL BE UNLEASHED...
WILL BE THE ONE THAT YOU'RE FEELING STRONGLY IN THAT MOMENT.
HOPE THAT HELPED!
I'LL SEE YOU ALL TOMORROW AFTER SCHOOL!
TOMOR-ROW AFTER SCHOOL? WHY?
WELL, IT SEEMS THAT TWO OF YOU ARE ABSENT FROM SCHOOL TODAY ...
SO I'LL CONTINUE MY EXPLA-NATION TOMOR-ROW.

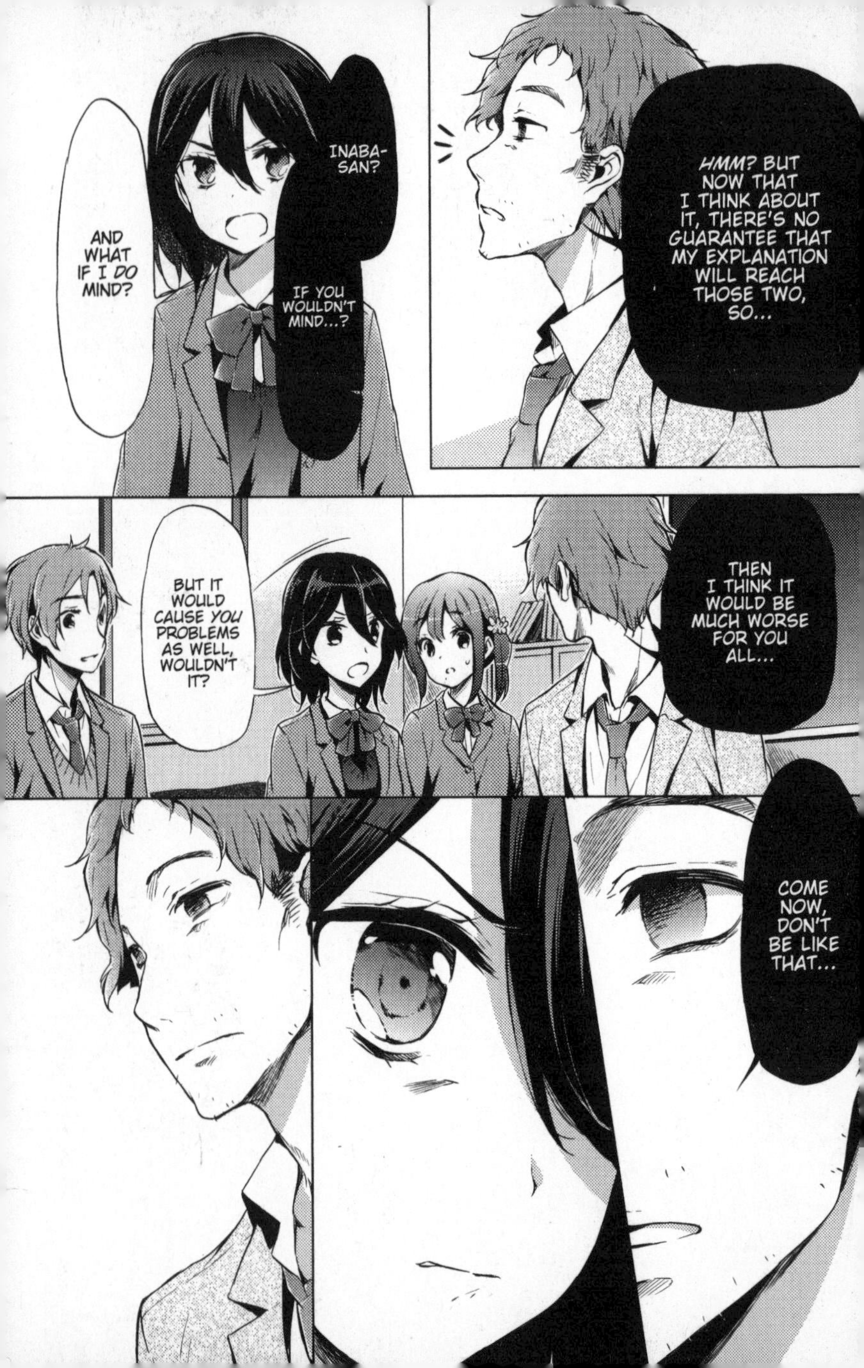
HMM? BUT NOW THAT I THINK ABOUT IT, THERE'S NO GUARANTEE THAT MY EXPLANATION WILL REACH THOSE TWO, SO...
INABA-SAN?
IF YOU WOULDN'T MIND...?
AND WHAT IF I DO MIND?
THEN I THINK IT WOULD BE MUCH WORSE FOR YOU ALL...
BUT IT WOULD CAUSE YOU PROBLEMS AS WELL, WOULDN'T IT?
COME NOW, DON'T BE LIKE THAT...

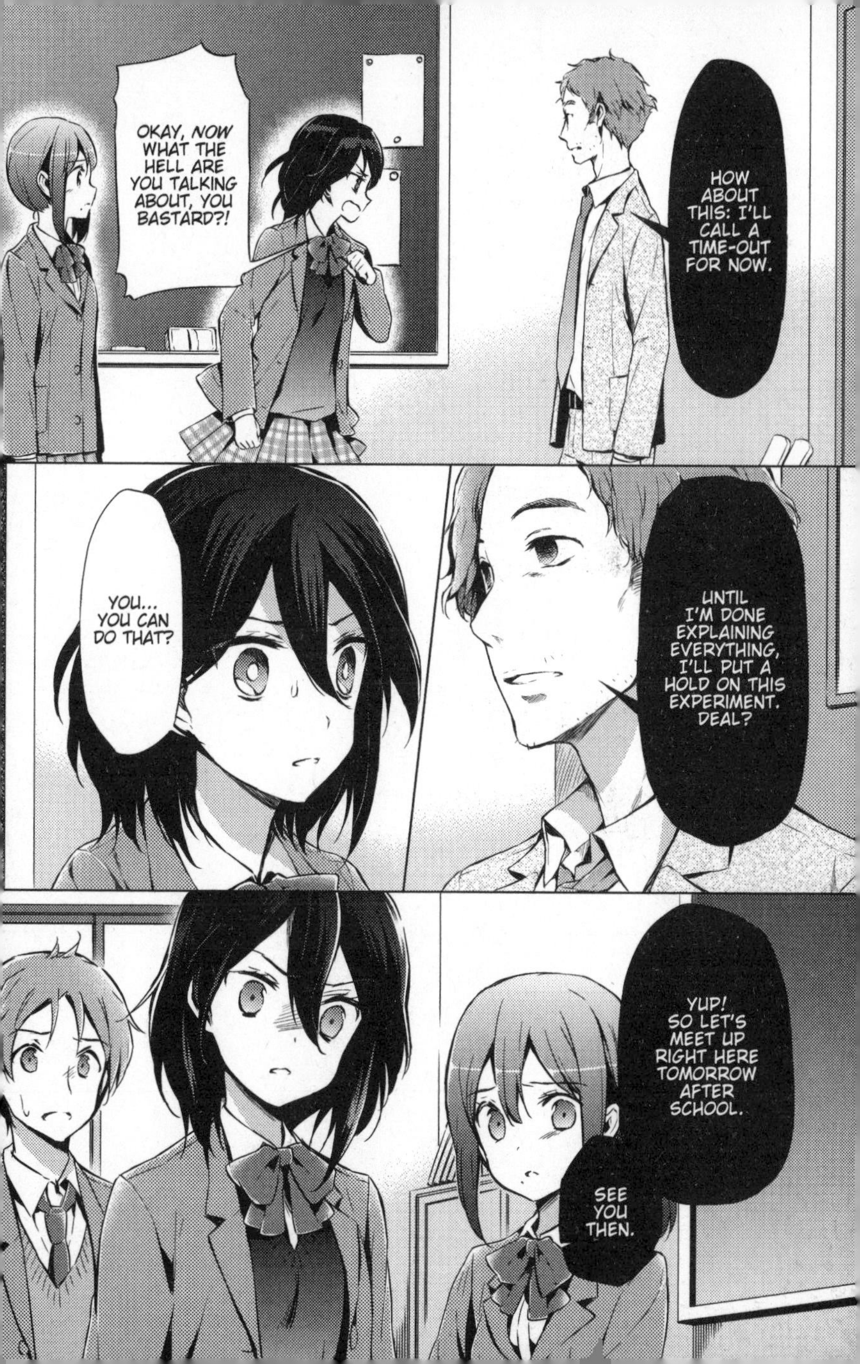
HOW ABOUT THIS: I'LL CALL A TIME-OUT FOR NOW.
OKAY, *NOW* WHAT THE HELL ARE YOU TALKING ABOUT, YOU BASTARD?!
UNTIL I'M DONE EXPLAINING EVERYTHING, I'LL PUT A HOLD ON THIS EXPERIMENT. DEAL?
YOU... YOU CAN DO THAT?
YUP! SO LET'S MEET UP RIGHT HERE TOMORROW AFTER SCHOOL.
SEE YOU THEN.

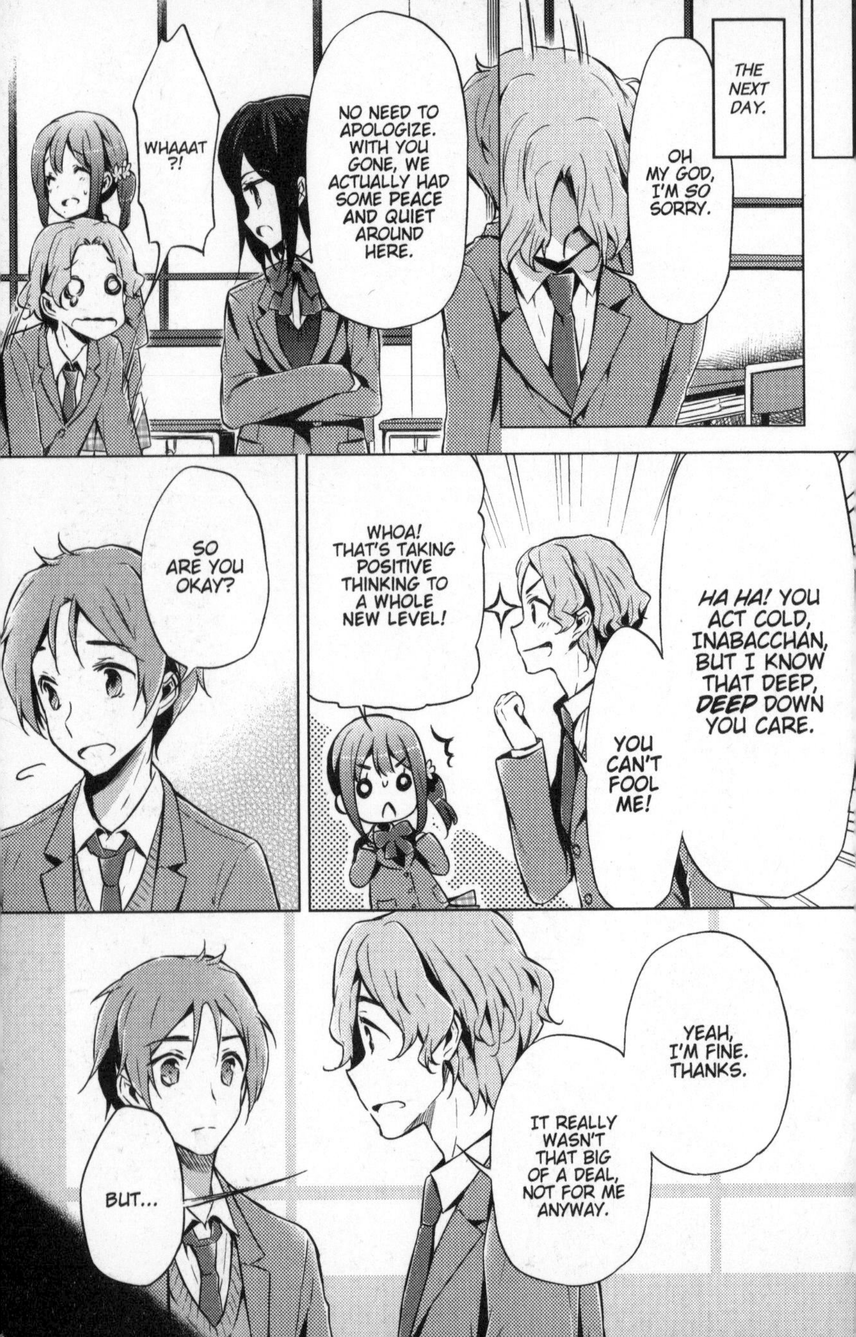
THE NEXT DAY.
OH MY GOD, I'M SO SORRY.
NO NEED TO APOLOGIZE. WITH YOU GONE, WE ACTUALLY HAD SOME PEACE AND QUIET AROUND HERE.
WHAAAT ?!
HA HA! YOU ACT COLD, INABACCHAN, BUT I KNOW THAT DEEP, ***DEEP*** DOWN YOU CARE.
YOU CAN'T FOOL ME!
WHOA! THAT'S TAKING POSITIVE THINKING TO A WHOLE NEW LEVEL!
SO ARE YOU OKAY?
YEAH, I'M FINE. THANKS.
IT REALLY WASN'T THAT BIG OF A DEAL, NOT FOR ME ANYWAY.
BUT...

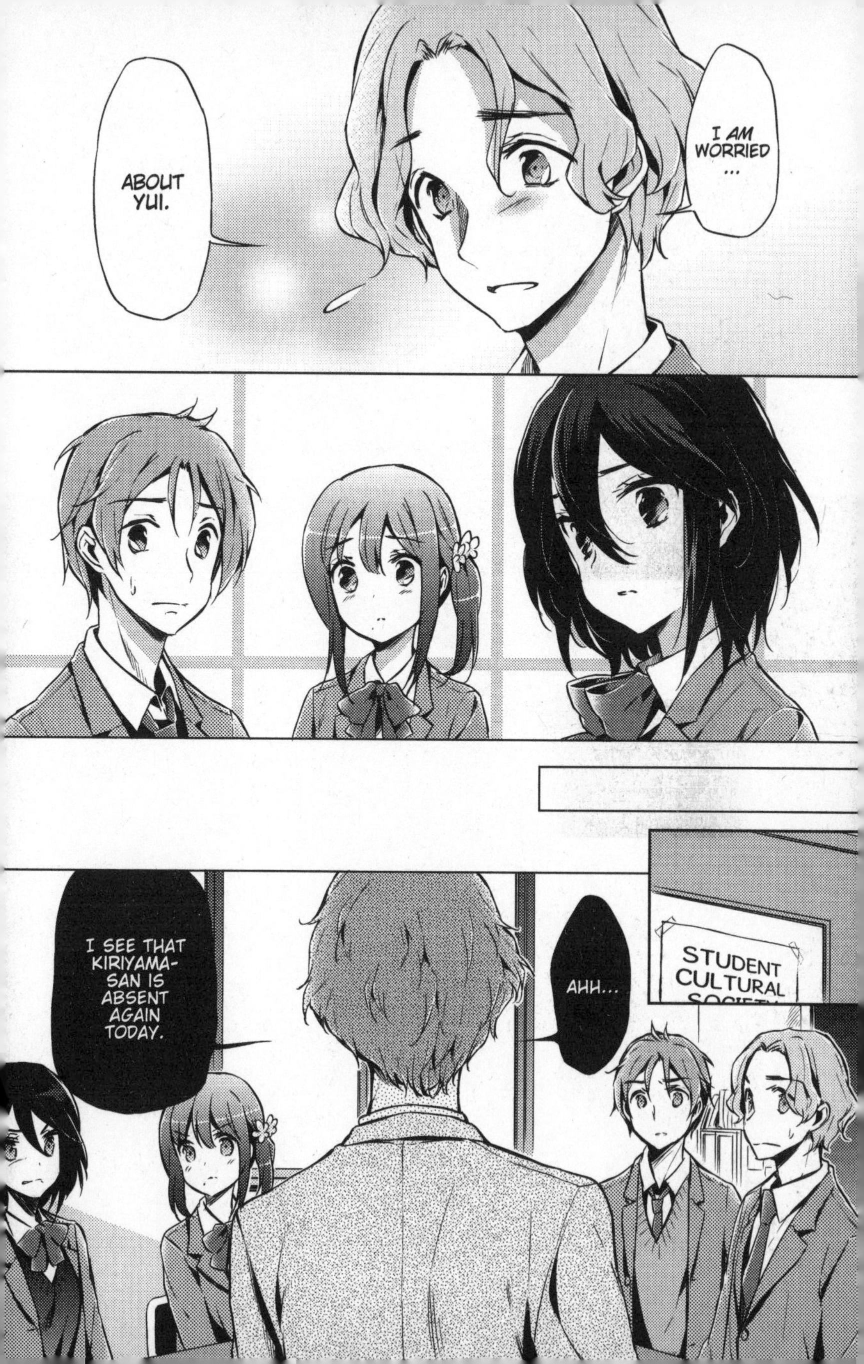
I AM WORRIED ...
ABOUT YUI.
STUDENT CULTURAL
AHH...
I SEE THAT KIRIYAMA-SAN IS ABSENT AGAIN TODAY.

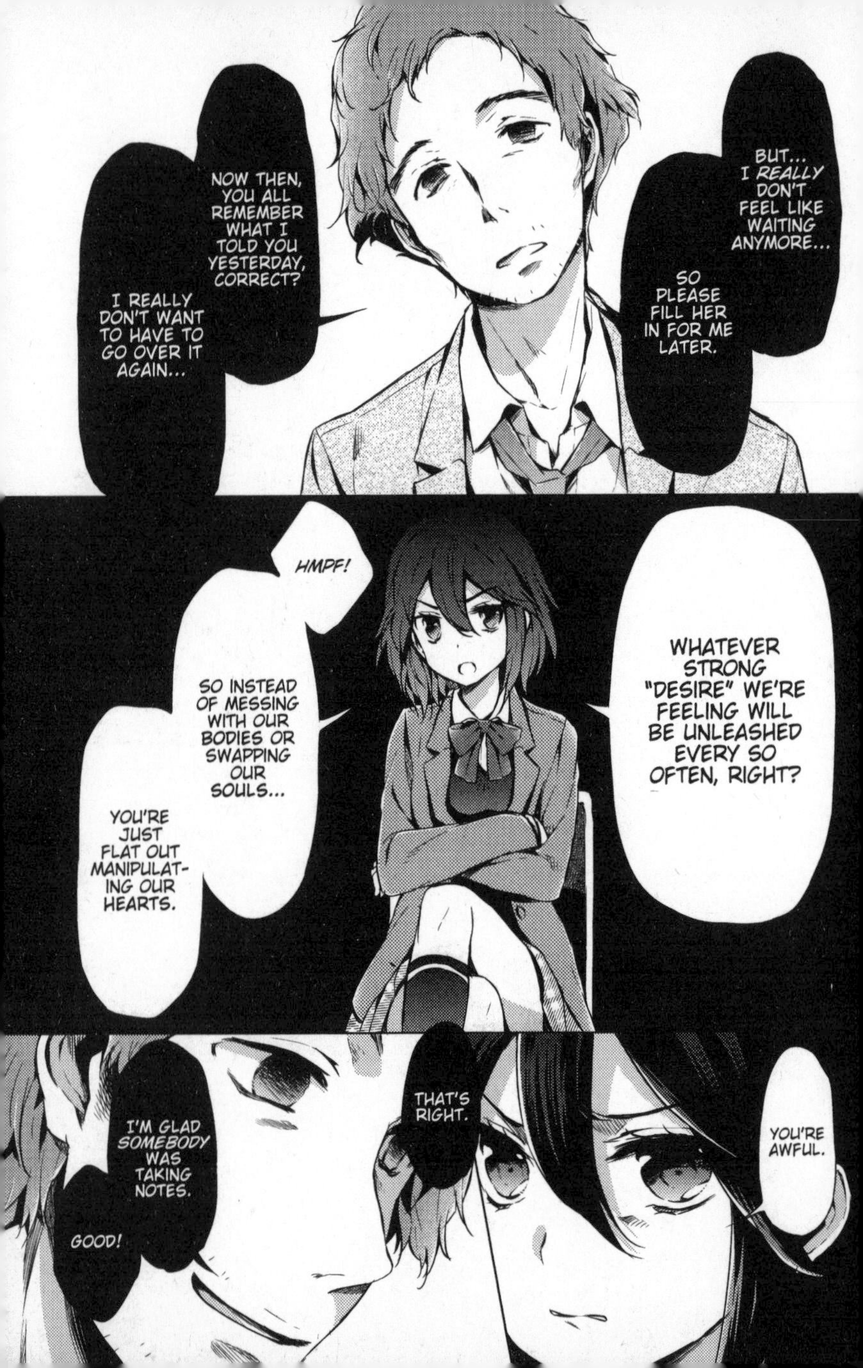
BUT... I *REALLY* DON'T FEEL LIKE WAITING ANYMORE...
SO PLEASE FILL HER IN FOR ME LATER.
NOW THEN, YOU ALL REMEMBER WHAT I TOLD YOU YESTERDAY, CORRECT?
I REALLY DON'T WANT TO HAVE TO GO OVER IT AGAIN...
WHATEVER STRONG "DESIRE" WE'RE FEELING WILL BE UNLEASHED EVERY SO OFTEN, RIGHT?
HMPF!
SO INSTEAD OF MESSING WITH OUR BODIES OR SWAPPING OUR SOULS...
YOU'RE JUST FLAT OUT MANIPULATING OUR HEARTS.
YOU'RE AWFUL.
THAT'S RIGHT.
I'M GLAD *SOMEBODY* WAS TAKING NOTES.
GOOD!

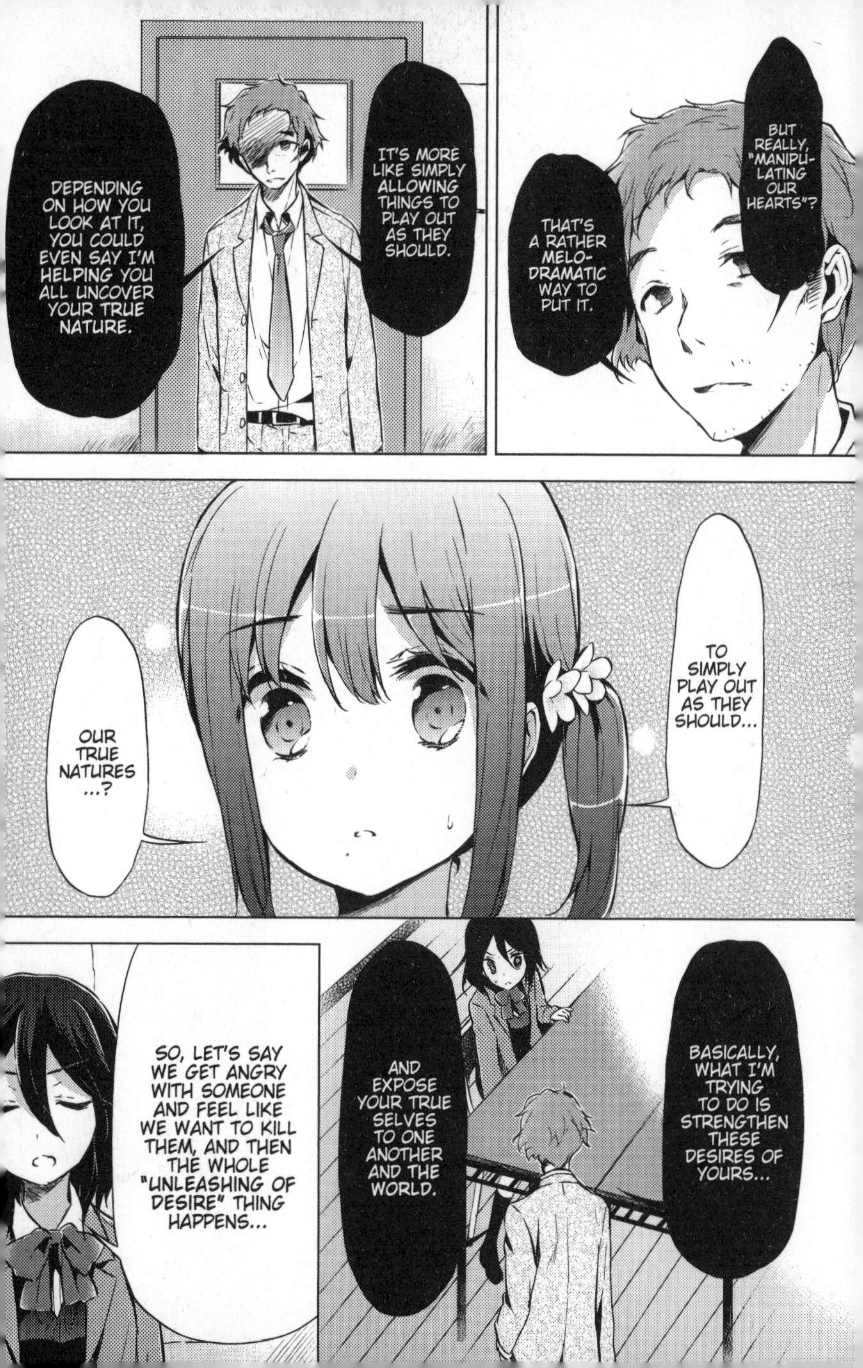
BUT REALLY, "MANIPULATING OUR HEARTS"?
THAT'S A RATHER MELODRAMATIC WAY TO PUT IT.
IT'S MORE LIKE SIMPLY ALLOWING THINGS TO PLAY OUT AS THEY SHOULD.
DEPENDING ON HOW YOU LOOK AT IT, YOU COULD EVEN SAY I'M HELPING YOU ALL UNCOVER YOUR TRUE NATURE.
TO SIMPLY PLAY OUT AS THEY SHOULD...
OUR TRUE NATURES...?
BASICALLY, WHAT I'M TRYING TO DO IS STRENGTHEN THESE DESIRES OF YOURS...
AND EXPOSE YOUR TRUE SELVES TO ONE ANOTHER AND THE WORLD.
SO, LET'S SAY WE GET ANGRY WITH SOMEONE AND FEEL LIKE WE WANT TO KILL THEM, AND THEN THE WHOLE "UNLEASHING OF DESIRE" THING HAPPENS...

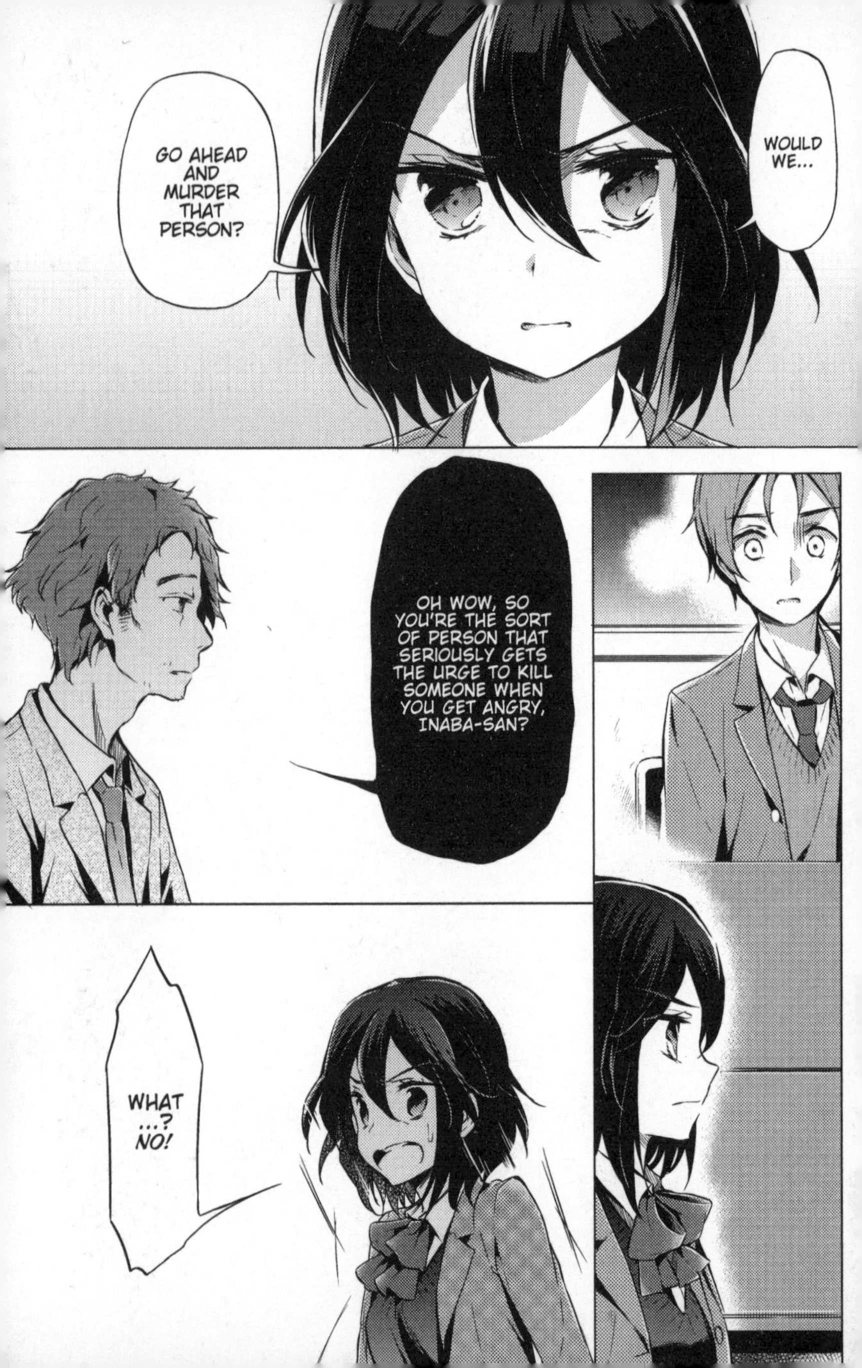
WOULD WE...
GO AHEAD AND MURDER THAT PERSON?
OH WOW, SO YOU'RE THE SORT OF PERSON THAT SERIOUSLY GETS THE URGE TO KILL SOMEONE WHEN YOU GET ANGRY, INABA-SAN?
WHAT ...? NO!

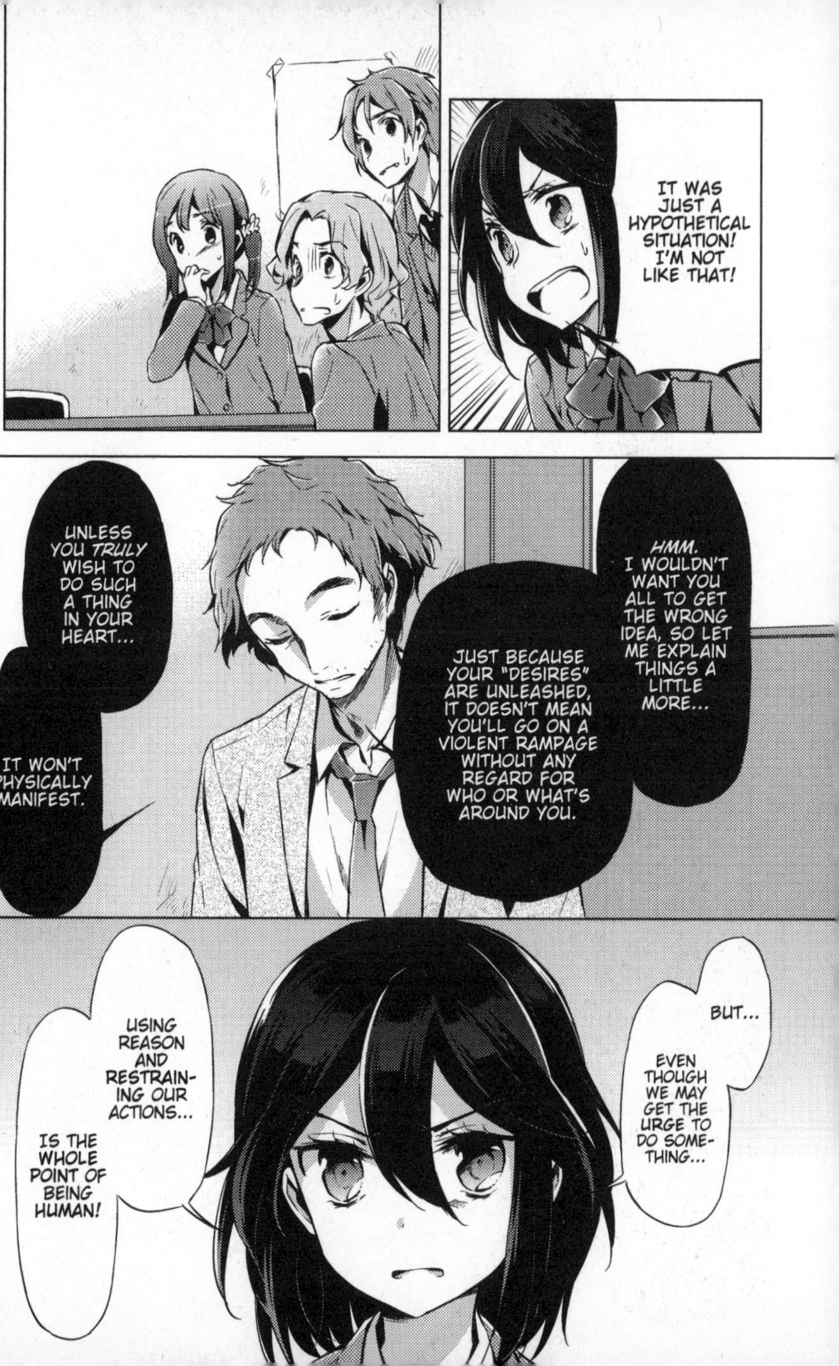
IT WAS JUST A HYPOTHETICAL SITUATION! I'M NOT LIKE THAT!
HMM. I WOULDN'T WANT YOU ALL TO GET THE WRONG IDEA, SO LET ME EXPLAIN THINGS A LITTLE MORE...
JUST BECAUSE YOUR "DESIRES" ARE UNLEASHED, IT DOESN'T MEAN YOU'LL GO ON A VIOLENT RAMPAGE WITHOUT ANY REGARD FOR WHO OR WHAT'S AROUND YOU.
UNLESS YOU *TRULY* WISH TO DO SUCH A THING IN YOUR HEART...
IT WON'T PHYSICALLY MANIFEST.
BUT...
EVEN THOUGH WE MAY GET THE URGE TO DO SOME-THING...
USING REASON AND RESTRAIN-ING OUR ACTIONS...
IS THE WHOLE POINT OF BEING HUMAN!

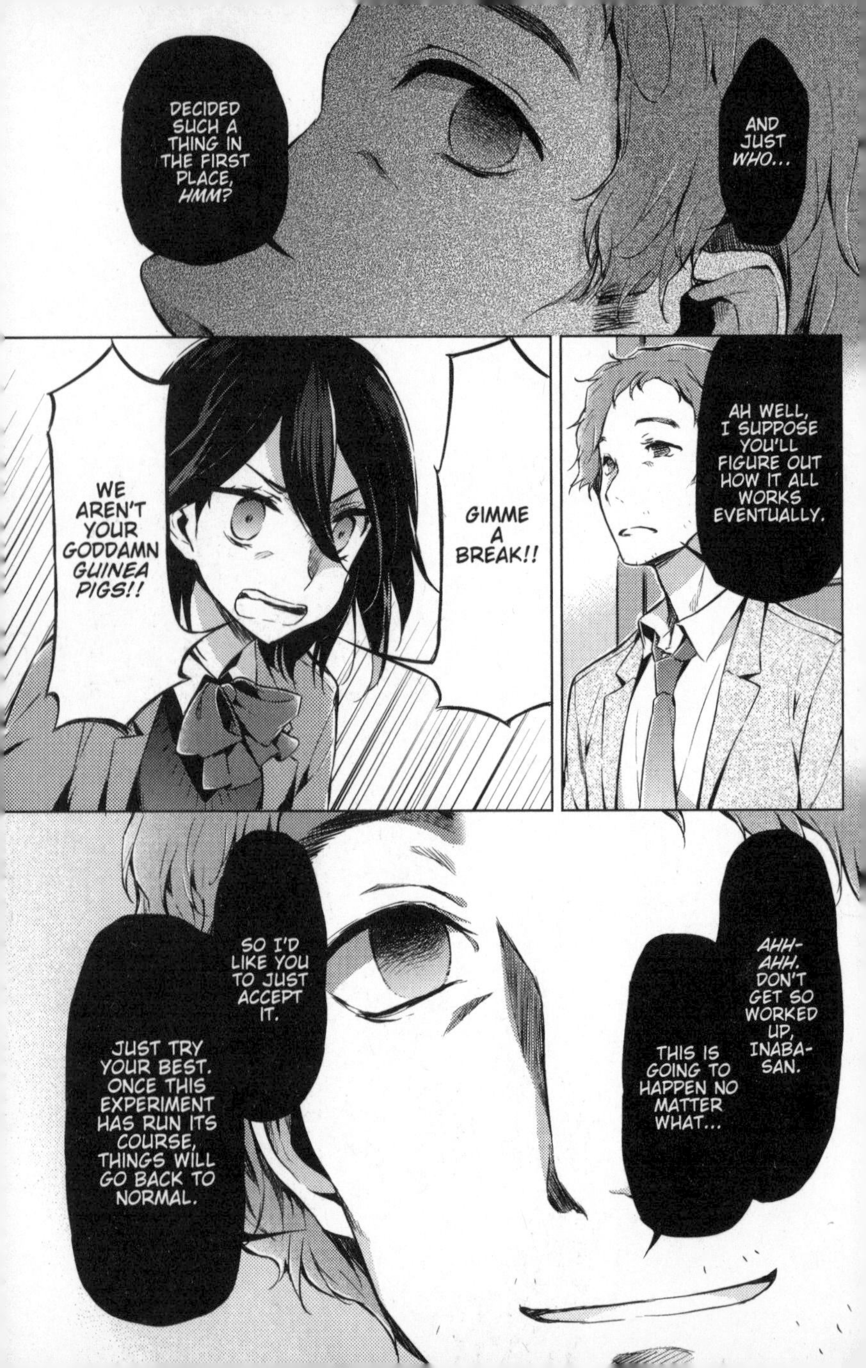
AND JUST *WHO*...
DECIDED SUCH A THING IN THE FIRST PLACE, *HMM?*
AH WELL, I SUPPOSE YOU'LL FIGURE OUT HOW IT ALL WORKS EVENTUALLY.
GIMME A BREAK!!
WE AREN'T YOUR GODDAMN *GUINEA PIGS!!*
AHH-AHH. DON'T GET SO WORKED UP, INABA-SAN.
THIS IS GOING TO HAPPEN NO MATTER WHAT...
SO I'D LIKE YOU TO JUST ACCEPT IT.
JUST TRY YOUR BEST. ONCE THIS EXPERIMENT HAS RUN ITS COURSE, THINGS WILL GO BACK TO NORMAL.

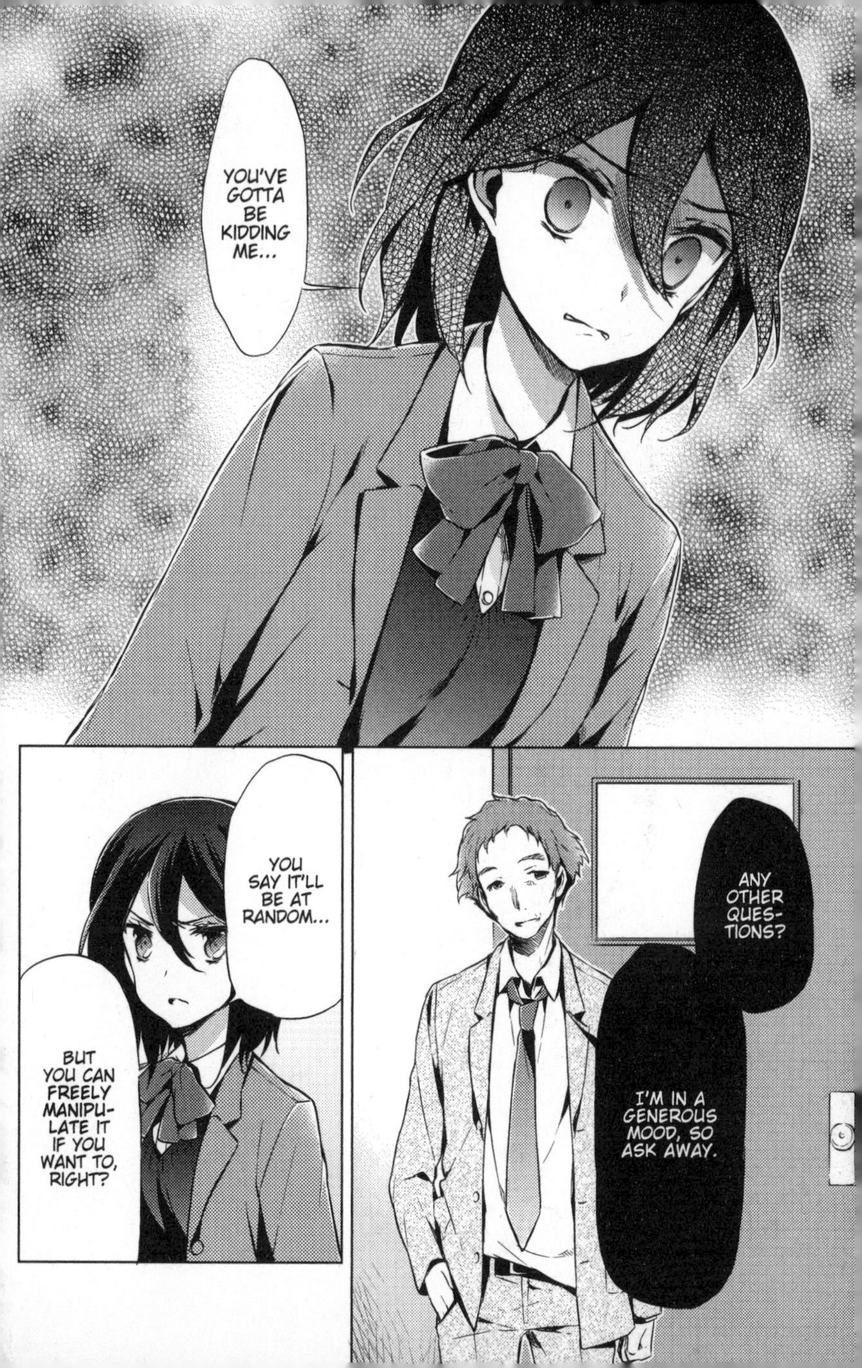
YOU'VE GOTTA BE KIDDING ME...
ANY OTHER QUES-TIONS?
I'M IN A GENEROUS MOOD, SO ASK AWAY.
YOU SAY IT'LL BE AT RANDOM...
BUT YOU CAN FREELY MANIPU-LATE IT IF YOU WANT TO, RIGHT?

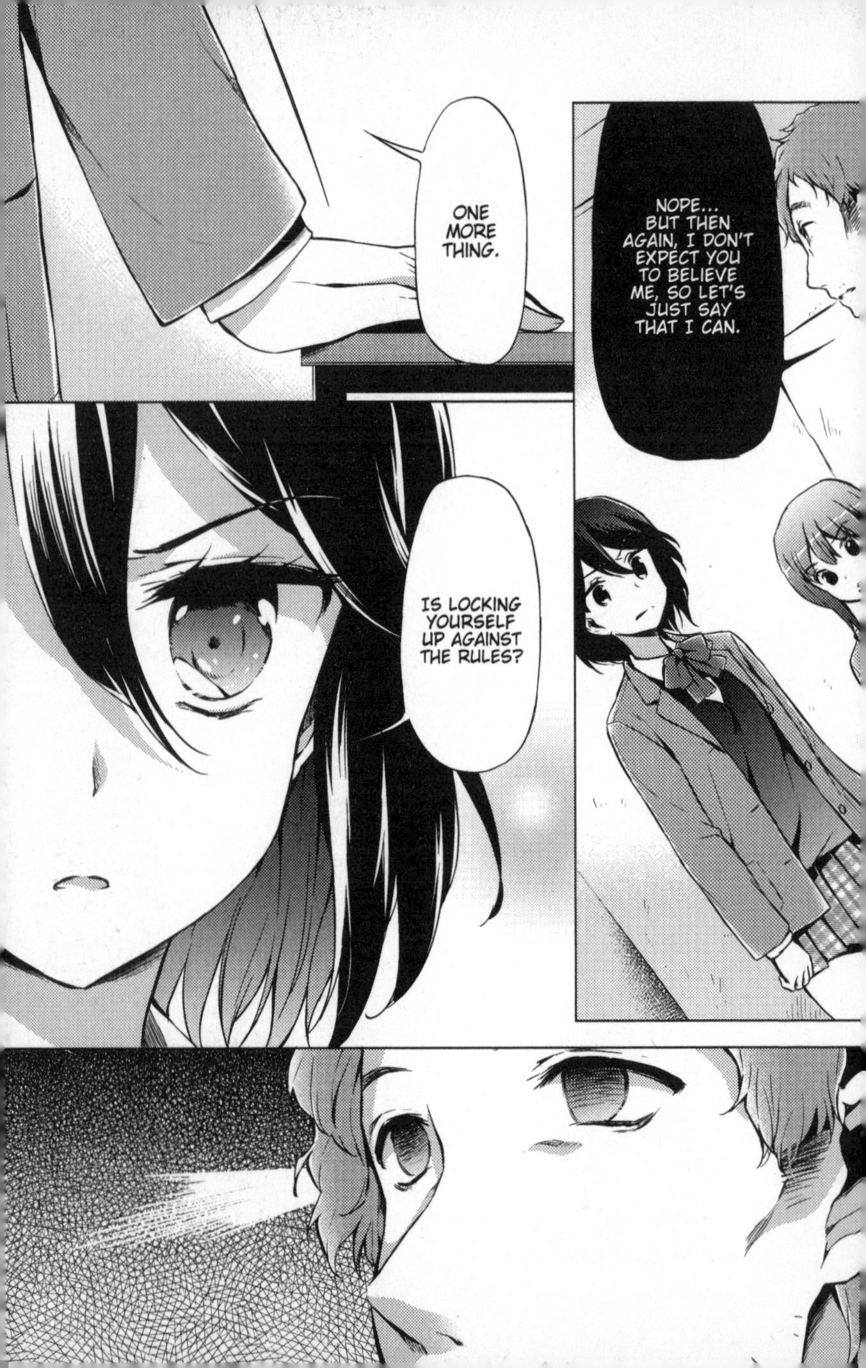
NOPE... BUT THEN AGAIN, I DON'T EXPECT YOU TO BELIEVE ME, SO LET'S JUST SAY THAT I CAN.
ONE MORE THING.
IS LOCKING YOURSELF UP AGAINST THE RULES?

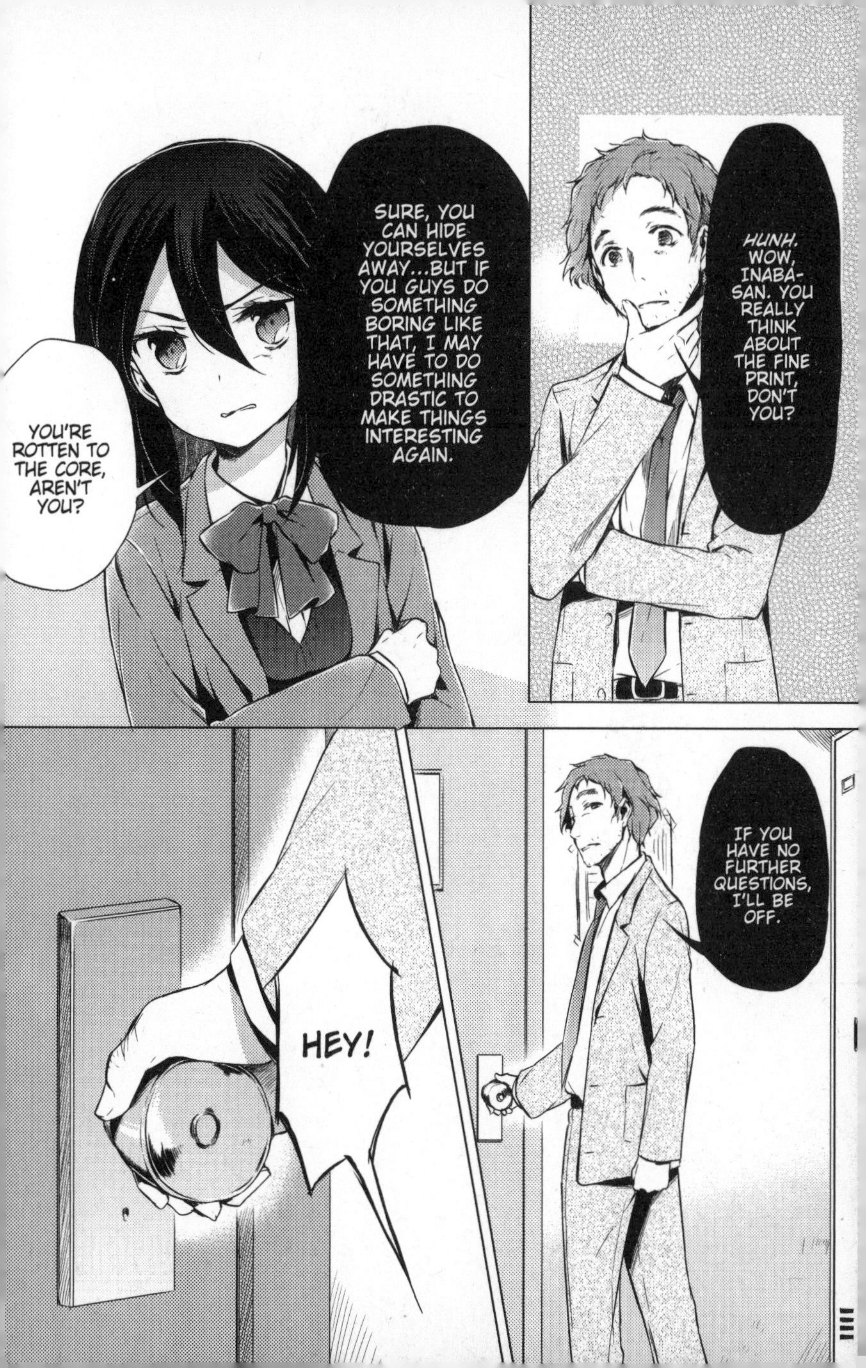
HUNH. WOW, INABA-SAN. YOU REALLY THINK ABOUT THE FINE PRINT, DON'T YOU?
SURE, YOU CAN HIDE YOURSELVES AWAY...BUT IF YOU GUYS DO SOMETHING BORING LIKE THAT, I MAY HAVE TO DO SOMETHING DRASTIC TO MAKE THINGS INTERESTING AGAIN.
YOU'RE ROTTEN TO THE CORE, AREN'T YOU?
IF YOU HAVE NO FURTHER QUESTIONS, I'LL BE OFF.
HEY!

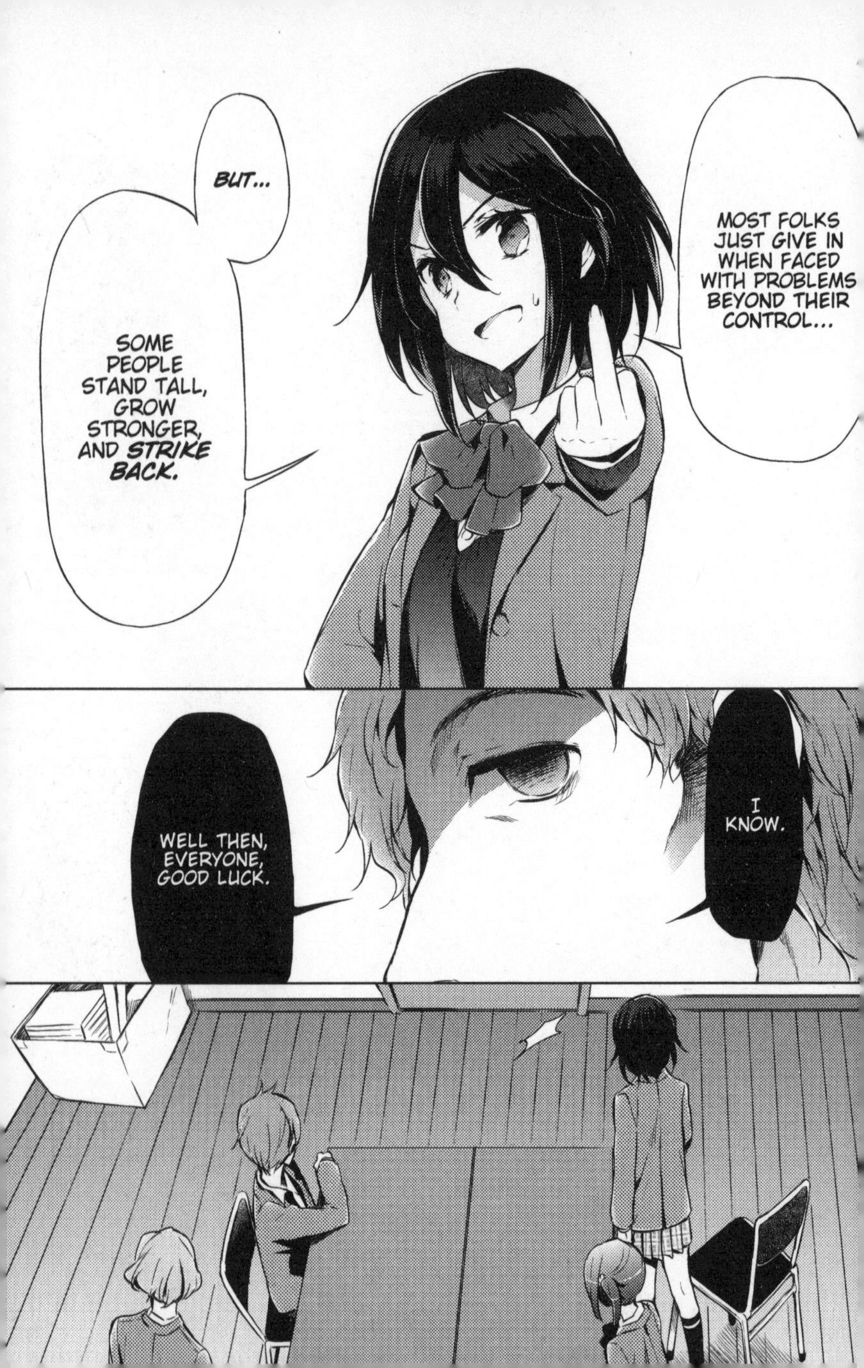
MOST FOLKS JUST GIVE IN WHEN FACED WITH PROBLEMS BEYOND THEIR CONTROL...
BUT...
SOME PEOPLE STAND TALL, GROW STRONGER, AND STRIKE BACK.
I KNOW.
WELL THEN, EVERYONE, GOOD LUCK.

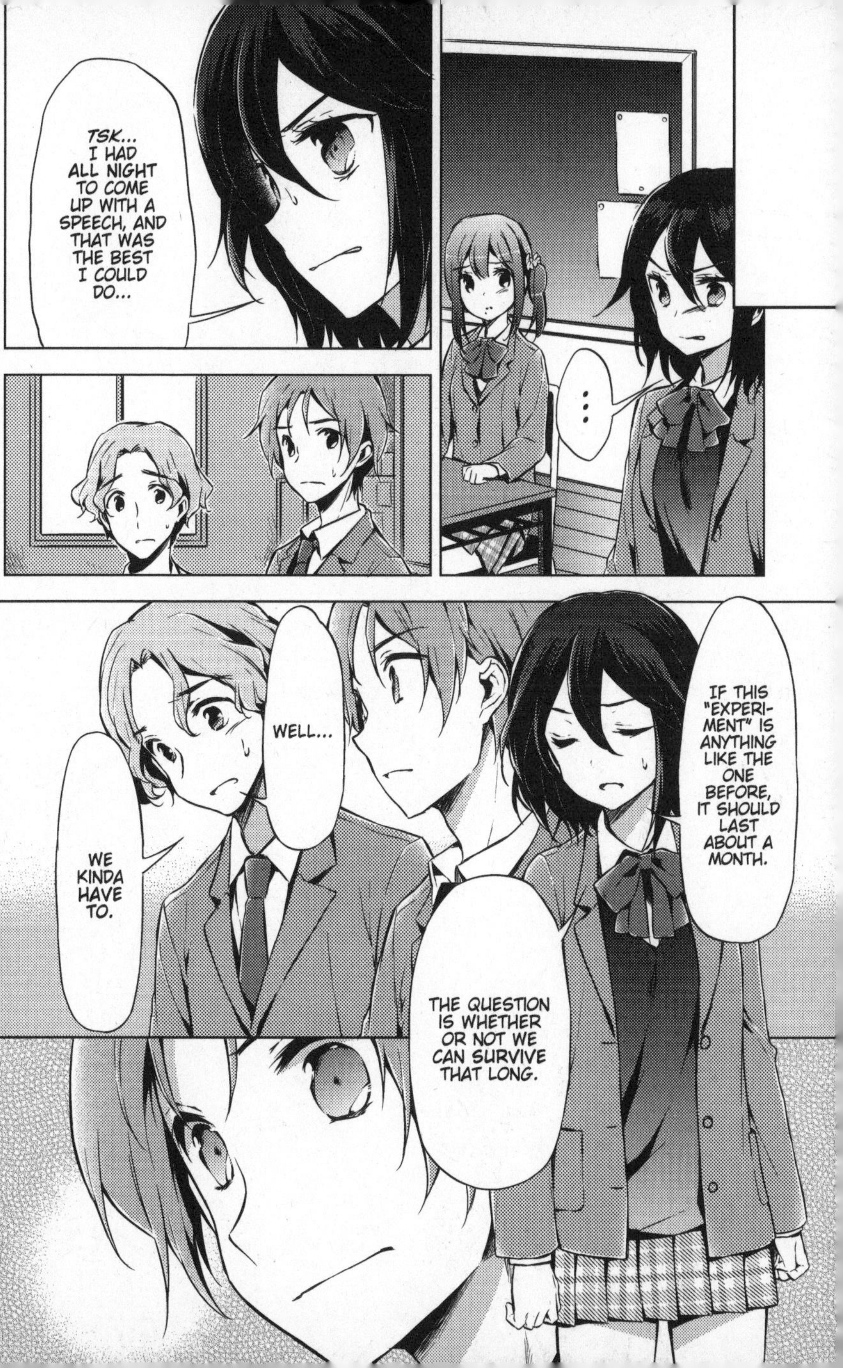
...
TSK... I HAD ALL NIGHT TO COME UP WITH A SPEECH, AND THAT WAS THE BEST I COULD DO...
IF THIS "EXPERIMENT" IS ANYTHING LIKE THE ONE BEFORE, IT SHOULD LAST ABOUT A MONTH.
THE QUESTION IS WHETHER OR NOT WE CAN SURVIVE THAT LONG.
WELL...
WE KINDA HAVE TO.

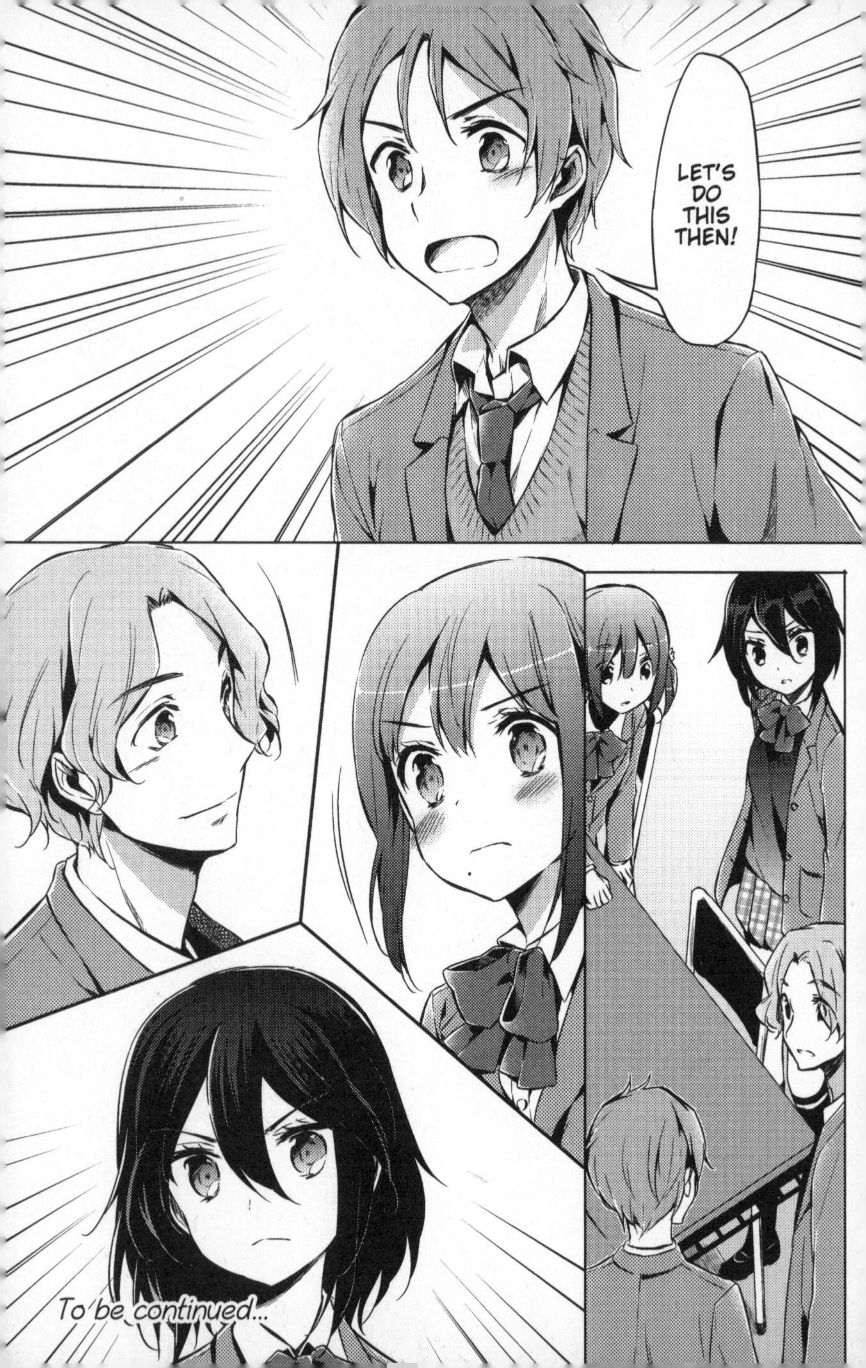
LET'S DO THIS THEN!
To be continued...

KOKORO CONNECT

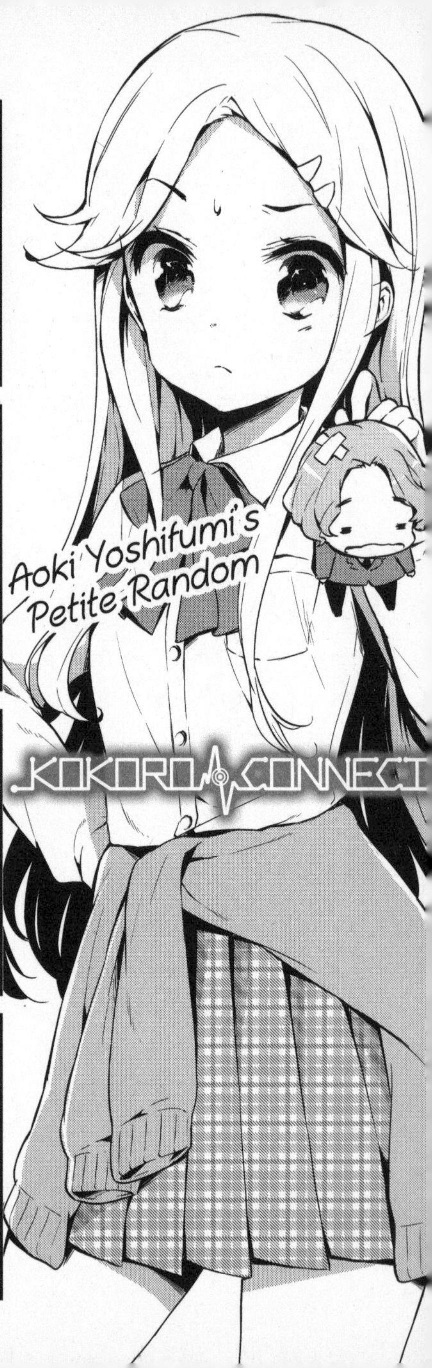
Aoki Yoshifumi's Petite Random
KOKORO CONNECT

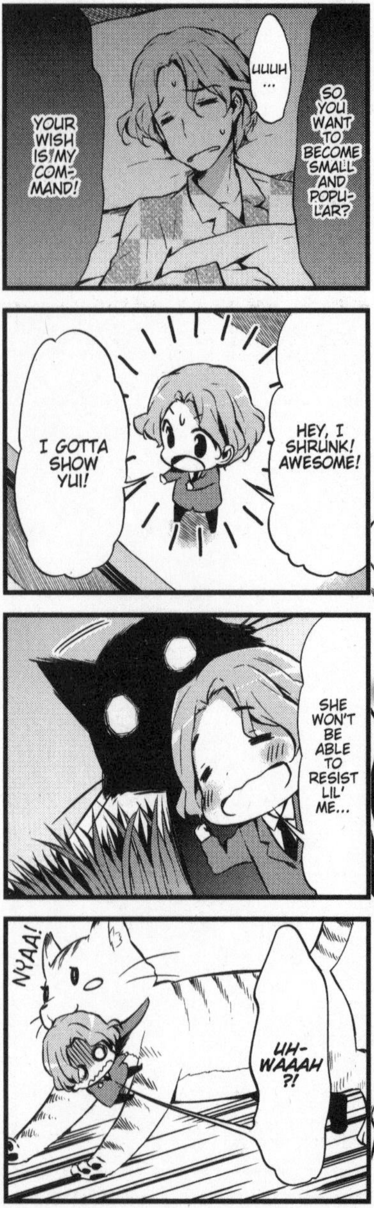
SO YOU WANT TO BECOME SMALL AND POPULAR?
UUUH...
YOUR WISH IS MY COMMAND!
HEY, I SHRUNK! AWESOME!
I GOTTA SHOW YUI!
SHE WON'T BE ABLE TO RESIST LIL' ME...
UH-WAAAH?!
NYAA!

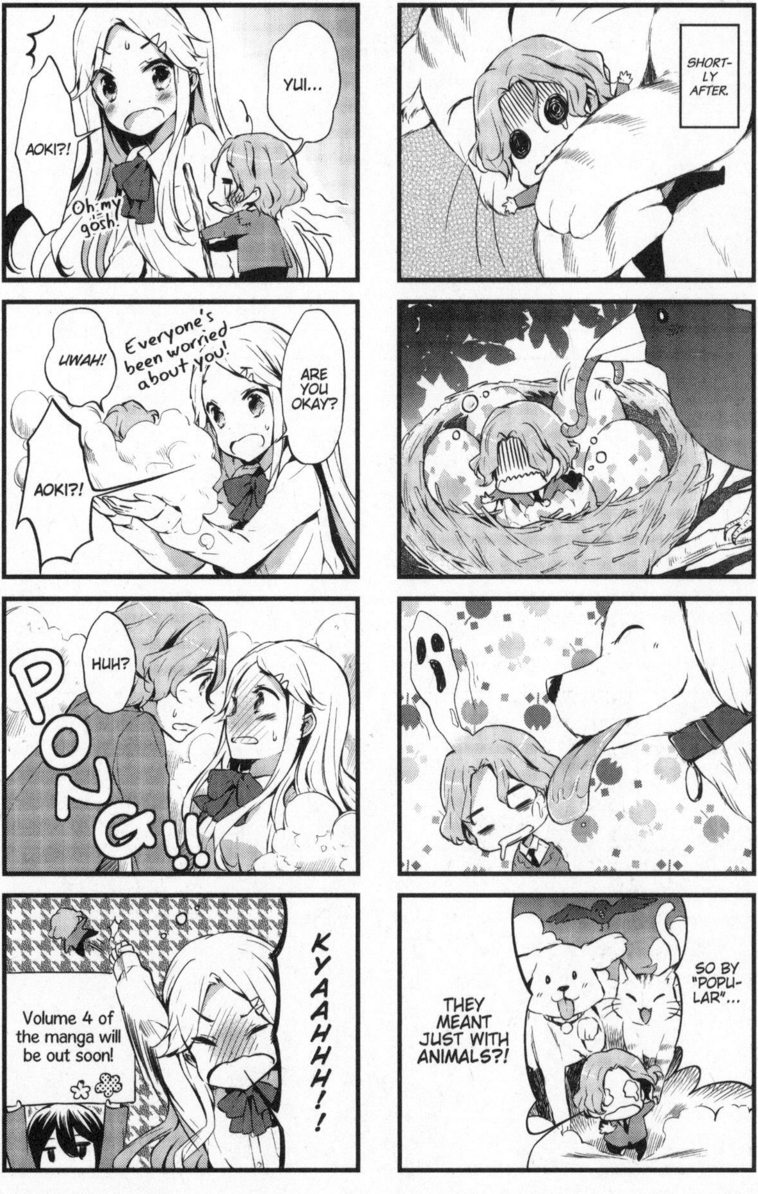
SHORT-LY AFTER.
SO BY "POPU-LAR"...
THEY MEANT JUST WITH ANIMALS?!
YUI...
AOKI?!
Oh my gosh!
ARE YOU OKAY?
Everyone's been worried about you!
UWAH!
AOKI?!
HUH?
PONG!!
KYAAHHH!!
Volume 4 of the manga will be out soon!

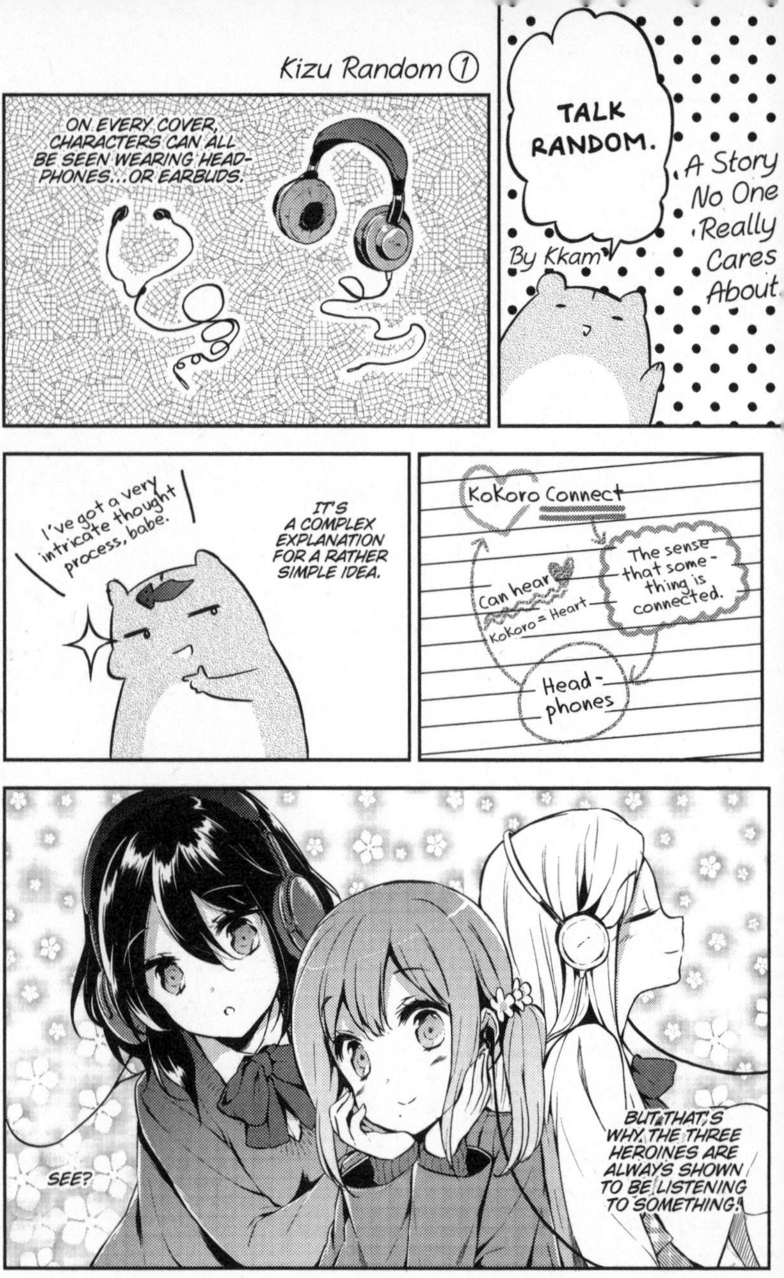
Kizu Random ①
TALK RANDOM.
A Story No One Really Cares About.
By Kkam
ON EVERY COVER, CHARACTERS CAN ALL BE SEEN WEARING HEADPHONES...OR EARBUDS.
Kokoro Connect
Can hear
Kokoro = Heart
The sense that something is connected.
Headphones
IT'S A COMPLEX EXPLANATION FOR A RATHER SIMPLE IDEA.
I've got a very intricate thought process, babe.
BUT THAT'S WHY THE THREE HEROINES ARE ALWAYS SHOWN TO BE LISTENING TO SOMETHING!
SEE?

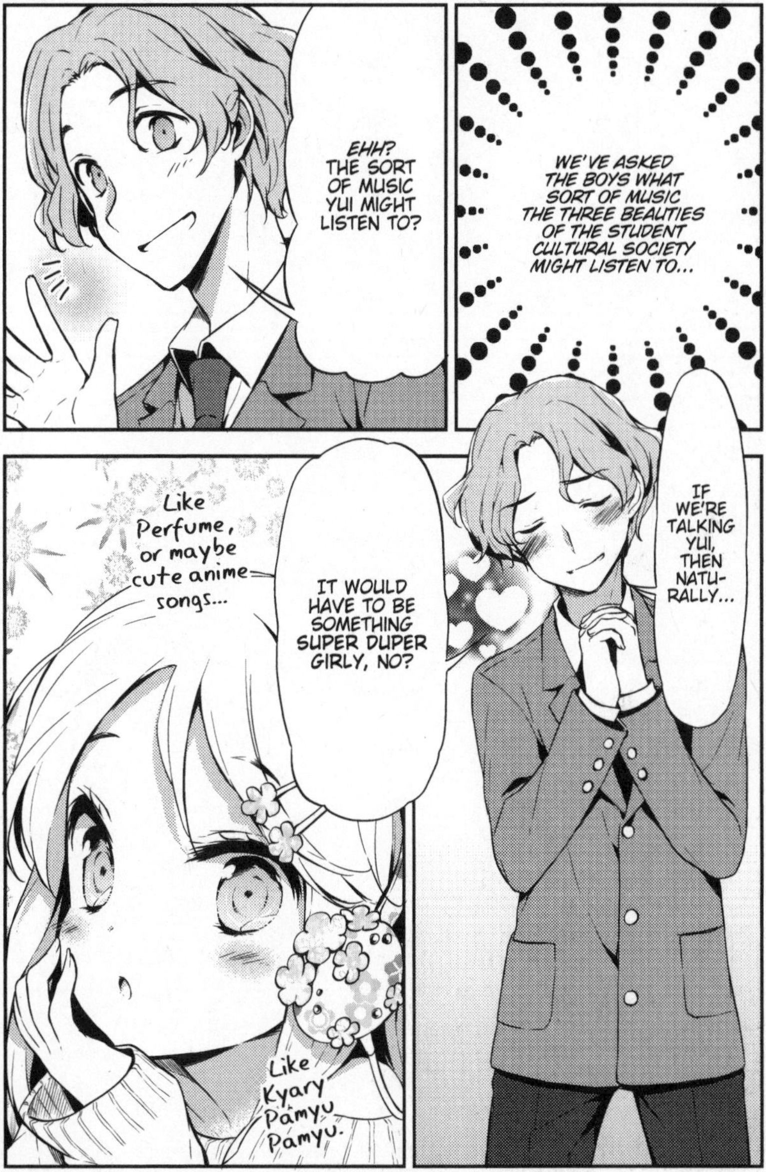
WE'VE ASKED THE BOYS WHAT SORT OF MUSIC THE THREE BEAUTIES OF THE STUDENT CULTURAL SOCIETY MIGHT LISTEN TO...
EHH? THE SORT OF MUSIC YUI MIGHT LISTEN TO?
IF WE'RE TALKING YUI, THEN NATU-RALLY...
IT WOULD HAVE TO BE SOMETHING SUPER DUPER GIRLY, NO?
Like Perfume, or maybe cute anime songs...
Like Kyary Pamyu Pamyu.

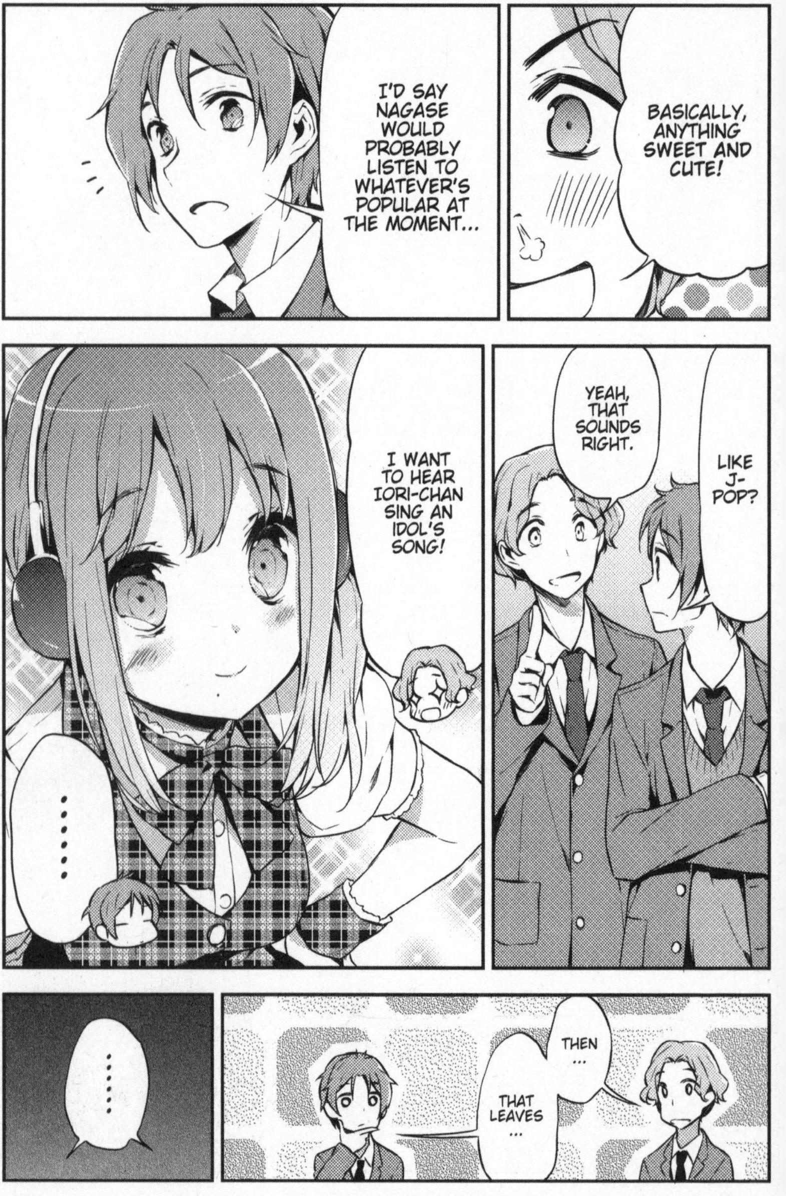
BASICALLY, ANYTHING SWEET AND CUTE!
I'D SAY NAGASE WOULD PROBABLY LISTEN TO WHATEVER'S POPULAR AT THE MOMENT...
LIKE J-POP?
YEAH, THAT SOUNDS RIGHT.
I WANT TO HEAR IORI-CHAN SING AN IDOL'S SONG!
......
THEN ...
THAT LEAVES ...
......

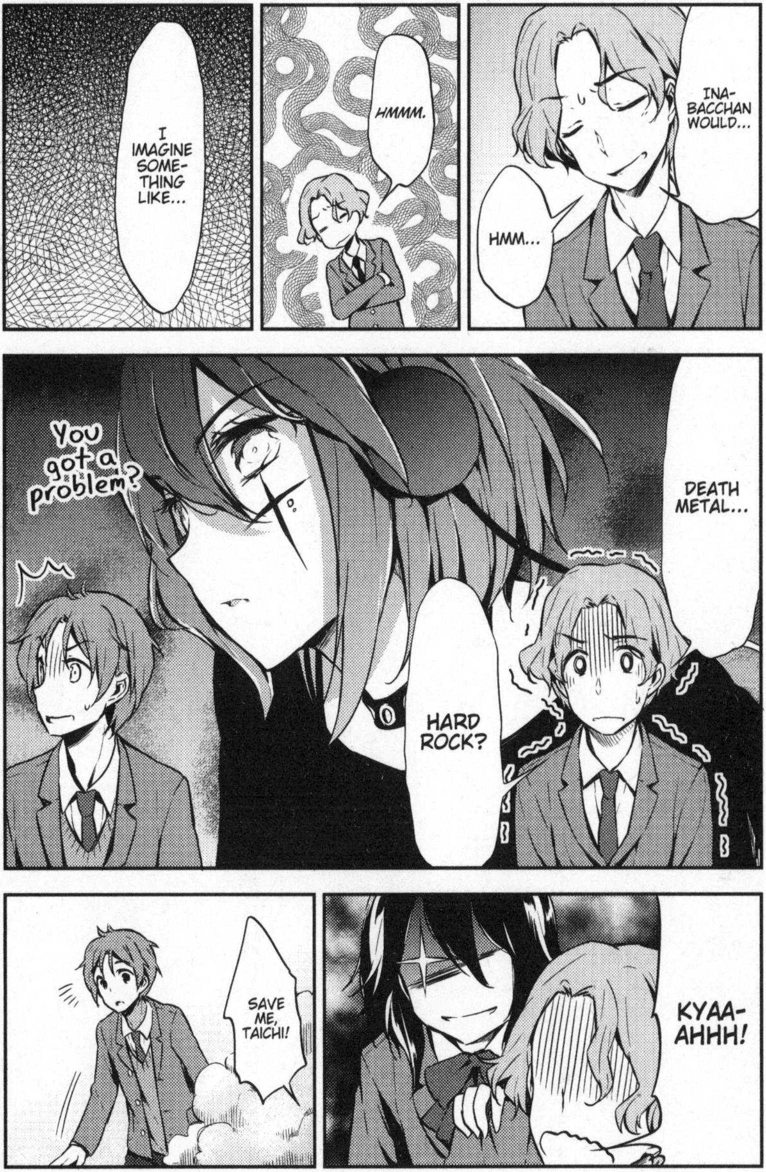
INA-BACCHAN WOULD...
HMM...
HMMM.
I IMAGINE SOME-THING LIKE...
DEATH METAL...
HARD ROCK?
You got a problem?
KYAA-AHHH!
SAVE ME, TAICHI!

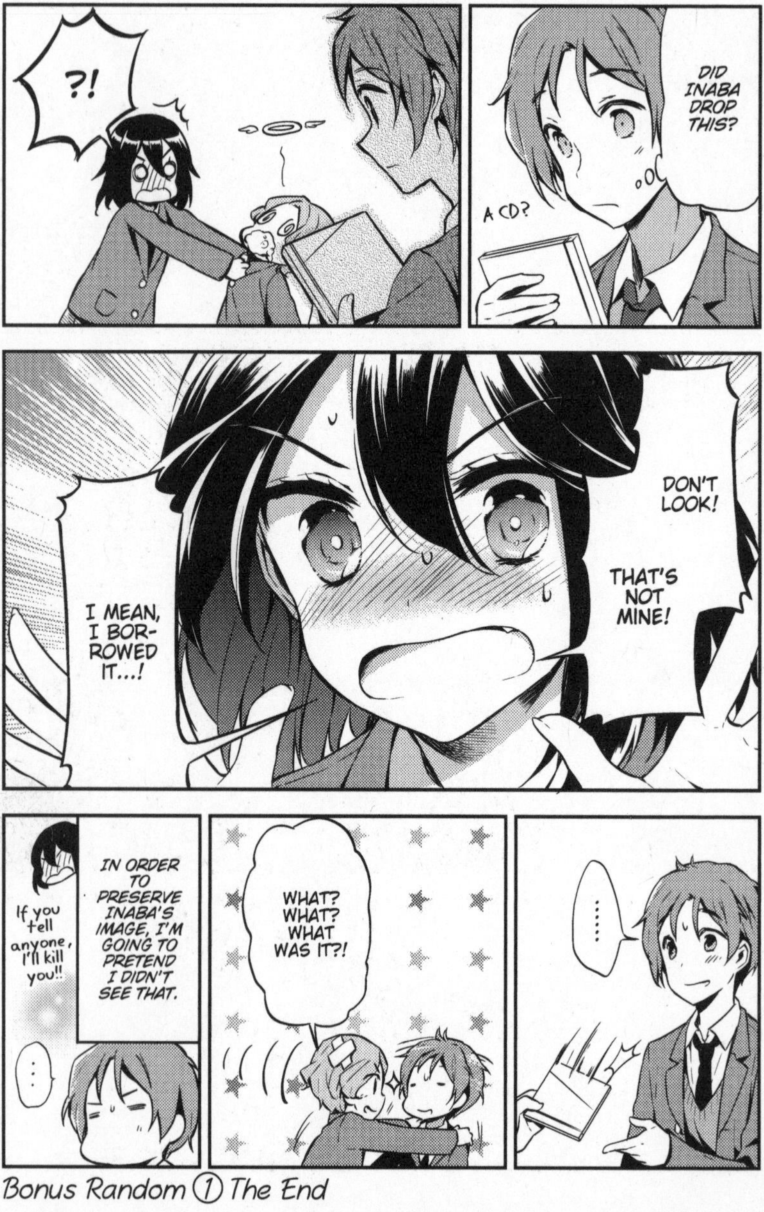
DID INABA DROP THIS?
A CD?
?!
DON'T LOOK! THAT'S NOT MINE!
I MEAN, I BOR-ROWED IT...!
......
WHAT? WHAT? WHAT WAS IT?!
IN ORDER TO PRESERVE INABA'S IMAGE, I'M GOING TO PRETEND I DIDN'T SEE THAT.
If you tell anyone, I'll kill you!!
...

Bonus Random ① The End

Bonus Random ②

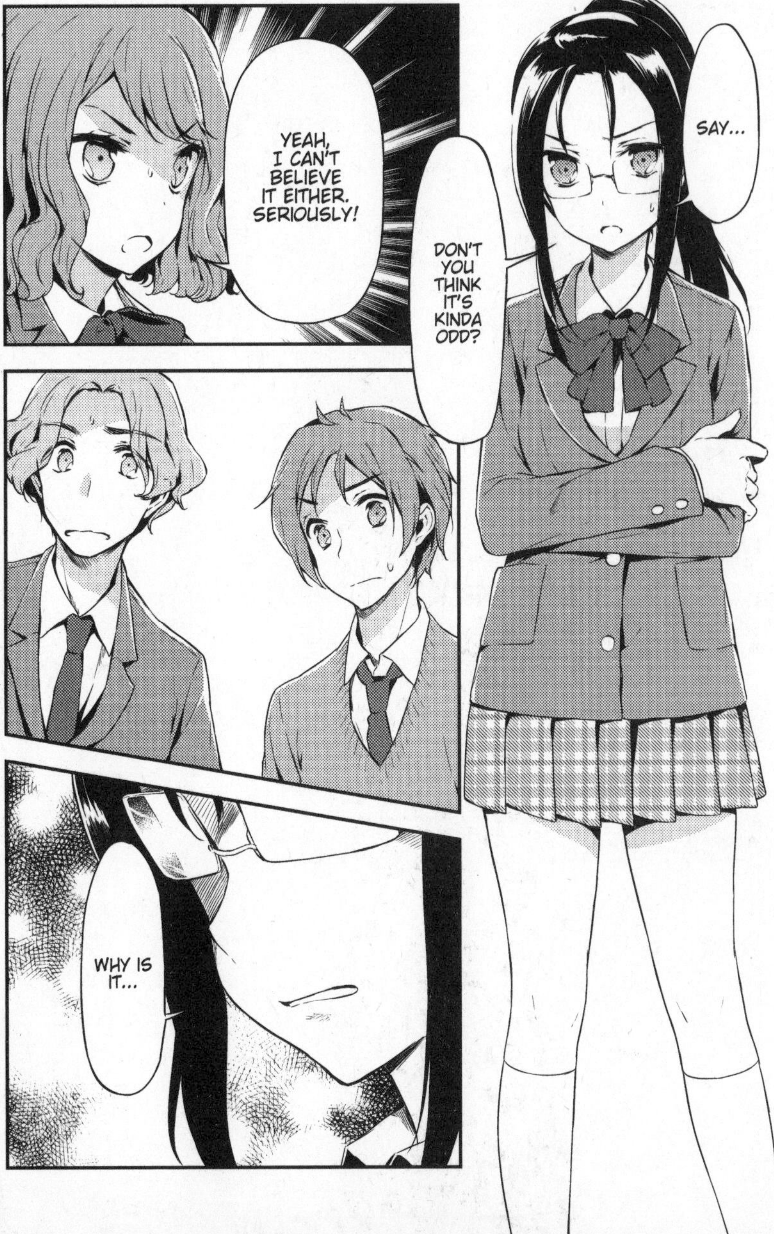
SAY...
DON'T YOU THINK IT'S KINDA ODD?
YEAH, I CAN'T BELIEVE IT EITHER. SERIOUSLY!
WHY IS IT...

AFTERWORD

Hello there! It's CUTEG (Kkam)! :)

Volume 4 of Kokoro Connect will be released soon and I can't help but feel like it's been such a long time since I last had a book come out (maybe that's just me?). At this point, the five members of the Student Cultural Society are involved in quite the serious story. Since Aoki's coolness will finally show up in the next few chapters, I've chosen him for the afterword illustration this time.

Thank you all so much for reading this volume all the way through to the afterword!

Special Thanks
Pai ti+L [ᵔᴥᵔ]

CuteG
2013. 03

2013
Those Mayans...
...are such liars!

2013 HAS MANAGED TO ARRIVE...

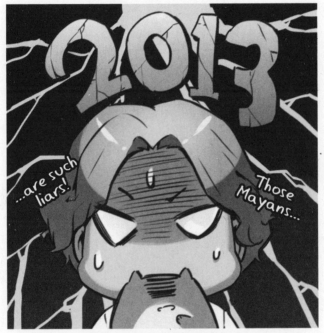